The Education
of the Heart

The Education
of the Heart

THE CORRESPONDENCE OF
Rachel Mordecai Lazarus
AND *Maria Edgeworth*

10 4441

EDITED BY
Edgar E. MacDonald

The University of North Carolina Press
Chapel Hill

Copyright © 1977 by
The University of North Carolina Press
Manufactured in the United States of America
ISBN 0-8078-1276-5
Library of Congress Catalog Card Number 76-29062

Library of Congress Cataloging in Publication Data

Lazarus, Rachel Mordecai, 1788–1838.
    The education of the heart.

    Includes index.
    1. Lazarus, Rachel Mordecai, 1788–1838.
2. Teachers—North Carolina—Correspondence.
3. Edgeworth, Maria, 1768–1849—Correspondence.
4. Authors, English—19th century—Correspondence.
I. Edgeworth, Maria, 1768–1849, joint author.
II. MacDonald, Edgar E. III. Title.
LA2317.L36A44   370'.92'2   76-29062
ISBN 0-8078-1276-5

FOR *Marie*

Contents

Preface

In the first decade of the nineteenth century, a remarkable occurrence took place in a small North Carolina town. When his business endeavors failed in the village of Warrenton, a Jewish merchant with a scholarly bent opened a school for girls. Jacob Mordecai's was the only family of Israelites in the area, but the esteem in which they were held led to the school's immediate success. In a day when the education of girls was considered of secondary importance, a matter of instruction by mothers or governesses, the idea of a sound education in a boarding school was visionary. And while Jews were a respected minority in southern cities, the stereotype of the Jew as Shylock was the universal literary image. But such was the response to the Mordecai School by the Protestant inhabitants of rural North Carolina that enrollment had to be limited to the available accommodations. Jacob Mordecai depended on his children to help run the school, in particular on his oldest daughter, Rachel. In preparing herself for her duties, she turned to the treatises on education by the Edgeworths, that remarkable family living in an isolated village in Ireland. *Practical Education* (1798) by Maria and Richard Lovell Edgeworth was considered the most scientific treatment of the subject since John Locke's *Thoughts*, which had appeared a hundred years earlier. In her very few moments spared from teaching, Miss Mordecai entertained herself by reading the charming novels of Miss Edgeworth.

When Maria Edgeworth visited London in 1813, she was the celebrity of the hour. Along with her father, she was accepted as an authority on the education of children. *The Parent's Assis-*

tant: or Stories for Children had established their reputation in 1796. In France as well as in England and America, the young were being raised on her *Moral Tales*; the finished product was entertained by her *Tales of Fashionable Life*. *Castle Rackrent* (1800) established her as a perceptive novelist who would influence later writers. From the sociological novels of the eighteenth century she had moved toward the pscyhological studies of the nineteenth; she first explored the psyche of children and the mind of the laboring class. Her delineation of Irish characters "supplied an impetus for the writings of all regional fiction, for Scott in Scotland, for Fenimore Cooper in America, for Turgenev in Russia" (P. H. Newby, *Maria Edgeworth* [Denver: Allan Swallow, 1950], p. 94). Her literary friendships embraced the intellectual elite in the Western world. In London she was sought after for her wit, sound sense, and modesty, a delightful contrast to her talkative father who was considered a boisterous bore.

One of Maria Edgeworth's most popular novels appeared in 1812, *The Absentee*. Miss Mordecai doubtless found the Irish characters charming, with all their wit and eccentricities. Then her eye beheld the name *Mordecai* in the novel, "a famous London coachmaker," a character described in unflattering terms who obviously played a villain's role. The young teacher, shocked to see the respected name of her family given to an unscrupulous character, even if in fiction, turned to her father for an explanation. Was this not a flagrant example of that anti-Semitism of which she had heard but never experienced? The benevolent attitude of Jacob Mordecai that endeared him to his family, friends, and students doubtless led him to suggest to his daughter that perhaps Miss Edgeworth followed a literary convention unthinkingly, that the Jew in literature was a stereotype, and where Miss Edgeworth had her Irish models before her discerning eye, she had to borrow from others her delineation of Jewish character. The question as to why the character in the novel had to be Jewish could be answered only by the writer.

On 7 August 1815, the young Jewish schoolteacher living in

the village of Warrenton, North Carolina, sat down and wrote the celebrated Miss Edgeworth a letter. In a long, respectful introduction she acknowledged her esteem for the entire Edgeworth family; then she got to her point. Why did British novelists, even the enlightened and benevolent Miss Edgeworth, write of the Jew in a derogatory manner? The young schoolmistress declared that the prejudice shown in the novels under question was not evinced in her provincial American society. Rachel Mordecai, the eldest daughter of Jacob Mordecai, thus commenced a defense of her faith and society that would extend to America itself.

Her letter struck the hearts of its recipients in Edgeworthstown, that small beacon of enlightenment in the chaos of Ireland. Richard Lovell Edgeworth, then on what he termed his "dying bed," characteristically snatched the pen from his daughter's hand and wrote approvingly to the Jewish schoolmistress. Maria Edgeworth wrote too and intimated that she was employed on a work to make amends. It was the novel *Harrington* (1817) in which a boy thoughtlessly instilled with a fear of Jews grows up and falls in love with a Jewess, Berenice Montenero. She and her father, a cultured gentleman from America, overcome Harrington's British prejudices. Then Harrington witnesses Berenice's anguish when she attends a performance of *The Merchant of Venice* and sees Jessica's perfidy cheered by the audience. Mr. Montenero explains to Harrington that never before has his daughter, raised in America, witnessed such prejudice. His words are those of Rachel Mordecai, taken directly from her letter to Maria Edgeworth: "Living in a retired village, her father's the only family of Israelites who resided in or near it, all her juvenile friendships and attachments had been formed with those of different persuasions; yet each had looked upon the variations of the other as things of course, or rather as things which do not affect the moral character—differences which take place in every society." Rachel Mordecai's heart was suffused with joy, but as the novel drew to a close, her joy was tempered.

Berenice is only half-Jewish; her mother, now dead, had been a Christian, and Berenice had been raised in that faith by the liberal-minded Mr. Montenero. The reason suggested in the novel for the "happy denouement" is that husband and wife, Harrington and Berenice, should be of one persuasion. Rachel Mordecai could not let Miss Edgeworth's easy generalization go unchallenged; the novel itself contained the all-too-obvious example of Mr. Montenero and his Christian wife. Again the careful respects from the schoolmistress in North Carolina to the celebrated writer in Ireland, but again the pertinent question. Why had Miss Edgeworth turned her "Jewish" heroine into a Christian? Miss Edgeworth confessed she had no ready answer, but accepted gratefully Jacob Mordecai's suggestion that she had wished to underline Mr. Montenero's nobility of character. And doubtless the nobility of Jacob Mordecai's explanation assured the continuance of a correspondence between the two ladies lasting twenty-three years, ended only by death.

The literary exchange grows into an extraordinary friendship, one that embraces a remarkable variety of topics. Into the warp of domestic life is woven the woof of literature, science, philosophy, gardening, politics, and a mutual veneration of Sir Walter Scott. But the psychology of the "emancipated woman" does not enter into their correspondence. Their increasingly affectionate friendship is based on their mutual respect for the father image. Rachel Mordecai's first and immediate appeal to Maria Edgeworth was her expression of respect for Mr. Edgeworth and for her own father. That letter arrived at a time when Maria Edgeworth was in despair at the prospect of losing her father. While Maria Edgeworth never married, both ladies prefigured the dutiful Victorian daughter who would seek in her husband the patriarchal image. Miss Mordecai married Aaron Lazarus of Wilmington, North Carolina, a widower with seven children.

In addition to the affection on both sides, Maria Edgeworth gained from Rachel Mordecai Lazarus an insight into American life that the writer learned to trust. For Mrs. Lazarus, with her multiple maternal duties and living in a quiet town in the South, the correspondence with Maria Edgeworth was a window upon the world for an intellectually superior woman. What may seem to a modern reader like effusive respect on her part for the older woman can be accepted as genuine; her letters to others attest to it. Mr. Lazarus recognized the intensity of his wife's feelings and took pride in her friendship with Miss Edgeworth. The depth of Rachel Lazarus's character is shown in the letter wherein she expresses the wish to visit the Edgeworths, despite fears of her own inadequacies: "I feel without fearing your infinite superiority, and in such society could taste the purest intellectual delight."

Their letters are presented here as complete as research could make them. Not every observation made by Maria Edgeworth or Rachel Lazarus is of unvarying interest; if they were literary, they were also "domestick." But the banalities are few, and even they attest to the breadth of interests the two ladies evinced in every phase of daily living. And what strikes one reader as banal may strike another as universal truth.

Transcribing these letters has posed several problems. After the first carefully composed letters to Rachel Mordecai, Maria Edgeworth began to write in the style in which she wrote to her family, rapidly as her thought flowed spontaneously through her pen. Sometimes words are run together in long clusters, the only break occurring where the pen went dry, frequently in the middle of a word. Almost her sole mark of punctuation was a short dash, marking brief pauses as well as period sentences. Somewhat more conventional punctuation has been supplied by the editor in an effort to clarify her thought for the reader. In reverse, Rachel Mordecai Lazarus employed an excess of commas. As though hesitant to express a complete thought boldly to one she considered her literary superior, she fragmented her thought into multiple phrases that sometimes render her meaning ambiguous. Many commas have been deleted by the editor, especially those between subject and verb, for a better flow of thought. In her later letters she perhaps unconsciously adopted

Maria Edgeworth's short dashes as substitutes for commas and periods alike. As Maria would draw to the close of a letter, she frequently touched on many ideas briefly so that some of her ideas appear run together, which in effect they were as she continued around the margins of her last page, then skipped to the margins of her first page. Sometimes, to the despair of the reader in its written form, after she had filled a page, she would turn it sideways and write down across her previous lines.

Maria Edgeworth was aware of the careless flow of her letters to Rachel, terming them her recreation as opposed to the careful letters she wrote other correspondents. As she made clear, she reposed complete trust in Rachel's discretion as to her private comments. She apologized for the appearance of one letter in which she had "scratched in and scratched out" excessively, but felt she did not need to waste time in recopying for mere "fairness" for an understanding friend. Nor did she take time to check her spelling of names or her facts; titles of books are approximate. In a letter to Sir Walter Scott she observed of her own letter writing, "As to accuracy, I can compare myself only to the sailor who 'would never quarrel for a handful of degrees.'" Titles in the letters are left as the two ladies wrote them; they are given correctly in the notes.

As will be seen in her letter of 22 March 1827 to Mrs. Lazarus, Maria Edgeworth strongly disapproved of the publication of private letters. She expressed these sentiments to a number of correspondents, feeling that the prospect of publication bred affectation in the letter writer and destroyed private confidence. But she admitted she liked to read old letters. "So I have no objection to treat myself to reading very old letters which come out from old recepticles, heaven knows how, and when I can wash my hands at all events of any share in the treachery." After the death of her sister Rachel, Ellen Mordecai treasured the letters of Maria Edgeworth. In a *Harper's Weekly* supplement of 6 May 1871 sketches of Edgeworth House and extracts from some of Maria's correspondence appeared. Knowing how both Maria and Rachel felt about the publication of private letters, Ellen Mordecai wrote Harriet Edgeworth Butler, a younger half sister of Maria's, "It almost made me frightened to think what I have safely in charge that these *Harpies* would be glad to obtain."

Ellen Mordecai was then eighty, and she consulted her brother Alfred, who had so captivated the Edgeworth ladies on his visit in 1833, as to what disposition should be made of the letters. They determined to send the originals from Maria back to Edgeworthstown; a friend, a Miss Maury, would soon be sailing from New York to Liverpool and could see them safely to England. Alfred Mordecai wrote Michael Pakenham Edgeworth, Maria's youngest brother, on 16 July 1871: "In taking out Miss Edgeworth's letters (with heartrending reluctance) from the portfolio in which they were arranged I have ventured to retain one or two unimportant notes, as mementos, and also her letter to my sister's husband after my sister's death." Ellen Mordecai wrote the same month to Harriet Edgeworth Butler, expressing relief in relinquishing her thirty-three-year guardianship of the letters. Almost immediately she had a change of heart. Her half sister Emma Mordecai convinced her that the letters should have become the property of Rachel's oldest daughter, another Ellen, now the mother of a large progeny. A month after writing of her relief, Ellen Mordecai requested the return of the letters. Harriet Butler complied, but before returning them she took a hasty copy of the greater part of Maria's letters to Rachel.

After the death of Rachel, Ellen Mordecai, unmarried and herself a teacher, continued the correspondence with Maria and later with Mrs. Edgeworth, the fourth wife of Maria's father, and with Maria's sisters until her death in 1884. Then her half sister Emma, likewise a maiden lady and a teacher, continued corresponding with the Edgeworth ladies until shortly before her death in 1906. A niece, Augusta Mordecai, carried on the correspondence until her death in 1939. Rosina Mordecai, a great-niece of Rachel's, continued writing until her death in 1942. On the Edgeworthstown side, the correspondence was continued after Maria's death in 1849 by her stepmother who died in 1865, followed by Maria's half sister Harriet (Mrs. Richard Butler) until 1881, then by Maria's half sister Lucy (Mrs. Thomas Romney Robinson) until about 1890, then by Maria's niece Harriet Jessie Edgeworth (Mrs. A. G. Butler). Thus Rachel Mordecai's first letter of reproach to Maria Edgeworth in 1815 resulted in a correspondence between the Mordecai and Edgeworth families that spanned 127 years.

Maria's letters to Rachel, along with Rachel's copies of her own letters, were sent a second time to Edgeworthstown. Ellen Mordecai died in 1884, and Alfred Mordecai probably sent them in 1886; on 19 September he noted in a letter that he had cut off a signature of one of Maria's letters as a memento. The letters were passed on by Maria's niece, Mrs. A. G. Butler, to her son, Harold Edgeworth Butler, and by him to his daughter, Christina Butler Colvin (Mrs. H. M. Colvin).

Thirty-seven original and holograph copies from Rachel Mordecai Lazarus exist; only two others appear to be missing. Thirty-four letters from Maria Edgeworth to Rachel exist, all originals except three, and no indications of missing letters can be detected. The copies taken by Harriet Butler in 1871 have proved of aid in checking the originals of Maria's letters and have provided the three letters missing from the originals. Most likely Alfred Mordecai retained the latter, and some member of the Mordecai family may still have them. Fewer originals from Rachel to Maria exist, for Maria passed on to other members of her family interesting letters that she received. Some fifteen or sixteen appear to be originals, but one cannot be absolutely sure as Rachel's copies in her hand were placed with the originals that survived at Edgeworthstown. As noted, only two of Rachel's letters appear to be missing, one for certain. That one is to be regretted as it gave her account of the Nat Turner insurrection. A letter to her brother George Washington Mordecai in Raleigh on this subject perhaps gives us some idea of what this missing letter to Maria Edgeworth contained and is partially quoted in the proper place.

While Rachel's first letter was an appeal against the injustice of racial prejudice as evinced by British novelists, it was directed in particular to Maria Edgeworth, for the Mordecais had learned to appreciate the humanitarian approach the Edgeworths had advocated in the education of children. The methods advanced by Maria and her father in *Practical Education* were in marked contrast to the prescriptive classical education that was the norm in their day. Their appeal was to the child's natural interests in things in a real world, and their approach can best be summed up in the phrase "the education of the heart" which the authors employed. In addition to contributing to our knowledge of educational theory and practice, the correspondence between Rachel and Maria presents an interesting record of literary tastes—and gossip—both in England and America, particularly concerning Sir Walter Scott, Lord Byron, Bulwer-Lytton, Washington Irving, James Fenimore Cooper, and Catherine Sedgwick. It likewise provides information on social and political conditions in Ireland and England during the first half of the nineteenth century, as well as in the United States. It adds evidence that there was much liberal feeling in the South toward the gradual emancipation of the slaves, and it underlines the attitude of ready acceptance of Jews in the South at a time when anti-Semitism was evidenced in the North.

The impression that is formed from reading this correspondence is one of surprise at how timely the letters appear. Political change, riots, violence, new inventions were their concerns as they are ours. Happiness and tragedy are as intermingled as they are in our present day. Another impression gained from reading the letters is how the disciplined mind finds joy in observing every aspect of life with interest and compassion. Whatever befell Rachel Mordecai Lazarus and Maria Edgeworth, no undue sympathy need be expended on them. They both lived fully, enjoying the variety of life, sharing abundantly. Though they never met, their correspondence made them the "family friends" they termed themselves, a friendship which proved that distance was no barrier for spirits such as theirs.

Acknowledgments

I am indebted to Mrs. Harold Edgeworth Butler for first giving me copies of several of the letters. As my interest in the correspondence grew, her daughter, Christina Butler Colvin of Oxford, England, made all the letters in her possession available to me. Mrs. Colvin was of incalculable aid in every way, in deciphering difficult passages, in identifying persons mentioned, in comparing ME's comments to RML with those made in other letters, in obtaining Xerox copies through the Bodleian Library, in providing nourishment for flagging spirits. The letters are published here with her kind permission. I am grateful to Mr. and Mrs. Robert Calder of Wilmington, North Carolina, for letting me read their family papers concerning Aaron Lazarus and his children. Mr. C. F. W. Coker of the North Carolina Department of Archives and History very kindly supplied me with copies of Mordecai letters. Mrs. H. L. Blomquist of Durham, North Carolina, and her brother Dr. Alfred Mordecai of Winston-Salem were helpful. Flavia Reed Owen, librarian at Randolph-Macon College, was ever encouraging, and Lelia Almond of that institution typed and retyped ever cheerfully. Richard W. Slatten proofread and maintained a truly remarkable interest over many months. These and many others have made editing the correspondence a happy chore.

Chronology

1768   1 Jan.: Maria Edgeworth (ME) born at Black Bourton, Oxfordshire, second child of Richard Lovell Edgeworth (RLE) and Anna Maria Elers.

1773   Death of ME's mother. Within four months her father marries Honora Sneyd of Lichfield. Maria's first visit to Edgeworthstown, the family estate in Ireland.

1775–80   ME at school at Madame Latuffiere's in Derby.

1780   Death of Honora, RLE's second wife. Within the year he marries her sister Elizabeth Sneyd. ME in school of Mrs. Davis in Upper Wimpole Street, London.

1782   ME goes to Edgeworthstown to live.

1787   *The Freeman Family* begun by ME; resumed as *Patronage* in 1809.

1788   1 July: Rachel Mordecai born in Goochland County, Virginia, the third child of Jacob Mordecai and his first wife Judith Myers.

1795   *Letters for Literary Ladies*, ME's first published book.

1796   *The Parent's Assistant*, a collection of children's stories.

1797   Death of Elizabeth, RLE's third wife, in November.

1798   RLE marries Frances Beaufort, a year younger than ME, in May. June: *Practical Education*, a textbook for children written by ME with RLE and other members of the family.

1800   *Castle Rackrent*, ME's first novel, published anonymously, still critically acclaimed.

1801   *Moral Tales*, a collection of stories for children. *Belinda*, ME's first society novel, a favorite widely translated.

1802   *Essay on Irish Bulls*, a study of Irish humor, written with help of RLE. Edgeworth family in Brussels and Paris during the Peace of Amiens. In Paris, ME receives her only proposal of marriage, from the Chevalier Edelcrantz, a Swedish courtier; she elects to remain with her family rather than live in Sweden.

1803   March: The Edgeworths return to England on eve of the resumption of the Napoleonic wars. ME's brother Lovell interned in France.

1804   *Popular Tales*, a collection of stories.

1805   [*Early Lessons*] *Harry and Lucy, Rosamond, Frank, and other stories; The Modern Griselda: A Tale*.

1806   *Leonora*, a romantic letter-novel.

1809   *Tales of Fashionable Life*, vols. 1–3 (*Ennui, Almeria, Madame de Fleury, The Dun, Manoeuvring*).
Death of Joseph Johnson, ME's publisher, succeeded by R. Hunter.

1812   *Tales of Fashionable Life*, vols. 4–6 (*Vivian, Emilie de Coulanges, The Absentee*).

1813   April: Visit to London where ME is received as a celebrity; among other writers she meets Byron.

1814   Oct.: Scott's *Waverley* reaches Edgeworthstown. ME is lauded in the preface; correspondence with Scott begins.
Continuation of Early Lessons, 2 vols.
Patronage, in 4 vols.

1815   7 Aug.: Rachel Mordecai writes first letter to ME.

1816   4 Aug.: RLE and ME both write to Rachel Mordecai.

1817   13 June: Death of RLE.
July: *Harrington* and *Ormond*, the former written to make amends to Jews, the latter written in part by the dying RLE.
Comic Dramas, three plays (*Love and the Law; The Two Guardians; The Rose, the Thistle, and the Shamrock*).

1820 *Memoirs of Richard Lovell Edgeworth, Begun by Himself and Concluded by His Daughter*, 2 vols.
ME's second visit to Paris, later visits Geneva and Italy, with sisters Fanny and Harriet.

1821 *Rosamond: A Sequel to Early Lessons*, 2 vols.
21 March: Rachel Mordecai marries Aaron Marks Lazarus.

1822 *Frank: A Sequel to Frank in Early Lessons*, 3 vols.

1822–1825 First collected American edition of ME's works, 13 vols.

1823 June: ME visits Scotland and meets Scott in Edinburgh.
Aug.: ME Scott's guest at Abbotsford for two weeks.

1825 First collected English edition, 14 vols.
Harry and Lucy Concluded, 4 vols.
Aug.: Scott visits Edgeworthstown.

1827 *Little Plays for Children*, vol. 7 of *The Parent's Assistant*; *Gary Owen: or the Snow Woman*.

1833 Alfred Mordecai visits Edgeworthstown.

1834 *Helen*, ME's last novel, well received.

1838 23 June: Death of Rachel Mordecai Lazarus.

1839 George Mordecai visits Edgeworthstown.

1849 22 May: Death of ME at Edgeworthstown.

The Education
    of the Heart

With respect to what is commonly called the education of the heart, we have endeavored to suggest the easiest means of inducing useful and agreeable habits, well-regulated sympathy, and benevolent affections.

——MARIA AND RICHARD LOVELL EDGEWORTH, *Practical Education* (London, 1798), preface.

. . . In the course of a walk in the park at Edgeworthstown [August 1825], I happened to use some phrase which conveyed . . . the impression that I suspected Poets and Novelists of being a good deal accustomed to look at life and the world only as materials for art. A soft and pensive shade came over Scott's face as he said: "I fear you have some very young ideas in your head. . . . We shall never learn to feel and respect our real calling and destiny, unless we have taught ourselves to consider every thing as moonshine, compared with the education of the heart." Maria did not listen to this without some water in her eyes—her tears are always ready when any generous string is touched . . . ; but she brushed them gaily aside, and said, "You see how it is—Dean Swift said he had written his books in order that people might learn to treat him like a great lord. Sir Walter writes his in order that he may be able to treat his people as a great lord ought to do."

——J. C. LOCKHART, *Memoirs of the Life of Sir Walter Scott*, 7 vols. (Philadelphia, 1838), 6:49–50.

The Correspondence

[Original]

Warrenton, North Carolina
U.S. of America
August 7th, 1815

A young American lady who has long felt towards Miss Edgeworth those sentiments of respect and admiration which superior talents exerted in the cause of virtue and morality never fail to excite, ventures, not without hesitation, to indulge a wish formed many months since of addressing her. If such temerity require more than an ordinary apology, it is to Practical Education[1] she must appeal as her intercessor; it is that, which by lately making her acquainted with the Edgeworth family, has gradually eradicated fear and in its stead implanted confidence.

With how much interest have I perused and re-perused the useful observations which those volumes contain. With what pleasure have I dwelt on the "anecdotes of the nursery," tho' it was a pleasure which on several accounts was tinctured with regret. First, as reminding me of deficiencies in my own mind and education, next, of my incapacity to impart lessons of equal utility, and lastly, I lamented that there were no more of them. But while reluctantly submitting to evils which are unavoidable,

1. *Practical Education* by Maria Edgeworth . . . and Richard Lovell Edgeworth, 2 vols. (London, 1798); 3 vols. (London, 1801); 2 vols. (New York, 1801); 2 vols. (Providence and Boston, 1815); later editions not listed. *Practical Education* grew out of RLE's interest in his own children's education. He raised his eldest son, Richard, according to the tenets of Rousseau. Richard grew into an undisciplined youth, and as a child of nature he emigrated to America. Disillusioned, RLE tried other approaches with his younger children. In 1778 he and his second wife, Honora Edgeworth, began to keep notes of circumstances in the

offered benefits should not be rejected; and I have resolved, that as far as my poor capacity will admit, these admirable lessons shall answer the benevolent intention of their authors and serve as models in the important business of education.

The eldest female of a numerous family, I find many claims on my diligence and exertion, and truly grateful am I to those who thus guide and direct me, in a course, by pursuing which, those who share my cares and my affections "may become good and wise and may enjoy the greatest possible share of happiness both here and hereafter."

To me the authors of Practical Education appear almost as individual friends, and friends the most disinterested; since, without knowing, they have assisted and encouraged me. I say *encouraged*, for I found both encouragement and comfort from the words, "A fond mother will tremble at the idea that so much depends on her own care in the early education of her children; but even tho' she may be unexperienced in the art, she may be persuaded that patience and perseverance will ensure her success; even from her timidity we may prophesy favorably, for, in education, to know the danger is often to a[*void it.*"]

True, I am *not* a mother, but if I were, I could hardly be

---

development of their children that they felt were worth recording. He continued this practice with his third wife, Elizabeth Edgeworth. Maria was drawn into the education of her younger brothers and sisters, and she studied the theories of Rousseau and Madame de Genlis. The work finally published in 1798 was the result of the collaboration of the whole Edgeworth family, from the recorded infant responses, the notes of the parents (the chapter "Obedience" woven around Elizabeth Edgeworth's notes), the chapter "Chemistry" by second son Lovell, to the general rounding out by Maria.

The word *practical* in the title can be understood to stand in opposition to *classical* with its emphasis on the memorization of arbitrarily chosen facts. The Edgeworths would eschew the prescriptive, and through sympathy and encouragement, they would stress the utilitarian and experimental.

The publication of *Practical Education* created a sensation in England, as well as on the Continent and in America. Not since Locke's *Thoughts* in 1693 had such a systematic treatment of education appeared. While widely admired, it was also condemned for its silence regarding religious education. It embodied the basis for modern education, and it made Maria and her father famous in their day.

more deeply interested; and with the consciousness of my deficiency, constantly rising in array before me, such an assurance came seasonably to my aid and encouraged me to *persevere*. In many of the opinions advanced, I found myself flattered, as they coincided perfectly with what had before been my own: of a far greater number which were new to me, I at once acknowledged the justness, and could not doubt the practical utility. May I not add, that the air of truth and candour which characterizes the whole work gave it in my estimation a value which without them, all its other excellencies would have failed to create.

How highly should I be gratified to know that the amiable and deserving family of Mr. Edgeworth are still as happy as they were, at the time that Practical Education was concluded; so far as depends on themselves, I think they must always be so.

The little volumes containing Early Lessons, the Parents Assistant, and Moral Tales,[2] I have read with pleasure, I trust with advantage, and am very certain they have contributed much to the improvement of the children in whose hands they have been placed. More of such works as the two first mentioned are much wanted; I seek in vain for successors of equal utility and merit. If I dared venture, I would ask if Laura, and my little friend Rosamond, are not real characters; and if the gentle, sensible Laura and the amiable Caroline Percy[3] are not drawn from the same individual. Such as the Caroline and Rosamond of Patronage[4] I should have supposed would be the characters of Laura and Rosamond when their minds had reached maturity.

With all my confidence in the benignant goodness of Miss Edgeworth I tremble at having said so much, and trespassed so

2. *Harry and Lucy, Part 1: Being the first part of Early Lessons, By the Author of the Parent's Assistant* (London 1801). *The Parent's Assistant: or Stories for Children*, 3 vols. (London, 1795). *Moral Tales for Young People*, 5 vols. (London, 1801).

3. Laura and Rosamond are characters in ME's stories for children. Laura is sensible and Rosamond romantic. Caroline and Rosamond Percy are characters in *Patronage*.

4. *Patronage*, 4 vols. (London, 1814); 3 vols. (Philadelphia, 1814).

very greatly on her patience and indulgence; still must I entreat that they may be extended to me yet a little longer.

Relying on the good sense and candour of Miss Edgeworth I would ask, how it can be that she, who on all other subjects shows such justice and liberality, should on one alone appear biased by prejudice: should even instill that prejudice into the minds of youth! Can my allusion be mistaken? It is to the species of character which wherever a *Jew* is introduced is invariably attached to him. Can it be believed that this race of men are by nature mean, avaricious, and unprincipled? Forbid it, mercy. Yet this is more than insinuated by the stigma usually affixed to the *name*. In those parts of the world where these people are oppressed and made continually the subject of scorn and derision, they may in many instances deserve censure; but in this happy country, where religious distinctions are scarcely known, where character and talents are all sufficient to attain advancement, we find the Jews to form a respectable part of the community. They are in most instances liberally educated, many following the honourable professions of the Law, and Physick, with credit and ability, and associating with the best society our country affords. The penetration of Miss Edgeworth has already conjectured that it is a Jewess who addresses her; it is so, but one who thinks she does not flatter herself in believing that were she not, her opinion on this subject would be exactly what it is now. Living in a small village, her father's the only family of Israelites who reside in or near it, all her juvenile friendships and attachments have been formed with those of persuasions different from her own; yet each has looked upon the variations of the other as things of course—differences which take place in every society. Again and again I beg pardon for thus intruding myself on Miss Edgeworth's notice; yet even now is my temerity about to appear in a new form while I give utterance to a very imperfect hope, that these lines may be honoured with a reply, and their author thus taught to believe herself not wholly unpardonable, in the liberty she takes in writing them. Should she be thus highly favoured, Miss Edgeworth will have the goodness to direct the letter according to the address, which a brother of the writer's, now in England, will annex.

With sentiments of admiration, esteem, and gratitude, Miss Edgeworth's

most respectful and obedient servant
Rachel Mordecai

Edgeworthstown, Ireland, August 4th, 1816

Whether I am addressing a real or an assumed character is more than I am able to determine; but the sentiments which your letter contained do honor to the understanding and to the feelings of the writer.

I have not seen the answer which my daughter sends to you with this, but I am certain that she felt real pleasure from the whole of your letter. We are used to receive compliments, but we have learned how to distinguish the value of the coin, by which we are repaid for our endeavours to be useful. I can assure you with great truth that we have steadily practised the precepts which we have published and that success has uniformly attended our exertions.

To praise my own is forbidden by the wise customs of society, but to acknowledge with gratitude the solace and delight which my declining health and age enjoy from the society and conduct of my numerous family may be permitted, as it holds out an encouragement to such generous minds as yours to persevere in the arduous task which you have begun.

If these letters reach you, pray make us better acquainted with your real self.

I have just heard that Miss Edgeworth has not mentioned to

you the subject on which she is now employed; it will I hope be an *amende honorable* for former misrepresentation.

I am Madam,
Your Obed. Servant
Richard Lovell Edgeworth

Edgeworthstown, Ireland

Dear Madam,

Your polite, benevolent and touching letter has given me much pleasure, and much pain. As to the pain I hope you will sometime see that it has excited me to make all the atonement and reparation in my power for the past. It was impossible to remonstrate with more gentleness or in a more convincing as well as persuasive manner than you have done. Your own letter is the very best evidence that could have been offered of the truth of all you urge in favor of those of your own religious persuasion. And the candor and spirit of tolerance and benevolence you shew, you have a right to expect from others.

Will you be so kind to tell me how I can send you what I am now preparing for the press? It probably will not be published till the end of the year, so that I shall have time for your answer. Is there any person in London to whom I can consign the book? Though you did not sign any name to your letter and though it seems an extraordinary coincidence that your brother's name should happen to be *Mordecai* (absentee),[5] yet I am persuaded from the tone of truth throughout the letter that you are a real living person and that you think and feel all you say. Perhaps I am credulously vain in believing all the gratifying things you say about Practical Education, but I own that they have given

---

5. As indicated in her next letter, Miss Mordecai's brother had erased her name. "Mr. Mordecai, a famous London coachmaker," plays a villain's role in ME's *The Absentee*. Her other Jewish characters are in the vein of Shakespeare's Shylock.

me great pleasure. Nothing can be more agreeable to my father and to me than to think that what we have written on education has been practically useful, especially to one so amiably intent upon the education of a family as you appear to be. I should tell you that tho' for convenience the word WE is used all through Practical Education, yet I did nothing in the education of the family of whom I there gave the history.

In answer to your very kind inquiry about the happiness of this family I can assure you that we enjoy perfect domestic happiness and except from anxiety about my father's health we have scarcely anything in this world to wish for.

> I am Dear Madam
> Your obliged and grateful
> Maria Edgeworth

[Addressed: To the care of Samuel Mordecai,[6] Richmond, Virginia, North-Carolina.]

[Original]   Warrenton, North Carolina, 25 September 1816

The twenty-fifth of September, if I kept a diary, should be noted as one of the most agreeable days I have ever known, and for its pleasurable sensations I am indebted to Mr. and Miss Edgeworth.

To express with simple truth the gratification derived from your letter, this morning received, would require terms which might appear exaggerated; I will therefore only acknowledge its politeness, its candour, may I not add, its friendliness, and return many thanks for a favor which I had scarcely permitted myself to think would be conferred. To those who, like you, delight in scenes of domestick unity, it would have been pleasing to see the animated countenances of my parents, brothers

6. Samuel Mordecai, Rachel's brother (see Appendix B).

and sisters, as they witnessed and participated in my gratification; fortunately for us, the joy of one is the joy of all.

With Mr. Edgeworth's flattering request that I will make you better acquainted with my real self, I readily comply. It was not indeed in the first instance my intention to conceal my name, and it was signed at full length to my letter* but Rachel, as well as Mordecai, formed so striking a coincidence, that believing it would give an idea of my character being an assumed one, my brother erased both.

Will you be interested to hear of one who, deprived of maternal care ere its value or its loss could be known or lamented, was for years dependent on nature and chance for the cultivation of her understanding and the forming of her heart and principles? To whom a second mother proved a blessing, and who in riper years learned patience, perseverance and cheerfulness in the school of adversity? My father, formerly a merchant, was in 1799 involved in the general ruin which attended the shippers of American produce, and after struggling under difficulties for several years, was prevailed on by many who had known him in better days to open an academy for young ladies. But just turned nineteen, I was sensible rather of requiring a governess myself than of possessing the capacity to become one, but the case was urgent, the best of fathers sought to encourage me, the confidence reposed by others inspired me with zeal, and with the commencement of the year 1808 we engaged in the all important business of education. A brother six years younger than myself,[7] but possessing information and steadiness far beyond his years, after the first six months be-

* That letter thrice crossed the Atlantic. My brother returning to America sooner than was expected and without visiting England, this letter was sent back and enclosed by him from Richmond. [*Miss Mordecai's note on the left margin of first sheet.*]

7. Solomon Mordecai (see Appendix B).

came our assistant, and the eighth year will now soon close on our labours. Labours they are indeed, attended with fatigue, anxiety and care. Yet have we abundant cause for thankfulness, since they have been uniformly successful. In the improvement of our pupils, acknowledged by their parents, we often receive a reward the most grateful, and the number of applicants constantly exceeding that to which we have limited ourselves gives a satisfactory proof of publick approbation.[8]

I should perhaps have been less minute in relating these particulars did they not tend still further to prove the estimation in which persons of our persuasion are held in this country. A charge of the most sacred nature would scarcely be committed for years to any who could not be regarded with entire confidence. I might add that my father has been for more than twenty years in the commission of the peace for the town and county in which we live. Two sisters younger than myself are employed in attending to domestick arrangements,[9] our mother having a young family that has generally occupied her time and attention. It is the improvement of these children which forms my principal pleasure, as well as my greatest anxiety. Four young brothers and sisters share the attention of us all and are, thank Heaven, good and promising children.[10] Eliza, a child of seven years has always been particularly my charge. She possesses an excellent disposition and a degree of intelligence which, while it delights, often causes me to sigh, at my incapacity to cultivate it as it deserves. I seek by fixing your principles and

8. Accounts of the Mordecai School in Warrenton are given in: Gratz Mordecai, *Notice of Jacob Mordecai, Founder and Proprietor from 1809 to 1819, of the Warrenton (N.C.) Female Seminary*, Publications of the American Jewish Historical Society, No. 6, 1897; Caroline Cohen, *Records of the Myers, Hays, and Mordecai Families from 1707 to 1913* (Washington, D.C.: Published for the family, n.d.); Lizzie Wilson Montgomery, *Sketches of Old Warrenton, North Carolina* (Raleigh: Edwards and Broughton Printing Company, 1924).

9. Two younger sisters, Ellen Mordecai and Caroline Mordecai (see Appendix B).

10. The four youngest of Jacob Mordecai's children at the time of the writing of this letter were Alfred, Augustus, Eliza, and Emma (see Appendix B).

precepts in my mind and making them as far as I can my guides, to supply in part my own deficiency.

What does Miss Edgeworth say of being "credulously vain" in believing all that I said about "Practical Education"? In acknowledging it my guide and director I shall gratify her less than by asserting, as I truly may, that to her and her excellent father *many children* are in a great degree indebted for their own happiness and their power of communicating it to those most dear to them. Since I last wrote I have met with the continuation of "Early Lessons," of which I had not before heard. I wish I could form a juvenile library of such books. It is principally by discovering how books ought to be written that we find the imperfections of such as we had before approved.

I must confess that I was rather gratified than surprised at Miss Edgeworth's frank admission of my charge (shall I call it) against her. It was my conviction of her being capable of a conduct so noble that first encouraged me to touch on so delicate a subject, but that she should immediately set about making what she calls 'atonement and reparation' was more than I could have hoped. Still do I rejoice at it, as it raises her character still higher in my estimation. We are told that authors at home and authors on our shelves are quite different persons; this assertion has often been a source of mortification to me, and I rejoice to find that in some instances at least it is erroneous. Your flattering attention in proposing to send me the book which you are now preparing for the press receives my warm acknowledgements. One of my brothers, who resides in Richmond, Virginia, and who forwards this will give a direction where it can be left so that (without accident) I shall receive it.

A tedious correspondent! am I not? And yet I cannot conclude without expressing a wish that the pleasure I have this day enjoyed may be repeated. A better feeling, I trust, than vanity gives rise to the wish of being allowed all the intercourse which a separation of three thousand miles will permit with such a family as the Edgeworths. Will you not let me know *you* better?

That Mr. Edgeworth's restoration to health may remove from his estimable family every cause of anxiety and that they may long live to improve mankind and to bless each other is the sincere wish of Mr. and Miss Edgeworths' obliged and grateful

R. Mordecai

[*Note at bottom of page*]

The original was sent to London by the ship Prince of Waterloo, under cover to Mr. Johnson, Bookseller, St. Paul's Church yard.

Any packet addressed to Samuel Mordecai, Richmond, Virginia, and left with Messrs. Marx and Wheattall, Merchants (Lime Street Square, near the India house, London) will be forwarded by those gentlemen.

[*Copy*]   Warrenton, October 28th, 1817

A few days since I had the pleasure of receiving the packet of books, for which I am indebted to the attentive kindness of Miss Edgeworth. Simple thanks are all the return that I can make for so great a favour, and I have to regret that I cannot to my own satisfaction express how much I am obliged. The publick papers had some weeks before given the melancholy information, which a note at the end of the preface to "Harrington" too surely confirmed, that the touching farewell was prophetick;[11] that the friend, the instructor, the benefactor of mankind was no

11. Two weeks before his death, Richard Lovell Edgeworth wrote a preface for *Harrington* in which he made a public farewell to his daughter's readers: "I have been reprehended by some of the public critics for the notices which I have annexed to my daughter's works. As I do not know their reasons for their reprehension, I cannot submit even to their respectable authority. I trust however that the British public will sympathize with what a father feels for a daugher's literary success, particularly as this father and daughter have written various works in partnership. . . . And now, indulgent reader, I beg you to pardon this intrusion, and with the most grateful acknowledgements, I bid you farewell for ever. Richard Lovell Edgeworth. May 31, 1817." He died two weeks later on 13 June.

longer permitted to dwell among us; he was summoned to receive his reward. None read or heard without emotion, for it was the concern of all; it seemed as if a luminary, which had shed its benignant influence over the world, was suddenly extinguished. I would not, dear and amiable Miss Edgeworth, probe the wound which filial affection united with confidence and tender friendship must too keenly feel, but I would convey that melancholy satisfaction which must arise from the assurance that in a foreign and far distant land, the worth of those we loved is known and felt, and that the tear of the stranger falls alike in sympathy with us, and in sorrow for his own individual misfortune. The last hours of the venerable and excellent Mr. Edgeworth must awaken, even in those most deeply afflicted, consolatory feelings: so calm, so collected, so amiable. What heart but must raise itself in the supplication, "May my end be like his." I fear to dwell longer on this painful subject. Miss E. requires not to be exhorted to submission and humble resignation to the Divine Will; and even while nature demands its tribute, she yields without repining, to the dispensations of the "Orderer of the Universe."

We have read both Harrington and Ormond[12] with much satisfaction; the former will, I hope by asserting the cause of toleration, reward the benevolent intentions of its author. In England, where from circumstances related in that work, we must believe prejudices carried to an excess, hardly conceivable by us in America, it will doubtless be productive of much good. If by scrutinizing the conduct of Jews, they are proved to fulfill in common with other men every moral and social duty, it is to be hoped that the stigma which habit has associated with the name will lose its influence. The eagerness with which Miss Edgeworth has sought for such characters, and such incidents, as were honourable to our unfortunate nation, evinces the sincerity with which she undertook their defence. It is impossible

12. *Harrington: A Tale*; and *Ormond: A Tale*, 3 vols. (London, 1817).

to feel otherwise than gratified by the confidence so strongly, yet so delicately manifested, by the insertion of a passage from the letter in which I had endeavoured to give an idea of their general standing in this country.[13] I say *in this country*, tho' I acknowledge myself but imperfectly acquainted with the opinions entertained in some parts of it. So far as regards some of the Southern States, I speak with confidence. The Northern might, I think, be included; the Eastern[14] are perhaps somewhat less liberal, but of this, I am not certain; and as for the Western they are yet in their infancy and have no determinate character.

To return to Harrington. The portrait of Mr. Montenero is rendered the more gratifying by its contrast with even the very few of those Israelites who have, in fictitious writings, been represented as estimable. I have met with none, that I recollect, but Cumberland's Shever.[15] And in Shever, tho' we find much to approve, there is still a want of respectability. He was a benevolent man; but in the profession of a *userer*, there is something against which correct principle revolts. Mr. Montenero is a good man, a man of science, and a gentleman whose acquain-

13. In the novel *Harrington*, the father of the heroine, Berenice, is discussing with the hero his daughter's shock in experiencing anti-Semitic prejudices in England. In this passage Maria Edgeworth borrows directly from Rachel Mordecai's first letter to her: " 'Till she came to Europe—to England—she was not aware, at least not practically aware, of the strong prepossessions which still prevail against us Jews.' He then told me that his daughter had passed her childhood chiefly in America, 'in a happy part of that country where religious distinctions are scarcely known—where character and talents are all sufficient to attain advancement—where the Jews form a respectable part of the community—where, in most instances, they are liberally educated, many following the honourable professions of law and physic with credit and ability, and associating with the best society that country affords. Living in a retired village [*Warrenton, N.C.*], her father's the only family of Israelites who resided in or near it, all her juvenile friendships and attachments had been formed with those of different persuasions; yet each had looked upon the variations of the other as things of course, or rather as things which do not affect the moral character—differences which take place in every society' " (chapter 8).

14. By Eastern states, Miss Mordecai refers to New England.

15. Richard Cumberland (1732–1811), English dramatist; Sheva is a character in his play *The Jew*, first performed in 1794. The author was praised for his intention to defend the Jewish character.

tance and intimacy anyone may covet. It is difficult duly to appreciate the greatness of mind which can relinquish opinions long indulged and avowed, and which has courage to recant when convinced that justice calls for recantation. The passage, page 30, beginning, "I have met with authors, professing candour and toleration, etc.," I read with peculiar satisfaction; such an instance of the candour, the superiority of Miss Edgeworth's mind and heart, I dwell on with a degree of pleasure, I may venture to say it, nearly equal to that which the reflection of having written it must yield herself. Many other remarks on this volume present themselves, but if I attempt to tell of all I found in it to give me pleasure, I shall say both too much and too little. Let me therefore, without dwelling longer on its many excellences, confess with frankness that in one event I was disappointed. Berenice was not a Jewess. I have endeavoured to discover Miss Edgeworth's motive for not suffering her to remain such; it appeared that there must be another, besides that of the obstacle it presented to her union with Harrington; and I have at length adopted an opinion suggested by my dear father, that this circumstance was intended as an additional proof of the united liberality and firmness of Mr. Montenero's principles. He had married a lady of different religious persuasion, without being inclined to swerve in the least from his own; and he had brought up his daughter in the belief of her mother, but with an equal regard for both religions; inculcating thereby the principle that, provided the heart is sincere in its adoration, the conduct governed by justice, benevolence, and morality, the modes of faith and forms of worship are immaterial; all equally acceptable to that Almighty Being, who looks down on all his creatures with an eye of mercy and forgiveness. It is not wonderful that I should, in the present instance, have adopted this opinion, for it is that in which all my father's children have been educated: we regard our own faith as sacred, but we respect that of others, and believe it equally capable of conducting them to the Throne of Grace. It would be gratifying to us to know how far our impressions respecting Berenice are correct.

In the character of Ormond, we found much to interest: its gradual development and formation, by casual circumstances, sometimes apparently adverse to its improvement, are happily delineated. This work forms a satisfactory contrast to "Vivian,"[16] a portrait, which tho' capable of proving eminently useful, leaves on the mind those unpleasant feelings which the view of such instability of character, whether real or fictitious, must always excite; while the firmness and decision of Ormond, united with good sense and nobleness of mind, promise every thing that we desire for our hero's happiness and respectability.

Miss Edgeworth will, I think, believe me when I say that I pause and hesitate, wondering at my own presumption in thus venturing, unasked, to offer my crude opinions; the confidence created by past indulgence alone encourages me to proceed. Still let me add, that I could not have ventured to trespass further than with acknowledgments on the receipt of the books, had I not been assured that Miss Edgeworth honoured my second letter with a reply, which unfortunately, I have never received.

The circumstance of my having addressed you, and obtained an answer, we had never mentioned, and we believed the secret confined to our family circle, till one of my brothers, travelling last summer to the northward, was astonished at being questioned respecting the letter mentioned in "Harrington," just then published in New York. The ladies who enquired perceived his unfeigned surprise and told him they had heard from Mrs. Griffith[17] of Burlington, a correspondent of Miss Edgeworth's,

16. One of the *Tales of Fashionable Life* (London, 1812), "Vivian," according to RLE's prefatory note, "exposes one of the most common defects of mankind. To be 'infirm of purpose' is to be at the mercy of the artful, or at the disposal of accident."

17. Mrs. Mary Griffith (d. 1877), American writer. She published two works anonymously, *Our Neighborhood* and *Camperdown: or News from Our Neighborhood* (Philadelphia, 1836). Widowed, she supported herself and her children on a farm in Charles Hope, New Jersey. Little is known of her, but her utopian story, "Three Hundred Years Hence," the first story in *Camperdown*, is the subject of an extended analysis by Vernon Louis Parrington, Jr., *American Dreams: A Study of American Utopias* (Providence: Brown University Press, 1947).

that his sister was the lady alluded to. They had also heard from Mrs. Griffith that Miss E. had again written to his sister. The last pleasing, and encouraging piece of information came very seasonably to divert my thoughts from the formidable idea of being an object of general conversation. I forgave Mrs. Griffith the pain in consideration of the pleasure. But what can have become of this much desired letter? By what conveyance was it sent, and could the direction be mistaken?

I will not abandon the hope of receiving a reply to these enquiries, and I ask yet more, to know the contents of that letter, which I fear will not reach me. While complying with this request, Miss Edgeworth will have the goodness to say, if in seeking an occasional intercourse with her, I have exceeded the limits of her indulgence. Sensible as I am of the selfishness of this wish, and that I can offer no equivalent for the gift to my individual self of moments so precious and so worthily devoted to the general benefit, I cannot prevail on myself to suppress it; yet I should be unworthy of the lessons I have received from Miss Edgeworth were I unable to submit to a disappointment, severe as this would be, without murmuring. I cannot conclude without repeating assurances of esteem and admiration; yet even these words do not express all I feel.

With every wish for Miss Edgeworth's prosperity and happiness, I have the honour of subscribing myself,

her very grateful friend and servant
R. Mordecai

[*Richmond, Virginia*]
March 3rd, 1821

[*Holograph copy*]

That I have this moment closed the volume containing the life of the admirable, the excellent Mr. Edgeworth,[18] is the only

---

18. *Memoirs of Richard Lovell Edgeworth, Esq. Begun by Himself and Concluded by his Daughter Maria Edgeworth*, 2 vols. (London, 1820).

apology I can offer for again venturing to address his daughter. The feelings awakened by viewing under various aspects, both publick and private, that character which I long since learned to love and venerate, have repeatedly risen to enthusiasm; and I find it difficult to believe that I have not at least some mental connexion with those in whose deep regret at the loss of *such a friend* I so truly sympathise. Pardon, my dear madam, the presumption which I am aware such a claim implies, but let it but plead for me that I have a heart capable of appreciating, even as it deserves, that superiority in talent and virtue, which governed by true wisdom sought its greatest enjoyment in domestick affection.

To express all I have felt, while perusing with deep interest the memoirs of a life so well spent, so happy in the capacity of imparting and of receiving happiness, would require an eloquent pen; mine can only tell that to the sensibility—which such departed excellence excites in all who can feel that it has been—a desire is added to imitate as far as possible those virtues which ensured happiness to everyone who shared the blessing of their benignant and fostering influence. The permission to become intimately acquainted with the annals of such a life is a high privilege, one which no inducement offered by modern literature could tempt me to forego. It is not my intention to speak of the style of this work; a consciousness of incapacity would forbid the attempt, even if inclination prompted it; yet let me be allowed to remark that the part written by Mr. Edgeworth has struck me as combining that sort of plainness, that noble simplicity, of which Dr. Franklin, where he appears as his own biographer, forms another instance, with a degree of ease and sprightliness and a freedom from egotism, which render the work peculiarly attractive.

Of the 2nd volume, by another hand, I dare only add that it has left on my mind an impression at once vivid and tender of the excellencies it has sought to portray. I might imitate the expression ascribed to your 4th Henry, in part at least; the delicacy of Miss Edgeworth will not be wounded by the allusion; she will unite with me in exclaiming, "But, far more happy the daughter, who finds in a parent such merits to record!"[19]

Ere I lay aside the pen, I must once more indulge myself in expressing my sense of obligation towards the authors of Practical Education, and of the other various works, for which the world is indebted to the same enviable co-partnership. They have been useful to me, both in the regulation of my own mind, and in forming those of others. At this moment, perhaps, I feel more sensibly than ever their claims on my gratitude, since a contemplated change of situation will render their precepts more than ever invaluable. In a few weeks, my fate will be united with that of an amiable and intelligent man, already the father of a family.[20] Should I prove myself capable of performing the sacred duties, which I am sensible will be incumbent on me, it is to these wise and benevolent friends that I shall be principally indebted for success. One more circumstance of family interest, I take the liberty of mentioning; that, in consequence of the declining health of a son and daughter, my father found it necessary to give up (in a very flourishing state) that seminary of education which he had conducted for ten years and has removed with his family to Virginia.

I am asked by a member of my family if I am not fearful of appearing to press myself on Miss Edgeworth's notice? I answer that I am not. I know too well how to appreciate the character of Miss Edgeworth to have any apprehension of her misconceiving mine.

Permit me to offer my best wishes for the continuance of health and happiness to yourself, and the amiable individuals by whom you are surrounded, and to express the affectionate respect with which I am,

Dear Madam, Your obliged and grateful servant,
R. Mordecai

19. Miss Mordecai seems to be paraphrasing a passage from Shakespeare's *Henry IV*.
20. Rachel Mordecai married Aaron Marx Lazarus on 21 March 1821.

Accept, my dear Madam, my warm thanks for the pleasure your letter has given to me and to all my family. My father used to love your letters and formed from them a high opinion both of the goodness of your understanding and of your heart. He would say, could he now feel for what is done on Earth, "Happy the man to whom she is to be united. She will make an excellent wife as she has been an excellent daughter." Could you know how the idea of what my Father would say or think or feel recurs to me always whenever I am interested by any circumstance strongly, you would be well pleased that I should thus congratulate you and your husband on your marriage, simply by thinking what he would have felt had he heard of it.

It was impossible for me to read your letter so full of respect, tenderness, and let me say it, *just* admiration for the memory of my beloved Father, without tears of pain and pleasure. It is most gratifying, touching, and soothing to his children and to his widow to find that he lives in the hearts of the good and wise, that his character is fully appreciated and that his virtues excite even at such a distance so much affection and such noble emulation. How you would have loved him had you known him as we did. I feared that I had never been able to represent him fully and fitly; yet you seem to understand his character so well that you have comforted me and strengthened my hopes that others may be as kindly disposed and as quick in comprehending even what is inadequately expressed.

We are truly grateful for your sympathy, and believe me that your claim of "*mental connection*" with us is willingly accepted. No earthly thing could dispose this family so kindly towards you as the respect and affection you have shown for my Father's character. If ever you should come to Europe, remember Ireland, remember Edgeworthstown, and be assured that there is a family who will give you a cordial welcome, and where you will find that domestic union which you rightly think the first of human blessings. Though without him we have lost [*much*] (this family never can be what it has been), yet in union and affection among all its members, it is and I trust ever will be the same, and we each and all make it the comfort and principle and ambition of our lives to follow his example and to pursue all his plans as far as possible. His representative, my eldest brother,[21] is indeed worthy to be his representative, and could he see all that his son has done these four last years he would give him the best reward that son could have upon Earth, his Father's full and affectionate approval.

My brother has established in this village a school for poor and rich where children of all religious persuasions are instructed together and live and learn to be good and happy. In a country like this where unfortunately much political and religious prejudice and party spirit prevail, such a school is a phenomenon. Above 170 boys now attend it. It will, I hope, do infinite good by its example and by the proof positive of its being possible to effect this much. His *integrity* in keeping to the spirit as well as the letter of his word, never to interfere with the religious opinions of those who come to his school, has been the principal cause of his success in an undertaking in which so many have failed. All the pupils go to their respective places of worship every Sunday and the Catholic priest, the Protestant clergyman, and the Dissenting minister each give religious instruction to their several parishioners without jealousy and without interfering with each other.

I will tell you my dear Madam since you are so kind as to be interested in all we write—(see how powerful habit is! I cannot bring myself to say *I* instead of *we*)—I have published two small volumes this summer called "*Rosamond, Sequel to Rosamond in Early Lessons,*" for young people from eleven to fifteen. If I had any opportunity, I should have pleasure in sending Rosamond to you.

21. Lovell Edgeworth (see Appendix A).

I have never, I believe, written to you since I received a very kind letter from you about Harrington and Ormond. It came to my hands when I was so unhappy that I could not write any answer. The feeling that my Father would have been so much gratified by it and that it came when he could no longer sympathise with me as he had done for so many happy years was dreadful. I have since read your letter again lately, after an interval of near four years, and feel grateful now for not having thanked you. I wish you would thank your kindhearted father for the reason he gave for my making Berenice turn out to be a Christian. It was a better reason than I own I had ever thought up. I really should be gratified if I could have any testimony even were it ever so slight from those of your persuasion that they were pleased with my attempt to do them justice. But except from you, my dear Madam, and one or two other individuals in England, I have never heard that any of the Jewish persuasion received Harrington as it was intended. A book or merely a print of any celebrated Jew or Jewess or a *note* expressing their satisfaction with my endeavors or with my intentions would have pleased—I will not say my vanity—but my heart.

I hope this letter will find you in the full enjoyment of all the happiness of domestic life which you appear so well formed to value, to share, and to adorn with all the treasures of a cultivated mind. As you do not tell me the name of the happy man who by this time calls you *his*, I must direct this letter to Miss Mordecai.

Believe me, Dear Madam, your grateful
Maria Edgeworth

[P.S.] I send you a sketch of Edgeworthstown—I mean of our house which is in a lawn at the entrance of our village. This little drawing is done for you by one of my younger sisters.

I have but lately returned from a tour to the continent of several months, four spent in Paris, three in Geneva, and two in England, and perhaps I may be in England and in London by the time this reaches you, but whenever you write, direct to me as usual at Edgeworthstown and your letter will be safe and will be forwarded to me by some of my family if I am not at home. If you should ever wish to send any book to me, direct it to be left for me at Mr. Hunter's, Bookseller, St. Paul's Churchyard, London.

[Holograph copy]

Wilmington, N.C., Sept. 16th, 1821

A few days since I had the pleasure of receiving Miss Edgeworth's kind and gratifying letter of the 21st June. To believe myself possessed of a place in the esteem of one whom reason had so long taught me to admire, whom I have learned to know, and whom to know is to love, is delightful alike to my mind and heart. The one would rejoice at a union with the intelligent, the other swells with emotion at the idea of being deemed worthy of affinity to the Good. Scarcely can I credit that such a distinction has been awarded me by the Edgeworth family, that their revered, their excellent father regarded me, so far as his knowledge extended, with sentiments of approbation! What an incitement to deserve the good opinion thus generously bestowed; to discharge every duty with cheerfulness, and to seek in the silent assent of my own heart that sanction without which even such praises have not their full value.

I feel, my dear Madam, in its full force the manner in which you offer congratulations on my marriage by imagining the expressions which would have been used on the occasion by your beloved father. None could be so gratifying, so touching to my heart; it is, believe me, capable of conceiving, of entering into the sentiments of yours; it comprehends how readily when interested, you recall the idea of him so much respected, so tenderly beloved, who had for so many happy years participated in your every emotion, at once the experienced guide, the kind companion of your way. A few words in your preface to his life had already familiarized this to my mind, and with you I lamented that he was no longer permitted kindly to aid, and with his judgment to give confidence to your exertions. Yet so far as my testimony may be admitted, this additional confidence was requisite for *your* satisfaction alone. To every mind free from prejudice and open to conviction, the character, the sentiments, the principles of the excellent Mr. Edgeworth are fairly and justly portrayed, and the mind which bears even a remote assimilation to his, by its capacity to admire his talents, to love his virtues, will acknowledge with delight how intimately, in the perusal of his memoirs, it has been permitted to enter into his thoughts and feelings. For my own part, long accustomed to view his opinions and precepts not blindly, but through convictions as a standard of truth and justice, I read with such a degree of interest as the ties of individual friendship might have inspired, and the letter I addressed to you on closing the volume was, after an interval of some days, revised because I feared that the warmth and enthusiasm of some expressions *might* occasion a doubt of their sincerity. "How you would have loved him, had you known him as we did!" Ah, my dear madam, I feel assured that I should, and how grateful am I to you for thinking thus kindly of me. Very, very often has the idea of personal intercourse with your family been permitted to charm my imagination, rather as a delightful chimera than as one of those probabilities which reason could venture to promise was in store for me. My change of situation (combining at once the duties of wife and mother) renders such a prospect more remote than ever, but should it ever be my lot to visit Europe, how gladly shall I remember Edgeworth's town, how joyfully accept the cordial, the more than flattering invitation which the letter before me so kindly conveys. I feel assured that I should behold domestick unity, combined with all the charms of intelligence and cultivation. It appears like vanity in me, even to *fancy* myself a member of such a group, the companion of—I dare only say, *Miss Edgeworth*. To you, who know so well what would have been viewed with pleasure and approbation by your revered father, it must indeed be a source of the purest gratification to see in your brother one worthy to be his representative, making usefulness his aim, and blest by finding in success the reward of his laudable endeavours. The school you mention must indeed from every account I have read of Ireland be a phenomenon there, nor do I doubt that its salutary effects will many, many years hence be even more generally felt and acknowledged than at present. The union of sects and parties in cordiality and good faith in a situation, where abstracted from those sources of dissention, the pursuits and interests of each individual are rendered the same, cannot fail to diminish prejudice, to promote good will and social order, and eventually to render merit the only criterion for bestowing friendship or preference. From the limits of a school, the precincts of a village, the benefit may extend to a whole community; perhaps in time to an entire country, which after long suffering, and struggling under oppression, may more than ever prove itself deserving of an equality of rights, of internal comfort and prosperity. I ought not perhaps to have thus far pursued a subject, with which I am but imperfectly acquainted; yet I believe I am not wrong in supposing that even such may be the result of institutions conducted on the wise and liberal principles of which your brother has given a meritorious example.

You greatly oblige me my dear Madam by mentioning the work in which you have lately been engaged. I have not yet been as fortunate as to obtain it, tho' if not already, it will shortly be published in this country. Yet tho' I shall procure it here, I cannot willingly relinquish the gratification of receiving it from yourself. Any packet directed to my brother Mr. Samuel Mordecai, Richmond, or to Mr. Aaron Lazarus, Wilmington, N.C. and given in charge to Messrs. Marx and Wheatall [London] will be carefully attended to. See how eagerly I avail myself of even an intended kindness, but is it not natural that we should covet proofs of the esteem of those whom *we* most highly esteem and admire?

The address above, you have already conceived to be that of my husband; it is so, and happy am I to add, a husband worthy of my tenderest affection. He had long possessed my esteem and approbation, but I hesitated in accepting a station which I was not confident of ability to fill consistently with my own comfort, with his, and with that of his family—two sons and five daughters! Still was I induced to yield, nor have I for a moment found reason to repent my decision. Surrounded by children docile, affectionate, and reasonable; accustomed to obey, and desirous of improvement, it is a pleasure to me to guide, to direct, and to contribute by every means in my power, at once to their present and future happiness. Fortunately Mr. L's ideas on the subject of education concur entirely with mine, and tho' he may have thought on it less deeply, and may consequently be less systematick, we are governed by the same general principles, and are in no danger of acting in opposition to each other. A younger sister just turned twelve whom I have perhaps mentioned in a former letter, as having been from her infancy my immediate charge, our kind parents have for the present permitted me to retain, and on leaving the parental roof, she was my companion. Possessing intelligence beyond her years, and uncommon sweetness of disposition, I have pleasing anticipations of what her maturity may prove. Still watchful solicitude perceives various errors, which to the best of my ability I seek to correct, and trust my cares may prove successful. My dear father often acknowledges himself happy in his children; the younger ones daily improving, promise to be a comfort to his declining years. The pleasure expressed by him on the receipt of your letter, which was forwarded to me from Richmond, increased the gratification it is so well calculated to impart. I will not apologise for this family detail; your goodness my dear Madam will suggest its excuse.

You kindly account for omitting to reply to my letter on the receipt of Harrington and Ormond; my wishes and the interest I shall ever feel in the Edgeworth family can alone give me a claim on any portion of your valuable time, but the hope you now give me of being occasionally permitted to enjoy an intercourse so highly prized is indeed delightful.

I regret that such testimonials of approbation have not been offered to the Author of Harrington as the candour and liberality of sentiment it evinces justly render her due. That none have proceeded from this country is readily to be accounted for, and should be attributed not to the work itself being undervalued, but to a certain degree of diffidence, which has probably prevented a direct address from any individual. None it seems would venture as I have done to address a letter to one of the most celebrated women in Great Britain. In me a sort of enthusiasm inspired by warm admiration of goodness, even more than of talent, gave rise to that temerity, which has been not only pardoned but so generously recompensed. I recollect seeing, about the time "Harrington" was published in this country, a letter from a Miss Gratz[22] of Philadelphia, a jewess distinguished by superior and highly cultivated understanding, expressing her approbation of the work, as well as her admiration of the amiable intentions of the Author. Were I a correspondent of Miss Gratz's, it would give me pleasure to write to her on this subject, but unfortunately for me, it is only through the medium of mutual friends that we are known to each other. Should I meet with any American publication deserving a place in your library, with how much pleasure shall I forward it as directed; this idea long since occurred to me, but I felt not altogether authorised to obtrude myself again on Miss Edgeworth's notice. It is almost superfluous to say that *I* have never written a line for publication, but in making notes on education for my own guidance, and on the plan suggested to me by your inestimable

22. Rebecca Gratz (1781–1869), philanthropist. She helped found the Philadelphia Orphan Society in 1815 and served as secretary for forty years. Sir Walter Scott's Rebecca in *Ivanhoe* probably was based upon Washington Irving's description of Miss Gratz's character. After the novel appeared, Scott wrote Irving, "How do you like your Rebecca? Does the Rebecca I have pictured compare well with the pattern given?"

work on the subject, how often have I wished that your better judgment could assure me I was pursuing a right course. To your precepts it is true I had ready access, and gladly have I resorted to them, pleased when they occasionally confirmed my opinions and practice.

Accept my thanks for the sketch of Edgeworth's-town house and offer them if you please to Miss Sophy Edgeworth[23] for her kindness in executing it for me. In looking at it I almost figure to myself the group of its amiable inhabitants, imagine their employments, and wish I could partake in their cheerful and improving conversation. May I say that with two countenances I have long wished to become acquainted. With *his* who now alas! no longer presides over his happy family; with hers, who while she mourns his departure, consecrates in her heart the remembrance of his virtues. The former I hoped to find prefixed to his memoirs and with that view endeavoured to obtain the English edition, but could not procure it, nor have I been able to learn whether or not it is thus enriched.

Your visit to the Continent has I hope been attended with benefit to your health and spirits, and I cannot help extending this hope so far as to anticipate pleasure from the appearance of some new work, suggested perhaps by scenes there presented to a mind fertile in its own resources, and gathering from each apparently trivial incident some valuable addition to its stores. My pen is very willing to proceed but I must no longer my dear madam indulge it at your expense. With every wish for the welfare and happiness of your whole family, let me beg you will accept the grateful and affectionate remembrance of

Rachel Lazarus

23. Sophia Edgeworth (see Appendix A).

[*Holograph copy*] Wilmington, July 29th, 1822

My dear Madam:

Various little circumstances have interfered with my inclination to address you, and caused me to delay much longer than I wished the acknowledgment of your kind and gratifying attentions. I have perused "Frank" with pleasure, a renewal of that pleasure for which I have been so often indebted to the pen of Miss Edgeworth, whose lessons I dwell on and treasure up in memory, solicitous to *imbibe*, if possible, sentiments and principles of which I feel so entirely the truth and the value. Both "Rosamond" and "Frank" have always been peculiarly interesting to me, from a belief that they in many instances trace family scenes, sketches from real life; the "Sequel" to each appears to me to convey this impression of reality, even more vividly than the preceding parts, and in the wise and benignant father, I constantly identify the excellent and ever-lamented Mr. Edgeworth.

It was very pleasing to me to remark the eagerness and delight visible in the countenance of each member of our young family when the packet was opened which contained "another of Miss Edgeworth's books." The younger girls regretted that they could not read the whole, but consoled themselves with the reflection that they could understand *some part* of it *now*, and by and by they could read the rest. The period has arrived when I may hope to look forward with increased delight and interest to the effect of these invaluable lessons. I am a mother, and for my sweet promising boy, now in his 6th month, I already begin to experience a mother's hopes, her fears, and her solicitude! Already are his dispositions and little habits to be formed and cultivated; and deeply sensible as I am, of the importance of training them rightly, it is not surprising that I should be watchful and diffident in undertaking a task so interesting.

The truth of your observation that children are sometimes injured by our too great anxiety to render them exactly what we wish, I have found verified in my own practice. This danger will now increase, and I must be more than ever vigilant in training *myself*, that I may become the more competent to guide usefully and judiciously the early years of my son. We have allowed ourselves the gratification of prefixing to the family name of Marx, that of *Edgeworth*;[24] to you, my dear madam, this liberty will not I hope be otherwise than acceptable.

I intended to mention above that "Frank" has been published in this country and is spoken of in terms of high approbation. Shall I be excusable in making a short extract from a review of this work which lately appeared in a library journal? "The impression Miss Edgeworth gives of society is so distinct and vivid, there is so much truth and precision in her portraits, she understands so perfectly and describes so accurately the language of polite conversation, that in reading her works the feeling of reality is seldom interrupted. With these talents for literary distinction, Miss E. has through life preferred the useful to the brilliant. Among her endowments there is such a predominance of plain, practical sense that we might perhaps describe her in a single phrase as the Franklin of Novelists."

Since my residence here, I have often wished that I could meet with an opportunity to send you several curious productions of our soil: among others, that singular species of Mimosa, the Venus's fly trap (Dionaea Muscipula)[25] which is found in great abundance in the open fields. The country around us, tho'

24. Marx Edgeworth Lazarus, b. 26 February 1822; d. 20 May 1896 (see Appendix B).
25. Venus's-flytrap (*Dionaea muscipula*). This somewhat rare plant was found in abundance in the Burgaw Savannah, some twenty-five miles north of Wilmington. "Insectivorous plants, including *Sarracenia flava* and *Dionaea muscipula*, added a note of drama to the extraordinary display of wild flowers on the Burgaw Savannah. The latter plant is known as Venus's-flytrap. It is almost entirely restricted in its distribution to a small portion of southeastern North Carolina, though it does also occur in a small section of South Carolina. . . . During the course of his travels in the 1770's, William Bartram observed extensive savannahs in southeastern North Carolina and noted the occurrence of Venus's-flytrap in them: Harper, *Travels of William Bartram*, p. 299. And in his in-

low, sandy, and sterile, abounds in beautiful perennials; the Magnolia grandiflora is seen in all its rich luxuriance, its large, white, tulip formed flower finely contrasts the thick dark green foliage. The wax myrtle,[26] indigenous to our soil, produces a berry of which candles, much resembling those of dark green wax, are made; to the poorer class of people it is an article of domestick economy. The foliage of various trees has in damp situations a singular appearance. A sort of long grey moss is formed on them, which, without destroying the verdure, suspends itself from the branches, and waving in the wind gives them a hoary and to me not uninteresting aspect. When stripped of its external coat, this moss exactly resembles horse hair; it is collected in quantities and buried in marshy spots, and when dried and cleaned, makes excellent mattresses. These productions were new and remarkable to me, and I mention them because I am inclined to believe that to Miss Edgeworth no species of information is unwelcome, how humble soever the source whence it flows.

Permit me, my dear madam, to offer through you for myself and Mr. Lazarus our respectful salutations to the amiable Mrs. Edgeworth and the other members of your much esteemed

---

troduction to the account of his travels, William Bartram includes an account of the insectivorous plants that he found in 'green meadows': *ibid.*, pp. liii–liv.

"Harper notes that Governor Dobbs of North Carolina was, in 1759, the first to announce the discovery of Venus's-flytrap: *ibid.*, p. 494. In a letter Dobbs wrote the following year, the governor described the plant as follows: 'But the great wonder of the vegetable kingdom is a very curious unknown species of sensitive; it is a dwarf plant: the leaves are like a narrow segment of a sphere, consisting of two parts, like the cap of a spring purse, the concave part outwards, each of which falls back with indented edges (like an iron spring fox trap); upon any thing touching the leaves, or falling between them, they instantly close like a spring trap, and confine any insect or any thing that falls between them; it bears a white flower; to this surprising plant I have given the name of Fly Trap Sensitive'" (Harry Roy Merrens, *Colonial North Carolina in the Eighteenth Century* [Chapel Hill: University of North Carolina Press, 1964], pp. 260–61).

26. Wax myrtle, also known as bayberry, candleberry, tallowshrubs. One species is classified as *Cerothamnus carolinensis*.

family, and to assure you of the sincere regard with which I shall ever be,

> Miss Edgeworth's grateful and affectionate servant
> R. Lazarus

> Edgeworthstown, January 15, 1823

Dear Madam,

For your persevering kindness in writing to me and depending upon my sympathy notwithstanding my silence, accept my cordial thanks. I have been travelling with two of my sisters[27] in France and Switzerland and England for the greatest part of the last two years and have had scarcely time to write any letters except to Mrs. Edgeworth[28] and my nearest relations. But though I have not told you so, depend upon it, I have rejoiced in your happiness, in your happy marriage and in the birth of your child. May he inherit all his mother's understanding and amiable, benevolent disposition. Your husband may add what he pleases of his own to this wish, but I think it will satisfy him just as it is.

Your frequent recurrence to my father's character and opinions is most kind and gratifying to me. I never can forget the pleasure your first letter to me gave him and the high opinion he formed of the writer. It was he who immediately excited me to write something to show you at least my wish to do justice to your people. I have always regretted that Harrington so imperfectly fulfilled my object. It should have been a strong picture of a great character resisting persecution. But that is past. You and your father accepted the will for the deed. Thank you. I have also received lately a gratifying acknowledgment from a Jew of considerable talents, Mr. Noah,[29] now High Sheriff of New York

27. Fanny and Harriet (see Appendix A).
28. Frances Anne Beaufort (1769–1865), fourth wife of RLE.
29. Mordecai Manuel Noah (1785–1851), American journalist. He published widely and was the author of several dramas. His best-known work was *Travels in England, France, Spain, and the Barbary States* (London, 1819).

and sometime ago Consul from the American Government to Algiers. With a very handsome letter he sent me his book of "Travels in England, France, Spain, and the Barbary States." It is a curious and lively book, tedious in some parts from his thinking it necessary to give a geographical description and historical view of every place he comes to, but independently of that shews much talent and conveys various information. It is besides peculiarly valuable to me as at once a proof of Jewish ability and of Jewish gratitude—for a very slight service or attempt to serve. I own that I should like to possess any book of merit written by any female of your persuasion or any mark of their ingenuity, even in needlework or any other way would be prized by me on the same principle.

I am very much obliged to you for the kind thought you had of sending me some of your beautiful American shrubs. The magnolia grandiflora we have in perfection and abundance in England and Ireland. The wax myrtle also is common. Our Irish bogs produce a plant very like it but does not produce wax in sufficient quantity for consumption. The Venus's fly trap is not common because of the difficulty of preserving it in hot houses. We have no hot house, only a green house. I should be more obliged to you for a little packet of seeds of any American flowers or plants, and if you would make a collection of insects, it would be valuable to our young people, with notes of their history and habitudes by yourself or your young people. Direct any packet you send to me at Mr. Hunter's, 72 St. Paul's Church-yard, London, if you send by a vessel bound for England, or if you send by a vessel bound for Dublin, direct to me to the care of Messrs. Hutton, Summerhill, Dublin. Direct your common letters undercover to Mr. Millar, Bookseller, Fleet Street, London.

I am very glad to hear that you like the sequels of Frank and Rosamond. You would oblige me by communicating any little remarks you may chance to hear on the different parts of these little books, for it is only by hearing the free observations of

copy be taken of it; I have just sent it under this restriction to Lord Bathurst,[30] one of our Cabinet Ministers.

There is at present in Scotland a Mr. John Hunter,[31] who has come from America to publish a book in London on the manners of the North American Indian tribes among whom he was born and resided seventeen years. His book is published and it has not succeeded I am told quite as well as was expected from his having, it is said, employed some literary person to correct and put it in form for him. It would have pleased more if he had allowed it to appear without correction in his own language; this would have given internal evidence of its being a genuine production of one who had lived among the people whom he describes. Mr. John Hunter does not know who his parents were; he took his name John from someone who was kind to him in his childhood and the name of Hunter he chose from his occupation of a hunter. Mrs. Griffith, a lady formerly of Philadelphia now of Charlieshope in New Jersey, who has for several years corresponded with me, wrote me an account of this man and gave him a letter of introduction to me. But as I was not in London he went to the lady at whose house Mrs. Griffith told him I had been the year before, Lady Elizabeth Whitbread,[32] and she introduced him to her brother Lord

30. Henry, third Earl Bathurst (1762–1834). Among other official positions he held the office of secretary for war and colonies until April 1827 and lord president of the council in the government of the duke of Wellington from 1828 to 1830. He was one of a number of officials whose franking privileges Maria Edgeworth availed herself of. She met Lord Bathurst in 1818 at Bowood, a great classical house created by Robert Adam, where they were the guests of Lord and Lady Lansdowne. In 1821, ME was the guest of Lord and Lady Bathurst at Cirencester Park, "an antient house with modern furniture and comfortable luxuries."

31. John Dunn Hunter (ca. 1798–1827), adventurer who claimed to have been kidnapped and raised as an Indian. His *Manners and Customs of Several Indian Tribes Located West of the Mississippi* (Philadelphia, 1823) was reprinted in London the same year as *Memoirs of a Captivity among the Indians of North America, from Childhood to the Age of Nineteen*. He was widely received in England but in America later was exposed as an imposter.

32. Lady Elizabeth Whitbread (d. 1846), daughter of the first Earl Grey and wife of Samuel Whitbread, English politician, heir to the Whitbread brewing for-

Grey[33] and several persons of literature and political consequence in London. I hear from them and from some of our friends in Scotland that he is a very interesting person, combining the frankness and raciness of character of a savage with the civility and benevolence of civilized life.

It is curious to observe how soon and easily a real savage takes the polish of what we call gentlemanlike manners and acquires what we call a fashionable air. They do this much more quickly than it is usually done by any civilized individual; a vulgar person, after a certain age, can never acquire a polite appearance or learn even the little forms and etiquette of the society of the higher classes. But in this instance of John Hunter and in that of Le Boo[34] and others I have heard the same remark from good judges. Indeed it may be accounted for by observing that our vulgar civilized people have many previous awkward habits to conquer and perhaps a sense of shame from an indistinct consciousness of this together with an awe from feeling themselves in what they think superior society which prevents their having full possession of their senses and faculties to observe what others in company do and to imitate their manners. The savage powers of imitation are perhaps for this reason among many others more undisturbed and quicker than ours.[35] I regret much that I have not myself seen Mr. Hunter.

---

tune. Maria Edgeworth was a frequent guest of Lady Elizabeth Whitbread's in Kensington.

33. Charles Grey, second Earl Grey (1764–1845), English statesman. He became prime minister in 1830 upon the fall of the duke of Wellington's government. He and his chancellor, Lord Brougham, forced the first Reform Bill (1832) through the House of Lords.

34. Lee Boo was a native of the Pelew Islands, on the western fringe of the Carolines in the Pacific. Captain Henry Wilson of the *Antelope* was wrecked on the Pelews on 9 August 1783, and while reparing his ship with the aid of the natives came to know Abba Thulle, the rupack or king. The king sent his second son, Lee Boo, to England to be educated. He charmed everyone with his delicate manners but died of smallpox on 27 December 1784, aged twenty. He was buried at Rotherhithe in London; a monument was erected by the East India Company.

35. ME here echoes a thought from her father's *Memoirs*: "Omai, a native of Otaheite, was then in England; he might well have passed for an European. It

We are at present reading *the Pioneers*. It is not in general liked so well as *the Spy*;[36] but I have not yet read enough to judge for myself.

By the by, I was surprised and shocked lately to see in an English paper copied from the New York *Gazette* (I think) an extract from a letter of Miss Edgeworth's to a female correspondent in America—at the head of the paragraph in large letters "Critique by Miss Edgeworth on Washington Irving's last work," and then came a passage from one of my letters, the words of which I recollected indeed but certainly never when I wrote it foresaw the possibility of being published.[37]

My dear Madam believe me I was quite convinced that it was not you or any one belonging to you who had been guilty of this breach of private confidence. I feel assured that your principles and your practice on this subject are and would always be the same as my own. The letter from which the passage was published was addressed to Mrs. Griffith, and I have written to her as strongly as I could to prevent a similar occurrence; a total cessation of all communication would be then the only remedy. I am sure that she did not publish the paragraph herself, but she must have lent my letter or read it to some one who did what appears to me unjustifiable.

I cannot guess from your last whether you have received a letter which I wrote to you about three months ago in answer to that most kind and amiable letter of yours to me in which you announced your marriage—and in which you were so good as

---

was an extraordinary circumstance observable in his manners, that he had after a few month's residence in England, more the air and appearance of a gentleman, than it would have been possible for a native of England, ordinary station, to have obtained, after he had grown up to be a man" (pp. 381–82). Dr. Johnson made the same observation of Omai. Omai figures in some detail in Fanny Burney's *Memoir* of her father (see note 235). She spells the name *Omiah*.

36. James Fenimore Cooper (1789–1851), *The Spy* (1821), *The Pioneers* (1823).

37. ME's letter "to an American Lady" appeared in several publications of the period, among others in *Port Folio* 16 (1823): 86. Extracts from this letter wherein ME comments on *The Spy* are contained in *Fenimore Cooper: The Critical Heritage*, edited by George Dekker and John P. McWilliams (London and Boston: Routledge and Kegan Paul, 1973), p. 67.

to mention some American seeds and plants which you thought of sending me if I wished for them. The Venus's fly trap in particular I wish for as it is difficult to obtain that plant here; it must be packed with great care in moss. Also I should wish for some of that grass which grows upon your large trees and which makes such a picturesque appearance. If you are so good as to send any thing of this kind to London direct to Mr. Hunter, Bookseller, 72 St. Paul's Churchyard for Miss E., and he will forward them to me, or if the vessel in which they are shipped comes direct to Dublin, for Miss Edgeworth to the care of Mr. Williams, Parcel Office, Sackville Street.

I have lately been taking with two of my young sisters[38] a tour in the Highlands of Scotland where the wild romantic beauty of the country and the frequent falls of water from the mountains resemble I should think parts of your country. We were amused and pleased with the frank feudal pride, honor and kindness of the heads of Clans and the sight of a fine hardy happy race of independent mountaineers in love with their own country. Dressed in their Scottish plaids and filibegs, *etc.*, and walking with a sort of peculiar elastic independence they seemed to suit the dells and mountains and to be there to ornament the landscape for our pleasure.

We spent three weeks in Edinburgh and saw all the bright constellation of wits in that city, itself well worth seeing, the most romantically situated city in Europe, very like the views of Athens. It was shewn to us by our great and amiable friend Sir Walter Scott.

We spent three weeks with him afterwards at his own home in the country, at Abbotsford, in a beautiful castle which he has built on the banks of the Tweed within a mile or two of Melrose, whose beautiful Abbey we went to see with him. That Abbey is well described in Peter's Letters.[39]

38. Harriet and Sophia (see Appendix A).
39. John Gibson Lockhart (1794–1854), Scottish writer and editor, is commented on with some frequency in this correspondence. A brilliant student at

Sir Walter Scott has built and planted with as much taste as you might expect from his writings. In the course of twelve years his plantations have grown up, and he now has walks of miles under the shades of his own trees. When I saw how much he had planted and built and how much he gives of his time to the pleasures of society and conversation, I was still more amazed at the quantity he has written. But as he said to me, "People can always have time enough if they will but use all they have."

He is delightful in his own family, with the most simple yet polite manners and with a constant flow of various original conversation such as I never heard equalled, without the least effort, never trying to shine, always pleasing, never fatiguing his hearers. I have compared him with all the men of the greatest talents in London of the present day, and in powers of memory, in humor, in variety and above all in the powers of inventive faculty, he in my opinion surpasses them all. He is besides quite free from all petty meannesses, including inordinate love of fame and fear of rivalship; he is the most benevolent and happy author living—most amiable in his own family.

But I am writing in the dark and cannot delay longer to finish my letter else I lose this packet.

Believe me dear Madam I am always glad to hear from you, so write to me freely.

Yours sincerely,
Maria Edgeworth

Glasgow and Oxford, he became a lawyer in Edinburgh in 1816. In 1817 the Scottish Tories established *Blackwood's Magazine* in opposition to the Whig organ the *Edinburgh Review*. Lockhart joined the staff of *Blackwood's* and is credited with some of the caustic articles published in that magazine. He married Sir Walter Scott's oldest daughter, Sophia, in 1820, and they had three children. Lockhart became editor of the *Quarterly Review* in 1825. An indefatigable writer, he is best known as his father-in-law's biographer, author of *Life of Sir Walter Scott*, 7 vols. (1837–38). The work referred to above, *Peter's Letters to his Kinfolk*, appeared in 1819.

Wilmington, Dec. 20th, 1823

How rich and how highly favored do I feel, my dear Madam, with two of your delightful letters before me. The one dated Jan'y 5th was by some means unaccountably delayed and did not reach me till late in October. The indisposition of several members of our family prevented its immediate acknowledgment, and a few days since I had the pleasure to receive its successor of Sept. 30th. I rejoice that the Indian treaty was acceptable, and shall deem myself fortunate whenever I meet with any thing capable of imparting pleasure to one who daily affords instruction and delight to me. How kind are your expressions of acknowledgment, and how truly do you estimate me in seeing yourself present to my mind, "on every occasion where I can show you regard and confidence." I am, believe me, fully sensible of the happiness of being permitted to express sentiments, not only of admiration, but of warmth and cordiality towards Miss Edgeworth.

I send with this "Schoolcraft's Journal"[40] of the expedition under Gov. Cass. Tho' in some parts tediously minute, and on the whole better calculated to interest the Geologist and Mineralogist than the general reader, yet there is, I think, sufficient merit in many of his descriptions of the country they were exploring and in the Indian anecdotes to render his book deserving a perusal. For his account of the Indian Hieroglyphicks see page 211. Capt. Douglass[41] whom he mentions is the gentleman from whom the Indian correspondence was obtained; his work it is thought will be superior to this and when published I

40. Henry Rowe Schoolcraft (1793–1864), American traveler, ethnologist, and writer. In 1820 he accompanied General Lewis Cass as geologist in an expedition to the Upper Mississippi and Lake Superior areas, and he published *Narrative Journal of Travels Through the Northwestern Regions of the United States: Extending from Detroit through the Great Chain of American Lakes, to the Sources of the Mississippi River, Performed as a Member of the Expedition under Governor Cass, in the Year 1820* (Albany, 1821).

41. David Bates Douglass (1790–1849), engineer, soldier, teacher, apparently did not publish an account of the expedition.

will transmit it to you. It is a pity that Mr. Hunter did not trust to simplicity of style and originality of subject for the success of his work, or that it had not been retouched by the pen of a De Foe.[42] Your mode of investigating why a savage acquires the ease and urbanity of gentlemanlike manners, more readily than a civilized but vulgar person, appears to me perfectly just, tho' requiring perhaps some limitation. There must, I think, be a foundation in natural kindness of heart and disposition, on which to scatter with success the seeds of civilisation and refinement. This was a trait in the character of Le Boo and it appears also to exist in that of Mr. Hunter. Several Indians have been educated at the U.S. Military Academy, but after remaining there some years, all, I believe, have returned to live and die among their own people. You mention "the Pioneers"; the character of the old woodsman is said to be drawn from real life. It is but a short time since I saw an account given by one of our exploring parties of a man by whom they were kindly treated in the wilderness, and who like Natty had retired as the country by degrees obtained new settlers. Col. Boon[43] too, the first white inhabitant of Kentucky, delighted in the handsome and flourishing towns, which were springing up around him, but regretted that hunting ground was becoming more rare and continually removed further into the forest land. Lord Byron has I see noticed his

42. Daniel Defoe (ca. 1659–1731), English author, presented his fictions as true accounts.

43. Daniel Boone (1734–1820), pioneer, became one of the most venerated American heroes. The character of Natty Bumppo in Cooper's Leather-Stocking Tales, particularly in *The Pioneers* and *The Prairie*, reflects aspects of Daniel Boone. Among other suggested prototypes one finds the names of several Indian fighters—Tom Quick, Tim Murphy, Nat Foster, Nick Stoner—in addition to various members of the Shipman family, neighbors of Cooper. Cooper himself denied that Natty was modeled on any one prototype. "In a physical sense, different individuals known to the writer in early life certainly presented themselves as models, through his recollections; but in a moral sense this man of the forests is purely a creation" (cited by Robert E. Spiller, *Fenimore Cooper* [New York: Russell and Russell, 1963]). Byron made him into a world-wide celebrity when he devoted seven stanzas (61–67) of Canto Eight of *Don Juan* (1823) to Boone, apostrophizing him as the hero of Nature as opposed to the hero of civilization.

singular habits as well as his unbounded hospitality, a trait, which, were not the fact well attested, would hardly be expected to exist in the disposition of one who avoided the vicinity of man. Col. Boon's death was characteristick; he was found leaning against a tree, his gun in his hand, having breathed his last while occupied in his favorite pursuit. To return to the "Pioneers," I found it less interesting than "the Spy." Neither the hero nor the heroine pleases me, and I am not fond of being forced to spend my time in low company, especially with one so self opinioned as the Sheriff. It was ill judged I think to portray an Indian, old and infirm, who is hardly interesting till the death scene. The descriptive parts appeared to me to be written with spirit and accuracy, and that in them consists the chief merit of the books. How largely must I calculate on your indulgence to venture my opinions thus. I express them in the hopes of being able to judge from their coincidence with yours of what claim they have to correctness.

I saw some time since the paragraph which you mention as being extracted from one of your letters; tho' pleased to know your sentiments respecting some American productions, I could not approve the medium through which they were conveyed, and your remarks to me on the subject confirm the opinion formed by Mr. Lazarus and myself, that such a publication could not be agreeable to Miss Edgeworth. I had learned from the papers that you lately visited Scotland; when you delightfully describe the Highland scenery with what may be justly styled its picturesque inhabitants, your visit to Edinburgh and enjoyment of its brilliant society, but above all, the three weeks spent with the "great, the amiable, the benevolent, the happy Sir Walter Scott," I not only imagine and sympathise in your enjoyments, but, presumptuous tho' it be, tho' it *is*, cannot but wish that such pleasures could be mine. Improving society is delightful to me, and under such circumstances I should have wished to concentre [*sic*] every faculty in the eye and the ear. You will readily believe that I do not attempt to steal upon your opinions, by what may be an inadvertent expression, yet when you say "the *quantity* that Sir W. Scott has written" I am pleased to imagine that you coincide with those who believe him to be the author of the Waverley novels. I cannot conceive such an identity of mind, of taste, and of a peculiar sort of knowledge to exist between any two individuals, as is discoverable in Scott's poems and the novels in question. Some passages of the introduction to *Quentin Durward* which, it has been alleged, bear evidence that Sir Walter is *not* the author, convince me but the more strongly that he is. He delights us by using the privilege of sporting with his pen even in the detail of his own merits.

I am pleased to hear from yourself of the book presented by Mr. Noah; he is a man of considerable talents and great respectability and has been for some years Editor of a Gazette in N. York. I sincerely wish that you could be gratified in your desire to receive a book written by some female of our persuasion, but I hardly think there is one in this country who has attempted more than perhaps some fugitive pieces. America does not yet abound with authors of either sex, nor do I believe that there are ten ladies in the U.S. who have ventured to write any book for publication. This does not probably arise so much from incapacity as from incidental circumstances. It is only within a few years that female education has been deemed an object of importance, and even now it is but imperfectly conducted. They marry so young (not unusually at 14 or 15) that there is not time to complete their studies; then, especially in the Southern States, circumstances and custom alike require that they devote themselves to their family and domestick duties, so that mental cultivation is almost out of the question. Here may be found numbers of women, on whom, according to Addison's idea, Rhadamanthus might smile and assign to them a portion in Elysium; but a very, very few resembling the wife of Bulaeus.[44]

44. Rhadamanthus in Greek legend became one of the judges of the dead because of his inflexible integrity. The wife of Bulaeus eludes the editor.

We have been much gratified lately to remark the spirit of liberality publicly evinced towards our Sect. An old Law of the State of Maryland excludes by means of a test act any Israelite from holding an office of trust or profit. It has been attempted during several sessions to abrogate this law. A candidate lately published a letter to his constituents stating that he should vote against the repeal. The illiberal spirit evinced in his mode of reasoning seemed to excite general indignation and elicited a number of well-written replies, signed by members of every Christian Sect, in which ample justice is done to ours. It may appear singular, but is perfectly true, that a Lady of the Episcopal Church lately bequeathed a sum of money to be appropriated to the erecting of a Church and appointed my eldest brother her Executor; while about the same time a gentleman of the Jewish faith in Boston where there is no Synagogue left Christian Executors to invest money for the repairs of a Synagogue.

You request me to mention any little remark I may hear on the different parts of Frank and Rosamond. Both are favourites that deservedly stand unrivalled with our young people but I heard one observe that she thought Godfrey was allowed to be too *provoking* and too little considerate of the wishes of Rosamond, for a boy so well and so wisely educated. The affair of the Palanquin, I believe, occasioned this remark. The incident of Frank saving the life of his mother and fainting from excess of emotion was objected to as being "like a novel" and making him too much of a hero, and they thought the project of making an orrery too high a flight for so youthful a genius. All were enraptured with the contents of the traveller's box which they declared they could almost *see* in the description, and a young sister of mine asked if we did not think Miss Edgeworth the Walter Scott of children? And the *Miss Edgeworth* of grown up people might have been the reply. You see my dear Madam how readily I comply with your invitation to "write freely" and yet I own that in addressing you, I always practice a degree of restraint because I fear to displease by simply expressing the sentiments with which such wit and talents, united with so much wisdom, with all the gentle virtues and with a yet more rare simplicity of character inspire me. Pardon me if I have said too much; to speak at all and say less were impossible. Our youngest daughter, nine years of age, has been reading some of the second part of Harry and Lucy, which I found perfectly adapted to her comprehension. She was much pleased to find on a reperusal that she could in almost every instance anticipate Lucy's replies. This will when completed be the most valuable scientifick work in our language for young persons. "Scientifick Dialogues" are excellent, but the style of H[arry] and L[ucy] will always render it more attractive to the youthful reader. We were much interested in the school established by your brother, and I thank you for the idea you have given me of the manner in which Arithmetick is taught; tho' unable to practise it with full advantage, I have already found an attempt beneficial.

I send a small collection of seeds and have written to a friend for others, which will be forwarded to you from New York. I do not know whether this is a favourable season for removing Venus's fly trap; I shall however try some now and send more in the spring; a light moist soil is most favourable to its culture. You will find some pods of cotton in its several stages of advancement; the younger members of your family may not be familiar with its growth. We have not the cotton tree here; it grows on a bush from two to four feet high. The flower of a delicate straw colour they have seen in botanical engravings. You greatly overrate my talents, my dear Madam, in thinking me capable of becoming an entomologist; still I thank you for directing our attention to a pursuit at once so fertile and so interesting; we will not neglect it, and should our observation produce any thing worth imparting, I need not I hope assure you with how much pleasure it will be communicated. You will find a rough sketch of the Formica-leo, or as the children call it, "doodle" in the fly state; it was sent to me some time since by a friend with the notice annexed. I have endeavoured to obtain the work on Entomology which you mention, but am told it is not yet published in this country. I wish very much to know the method you employ in teaching History. It cannot, I think, be entirely by a regular course of reading that children like those in your little Books acquire such general and correct information. Both Mr. L. and myself sincerely thank you for the interest you so kindly express in our happiness and in the future welfare of our little son. My husband is but too ready to acquiesce in the limits which your very flattering opinion of the mother would set to the excellence of her offspring; pardon me, if I, my dear Madam, conscious of the imperfections of such a standard, am less easily satisfied. Our little Edgeworth (may the name impart to him some portion of those rare qualities so intimately associated with it) is now nearly two years of age; he speaks quite plainly and to us his conversation is already interesting. He is a lively, docile, affectionate little fellow, and will I hope continue a joy and comfort to his parents. Have the goodness my dear Madam, to make the best respects of Mr. L and myself acceptable to the several members of your amiable family and permit me once more to assure you that I am

Your obliged and affectionate friendly servant
R. Lazarus

Rough sketch of the myrmelion or formica leo in the fly state. (Here follows a draft which the reader must imagine). I took two of the largest I could find, put them in sand and fed them with insects. They soon refused to eat and entombed themselves, each in a ball of sand as large as a common marble. In this state they remained 29 or 30 days and then burst from their confinement, four-winged insects about 1 ½ inches long.

[*Sketch is over description*]

Your kind letter and your most judicious and interesting presents have just arrived here. We have unpacked them this day and I hasten to tell you that they are all perfectly safe and well after their journey and voyage. The Dionae is all alive in its native earth; it was so well packed that it could have had no excuse for dying and we shall take the greatest care of it. We have just been taking the best advice our books afford and Rees *Encyclopedia*[45] tells us that it likes shade, moisture, and warmth. All these it shall have and lodgings in greenhouse in summer and hot house in winter. But all our accounts agree in describing it as a plant which though it may live through the summer can scarcely survive a winter in these climates except under the care of professed Botanical gardens. I have great hopes however from Mrs. Edgeworth's care under which all the vegetable as well as animal world flourish. I shall give some of the young plants to the gardener of our Dublin Botanic garden who has been very obliging to some of my intimate friends, two sisters of Mrs. Edgeworth's. They rejoice that I have this rarity to offer him. I shall give another to another relative who is particularly fond of rare plants, and whom I particularly wish to gratify, the father-in-law of my youngest sister (Sophy) who was married a fortnight ago. You see my dear Madam how many people you have put it in my power to oblige.

I kept the unpacking of the little box of treasures for my sister Sophy, the happy and I must say pretty, graceful, amiable, dear little bride. We all gathered round her and it would have given you pleasure to have seen how much you afforded us. Your having so carefully and nicely packed and docketted all the articles delighted us on first opening the lid. You must know I am a rival packer and therefore my admiration must be well deserved before it can be obtained. Whenever I travel with my

45. Abraham Rees (1743–1825), *The New Cyclopaedia: or, Universal Dictionary of Arts and Sciences . . . Biography, Geography and History,* 44 vols. (London, 1802–20).

sisters, I always insist upon packing imperial and capbox with my own hands and pique myself upon the skilfulness of my arrangements—not a ruff, not a pleat spoiled! You may then be proud of my testimony in favor of your packing of the creeping leaf and the grasshopper and the spider all in their little box. There is however in that box a superfluous quantity of legs. After the white case of the grasshopper, the coaty-did [*katydid?*] has his full complement of two; there remains a green and a brown leg, one beautifully jointed and serrated. To whom or what does this belong? [*A small drawing of an insect's leg.*]

We have excellent magnifying glasses and have been in admiration as we looked at the head and eye of the withered grasshopper and the jointed serrated leg, and the spider's body. The creeping leaf is most curious; I have seen this in museums; but I am particularly glad to possess one for a little brother, Pakenham, who is fond of natural history. The cotton plant in all its stages he will also prize very much. All together these look like a white province rose and a half blown and a bud. The Palma Christi is common in our conservatories, from which the castor oil is obtained. Syringa is a shrub common in all our shrubberies and very hardy and as you say a graceful and beautiful shrub with cream coloured flowers, something like orange flowers, and smelling like cucumbers and orange flowers mixed. Lady's Slipper and Clematis of various kinds we also have. The evergreen daily rose I suspect is what we have and call the everblowing Chinese rose. We are curious to see whether there will be any difference between the Carolina Eglantine and any of our eglantines and eager to see the Yapon or Cassine;[46] as you say it is a tree, however, we must take patience. I am naturally impatient and am at this instant afraid I shall be dead before its bright scarlet berries cover it in this country. Mrs. Edgeworth will sow them this day however. The branch you sent had, as you foresaw, lost its beauty before it reached us, but

46. This plant was probably the *Ilex cassine*, a member of the holly family, known as yaupon or cassena.

the leaves were green and had the smell and taste of the inferior kind of tea. This we suppose is what Franklin in his journal speaks of as *tea of the country*.[47] We expect much from the Cherokee, evergreen, Georgia, or Nondescript rose; Rosamond was never more curious than I am to see what this Nondescript will be. What you call Indian arrow wood, American strawberry tree, or burning bush is common here under the name Euonymus. All the seeds common and uncommon shall be carefully sown and we shall see what comes of them. All the sods round the Dyonae shall also be put down carefully where any seeds that may chance to be in them may be noticed. I remember in Peyrouse's voyage some of the plants and shrubs which he sent to Paris in their native earth from the countries he visited died, but the gardener at the Jardin des Plantes had the good sense to preserve the earth and from which sprung up many grapes and plants new to the French.

Your grass or moss that grows as you describe from the branches of trees must give them a most curious, hoary appearance. It is I think the most extraordinary to us of anything you have sent us, and I thank you for having sent two specimens, one in its natural and one in its dressed state. It must make delightful mattresses and would I should think be worth exporting as it would compress into small bulk. If you do not forbid me I shall take the liberty of introducing your description of this in the sequel to Harry and Lucy which I am now writing and shall mention that a specimen of it was sent to me by an American friend.

The ground puppy seems to be a species of lizzard. The cases made by an insect in the leaves of the pine tree we hope are chrysali and may perhaps bring forth some living creatures in good time and with good warmth which they shall have.

The speech of the Indian who killed the white man by accident is admirable—magnanimous and eloquent. We are all

47. A decoction made of the leaves of the *Ilex vomitoria*, also termed yaupon or cassena, was the ceremonial drink of the aborigines.

much interested about him, and we request you will tell us the end of his history. Was he tried? And what judgment was pronounced? Tell us all about it.

Schoolcraft I have just turned over and from the dips I have made in the work it appears to me just what you describe it, too full of geological details for all but a geologist, yet interspersed with some curious facts on other subjects. The hieroglyphics especially are curious; the horrible account of Mr. D. whose feet were frozen off and whose wife deserted him in that condition made me shudder. I am glad that Mr. Schoolcraft and his companions sent him some relief as humanity required.

I fear you may be vexed by finding nothing new in this letter but an account of the safe arrival of your own presents; and yet I think after having taken so much pains to send them you must feel it satisfactory to have even this long-winded detail of their unpacking and of the pleasure they have given and give us in prospect. As soon as I can get an opportunity I will send you the little work on *Entomology*, which I mentioned, in which you will find the Lion Ant (I never saw a real one). I will also send you *Dialogues on Botany*. These two books are written by Mrs. E's two sisters,[48] but their names are not put to the works and you will keep them to yourself.

I forget whether in any of your letters you ever mentioned to me a novel of Sir W. Scott's (*Ivanhoe*) in which there is a charming Jewess, Rebecca; pray tell me again, even if you have told me once, how you like her. I have no doubt whatever from the internal evidence afforded me by the likeness between his conversation and the Waverley novels that he is the author of them. Indeed I know of no other person of talents and knowledge of Scottish manners equal to their production; yet he never will acknowledge them and he finds innumerable forms of eva-

48. [Harriet Beaufort], *Dialogues on Botany, For the Use of Young Persons; Explaining the Structure of Plants, and the Progress of Vegetation* (1819); [Louisa Beaufort], *Dialogues on Entomology, in Which the Forms and Habits of Insects Are Familiarly Explained* (1819).

sive speech by which he disavows them without telling perhaps what he conceives direct lies. His own Effie Deane[49] however would have died the death of the righteous or at least have suffered her sister to die the death of the unrighteous before she would have on the most urgent necessity have so far paltered with the truth. I own that I am very sorry that Scott should from any motive have condescended to such evasions. He first was driven to the denial by the King's drinking to him from the Bear of Bradwardine when Waverley first came out and before Scott was sure perhaps whether it would stand its ground. After having once denied it to the *King*, he could not acknowledge it to the *subject*. And doubtless the mystery has increased public curiosity about the works so that Scott and his publisher have found their account in keeping up the farce. A farce it is now. In this country few who know him or who can judge of literature and of probabilities can doubt his being the author. He enjoys the jest and as he loves diversion I think the amusement is now and has been all through *his* chief motive. Of course when we were with him we never directly or indirectly touched upon the subject as we deemed it a point of good faith and good breeding not to force his confidence, far less to steal upon or surprise it. Therefore the more he laid himself open the less we took advantage. My American correspondent Mrs. Griffith however lately wrote to me to desire I would let Scott know that he would lose all his popularity in America if he did not immediately come forward and avow the Scotch novels, because as she says they are now attributed to some Mr. Greenfeld[50] who is as she says a person whose character is so bad that he cannot reap the fruits

49. ME here means to write *Jeanie Deans*, the heroine of Scott's *Heart of Midlothian*, who cannot bring herself to tell a lie even to save her innocent sister, Effie, from hanging. She does, however, walk to London from Edinburgh to beg the queen's pardon for Effie.

50. ME writes Greenfeld; RML writes Greenfield. William Greenfield (d. 1827), who was an assistant professor of rhetoric at Edinburgh, 1784–1801, was credited by Mrs. Grant (see following note) as the author of the anonymous *Essays on the Sources of the Pleasures Received from Literary Compositions* (London, 1809, 2d ed. 1827). He may be the writer that Mrs. Griffith alludes to.

of his own talents, dares not avow himself the author because he knows that none would buy the books if they were known to be his. Therefore as the story is strangely stated, he has bribed Walter Scott to let them pass for his.

Mrs. G. further tells me that a story is current in her neighbourhood of Mrs. Grant[51] the Author of *The American Letters* having said that Sir W. Scott confessed to her that he is the author of these novels. As Mrs. Griffith expressly desired that all this should be made known to Sir W. and as I could not undertake to do this in any words but her own I sent her letter to him. His answer was admirable as far as it regarded Mrs. G.: "Give my respects to your American correspondent and tell her that I hope she will not attribute to me any share in any dishonorable transaction respecting this or any other matter until she finds in some other part of my conduct some thing that might justify such an accusation or suspicion." He adds, "I have for these twenty years past been pretty well known and have maintained an indifferently good reputation as a lion in my own deserts."

He says moreover that he has never seen or had any communication whatever with this Mr. Greenfeld and that if he is the person he is supposed to be he could not without a total loss of reputation have had any communication with him. Then he says what I did not repeat to Mrs. G. as I was not sure that he meant it should be repeated, that the story of Mrs. Grant is quite absurd: "Why I should choose Mrs. Grant for my Mother Confessor it would be hard to tell. If it had been you or Joanna[52]

51. Anne MacVicar Grant (1755–1838), Scottish author. As a young girl she lived in the United States for ten years, and her best-known work was *Memoirs of an American Lady* (London, 1808), admired by Scott. Living in and writing about the Scottish highlands, she was credited with the authorship of the earlier Waverley novels. She corresponded with many American friends.

52. Joanna Baillie (1762–1851), British poet and dramatist, born in Scotland. Among her works are *Fugitive Verses* (1790), *A Series of Plays* (1798), *Miscellaneous Plays* (1804), *The Family Legend* (1810), and *Dramas*, 3 vols. (1836). ME was frequently the guest of Joanna Baillie and her sister at Hampstead. They first met in 1813, and Joanna recorded her impression of ME to Walter Scott: "I have found

there might have been some probability in the story." He yet further says, and this is the passage which I cannot approve though it is worded with the care of a special pleader to avoid the lie direct,

"I have repeatedly answered to all who had the slightest title to ask the question that I have nothing to do with these novels."

Now here are two things to be remarked on this, that he may shelter himself behind the plea that no one has any right to ask the question, and that he may safely say "I *have* nothing to do with these novels" because he has sold them.

His publisher spoke more openly to me, but I do not think it right to repeat how openly. I conclude upon the whole that some other person or persons have written parts of each book, just enough to allow him to declare that they are not all his, just as great painters allow inferior hands to do the drapery. You know that many more pictures are *undoubted Raphaels* than the life of Raphael had he never one instant had the pencil out of his hand could have finished, even if he had neither allowed himself to eat, drink, or sleep. In all these pictures connoisseurs recognise touches of the master's hand.

In the last of the Scotch novels, St. Ronan,[53] there are many touches which could be from none but the mighty master; yet the public complain and we his most sincere friends are forced like Mrs. Candour to acknowledge that there are fewer of

---

Miss Edgeworth a frank, animated, sensible and amusing woman, entirely free from affectation of any kind, and of a confiding, affectionate and friendly disposition that has really gained upon my heart. . . . She has been received by everybody, the first in literature and the first in rank, with the most gratifying eagerness and respect, and has delighted them all. She is interested in every subject that comes into play, and tells her little anecdote or story (when her father does not take it out of her mouth) very pleasantly. . . . You would have been amused if you had seen with what eagerness people crowded to get a sight of Miss E.—who is very short—peeping over shoulders and between curled *tetes* to get but one look. She said herself at a party where I met her that the crowd closed over her" (quoted in Elizabeth Inglis-Jones, *The Great Maria* [London: Faber & Faber, 1959], p. 114).

53. Scott, *St. Ronan's Well* (1824).

these than in former works. He will indemnify us in The Crusades which is soon to come out.

I daresay you are right in your judgment of the Pioneers, yet I cannot have the merit of having formed the same opinion after the first perusal of the two works. I preferred the Pioneers, but for reasons which could not be yours: because it described more what was new to us in American manners, customs, habits of living and scenes of the country. Other talents for drawing character *etc*. I could find in European novels, but these parts have the merit to us of novelty and of pictures of national manners—the furniture even of the house, the dinner, *etc.*, tho' the most trivial circumstances, have in this view merit, not positive perhaps but relative. Also the maple sugar manufacture, clearing the wood, pigeon shooting, aiming at the goose, the panther, the view of the vindictive feelings of the original inhabitants of the country against the newcomers, I think strongly drawn; the making the Indian go off at last from civilized society is a master stroke.

We have been much pleased with a book which can hardly please you Americans, "The Siege of New Orleans and the Taking of Washington" by an Officer.[54] It tells us much of the small circumstances which grand military writers often make it a principle to omit—more fools they. Griscom's *"Year in Europe"*[55] which he sent me from America is a faithful but not lively picture, not by a master's hand but by a hand whose truth and accuracy may be depended [*on*]. Tho' the book is heavy in form and substance and tho' all my family laughed at me for wading through what was too commonplace for them, yet I went on and it had an interest for me; I was interested in seeing how things familiar to us strike Americans, in what relative value he holds

54. [George Robert Gleig] (1796–1888), *A Narrative of the Campaigns of The British Army at Washington and New Orleans. . . . By an Officer, Who Served in the Expedition* (London, 1821).

55. John Griscom (1774–1852), American educator (chemistry and natural history), author of *A Year in Europe* (New York, 1823).

our various improvements in manufactures, machinery, works of art, and refinements of manners, *etc*.

We are reading aloud in the evening (I mean that my sister Harriet who excuse me for saying so reads admirably) is reading to us an amusing book, Hajji Baba.[56] It is a sort of Persian Anastasius,[57] but there is not a word in it offensive to morality or good taste, and the style is free from all that affectation of wit which sometimes appears in Anastasius. Besides the hero is not such a vile, incorrigible, ungrateful profligate. This may have nothing to do with the merit of the work as I have often urged on the other side of the question in favor of Zeluco,[58] yet still it diminishes the pleasure of the reader because a villain hero cannot interest. Mr. Hope the author of Anastasius is a friend of mine and I should be proud to find out that Hajji Baba were written by him. It is worthy of him and of his improved taste. It is given however to Mr. Morier, author of Travels in Persia. If Morier wrote it he has infinitely more genius than I suspected.

"O'Driscol's letters [*Written above* Letters *"or view of"*] on Ireland"[59] I recommend to you, tho' it has many Irish *flowery* faults of style it is a work of genius and virtue, written and felt and thought with great liberality, and it is in some passages as

56. James Morier (1780–1849), English traveler and author, published accounts of his travels to the Near East, then wrote several romances based on Eastern life and manners, among them *The Adventures of Hajji Baba of Ispahan* (1824) and *The Adventures of Hajji Baba of Ispahan in England* (1828).

57. Thomas Hope (ca. 1770–1831), English art collector and author of *Anastasius, or Memoirs of a Modern Greek* (1819), published anonymously. ME was a frequent guest of the Hopes at their Duchess Street house in London, renowned for its furniture and art in the "English Empire" style, and at Deepdene where she cared not at all for the "frightful monsters in bronze or stone or plaister" that lined the halls.

58. John Moore (1729–1802), Scottish physician and writer. His *Zeluco: Various Views of Human Nature, Taken from Life and Manners*, 2 vols. (1789) has as its theme the proposition that people who behave wrongly and selfishly are generally punished in this world for their misdeeds. Byron said that he intended Childe Harold to be "a poetical Zeluco."

59. James Doyle (1786–1834), R.C. bishop of Kildare and Leighlin, *Letters on the Reunion of the Churches of England and Rome, from and to Dr. Doyle . . . , J. O'Driscol, A. Knox, and T. Newenham* (1824). John O'Driscol, *The History of Ireland*, 2 vols. (1827), and *Views of Ireland, Moral, Political, and Religious*, 2 vols. (1823).

fine in its eloquence as Burke, and as patriotic in its views as
Grattan or Berkeley, that most amiable man and bishop perhaps
that ever existed. If you have his works read his *Querist*;[60] the
queries are all or almost all applicable at the present day to the
state of Ireland.

Doblado's Letters on Spain[61] I also recommend as a strong
and I am afraid true picture of Spain. It is written by a Mr.
Blanco or White who resided many years in that country—was a
Catholic, is a Protestant, and is now an English clergyman. He
had best keep where he is, for if the Inquisition catch hold of
him they would not only cut off but broil and mince his ears.

But to return to my own family. I told you in the beginning
of this letter that one of my sisters is just married. I am sure you
will be glad to hear that there is every human probability of its
being a happy union. She has married a man whom we have
known from childhood, with good principles, good name, good
manners, good family, and good fortune. It is a marriage completely of her own inclination and entirely of her mother's approbation and to the joy of all her family. Her husband's family,
also his four brothers and two sisters and father are particularly
suited to ours by their domestic tastes and family union, and all
are fond of our dear Sophy and know how to appreciate the
wife Captain Barry Fox has and has deserved by the strength of
his attachment proved by three years constant efforts to improve
in everything that could render him more and more worthy of
her. When he was first attached and first proposed for her she

60. Edmund Burke (1729–97), statesman. As a member of Parliament he
spoke against the British employment of Indians in the American Revolution
and advocated the abolition of the slave trade. Henry Grattan (1746–1820),
statesman, member of Parliament. George Berkeley (1685–1753), Irish bishop
and philosopher. *The Querist*, a practical treatment of social and economic
philosophy, appeared in three parts, 1735, 1736, 1737.
    61. Joseph Blanco White (1775–1841), theological writer of Irish descent was
born in Seville and christened José María. He was ordained a priest in the
Roman church in 1800, but became a skeptic, fled to England, and qualified for
Anglican orders in 1814. He became a Unitarian in 1835. His publications are
numerous. *Letters from Spain, by Don Leucadio Doblando* appeared in 1822, a second edition with his name in 1825.

was too young to marry—she is not yet of age—but so steady, so gracefully composed, and yet so feeling a young bride I never before beheld. Forgive my family egotism.

Barry Fox was for some time in America, in Canada, and if he had not married would have returned there as he says to live unmarried and alone in despair. But happily for all he will now settle in this country and her mother will not lose a daughter's society nor we a sister's.

They are going to England in a fortnight and to take a tour in France and Italy if he can obtain a few months leave of absence.

I am so much hurried that I can only huddle together the end of this letter.

I will send you as soon as it comes out a work now in the press by a lady of our acquaintance, a history of England for young people.

My poor invalid sister Lucy begs that in your next letter you will tell her what history of the Jews you would recommend to her after the time of Josephus?

My sister Harriet begs you will tell what is the meaning of the mark at the end of this advertisement: "for the operations on the place and terms apply to Samuel M'Culloh, eotf."

Abruptly but very affectionately and gratefully

Your obliged friend
Maria Edgeworth

Why should not you come to Edgeworthstown and visit us? *Answer this*.

[*Appears to be original,*
may be holograph copy]   Wilmington, July 17th, 1824

Your letter my dear Madam of the 9th of April has been perused and reperused by me with the greatest pleasure, a pleasure which I am ever proud and happy to acknowledge, tho' conscious of inability to bestow an equivalent in return. But I love to be obliged to you, and while your indulgence continues, shall always hasten to renew my obligation.

Your approbation of the contents of the box is most kind and gratifying, each article so carefully noticed as to attach to the veriest trifle a degree of value and importance. It was you, my dear Madam, who first put into words a sentiment which I had often felt, that there are more who know how to give than how to receive, and it is in you that I find the exemplification, in all its grace and reality. I was particularly glad to hear that the fly trap arrived in good health; because from the severity of the weather after the plants left here, I had little hopes of their surviving. I have just been collecting some seed from a fine one, which I have watched as it budded, bloomed, and came to maturity; you will find them inclosed, and should you lose the plants, others raised from the seed in your climate may prove more fortunate. The seeds that I before sent under that name were given to me, and now I find were not those of the Dyonaes. Tho' not fearful that your stock of patience would be exhausted while awaiting the growth of the Non-de-script rose and the Yapon, I shall endeavour to prevent its being exercised on this occasion by sending you some specimens of each. I have several thriving suckers, which with their roots will I think bear removing in October or November. The Non-de-script is very hardy, its growth rapid and luxuriant. The foliage, a bright and glossy green, is beautifully contrasted in the spring by innumerable white buds and flowers. It requires to be led over an arbour or trellice. The person, to whom I mentioned to you I had applied for a collection of seeds, declined sending them until the ensuing fall; by some delay the letter did not reach him till long after it was written, and judging it then too late to send them for the present year, he tells us we shall have fresh ones this fall which will be more sure to thrive. Your encomiums on my packing, tho' they made me smile, are I assure you duly estimated. Of the brown serrated leg, I intended giving you the history. My sister Ellen found on a privet bush a grasshopper that had evidently just effected its enlargement from its last years covering which lay near it. There was also the leg of another exactly resembling it, which she supposes had been torn off by accident. She took possession of all. The little animal ate leaves and crumbs of bread and continued well and lively for some months. It seemed however to have an intuitive dread of being sent from its birth place, for on the morning when with its case and some other little articles it was to be sent to me, it was sought for in vain in its usual abode. Soon after the departure of the messenger, it was seen hopping from under a set of drawers, in one of which its box had been kept. It did not survive the winter, but my sister has preserved [it] and will send it to me. You will find that the joints in the leg which you have correspond exactly with the delicate indentures of the covering. I did not know that our evening chatterer, the Caty-did, was called "the creeping leaf," tho' the veins in its green wings render the name appropriate. I inclose for your little brother, who is fond of natural history, an account which I met with yesterday in a newspaper, of a battle between a spider and a frog; he will perhaps wish as I did, that the gentleman had described it more particularly; the fact however is curious. The Syringa that you describe is probably similar to ours, except that ours, I think, has no scent whatever. Moss is exported in considerable quantities from this to the Northern States; did you observe something on it of a rather darker colour that has the appearance of a blossom? Can such a species of vegetation produce seed? It seems merely to suspend itself from the branches of trees, and the root if there is any, eludes my observation. I will send a small branch that you may examine it in a more satisfactory manner, especially as you propose inserting some account of it in your "Sequel to Harry and Lucy." It cannot be otherwise than gratifying to me that you should thus employ the little information I have given on the subject, or that anything I have said has proved useful or agreeable to you. Be so good as to tell me if your Chrisali become animated. I have several times kept some of the same kind, but the worm (I fancy it is) has never left its envelope.

I am sorry it is not in my power to give the information you desire respecting the Indian; I too felt anxious to know the result, but we saw nothing further of the trial, as I am inclined to think we should had he been condemned, so we may reasonably hope that if tried he was acquitted. I lately saw another very sensible and well written letter from an Indian, in reply to one that made some enquiries relative to the situation of his tribe. He says they are fast advancing in civilisation, that exclusive of Missionary schools, they have established several for the education of their youth; that many of them have embraced the Christian Religion, and that there are among them several men of property, who cultivate flourishing farms which exhibit every appearance of neatness and comfort. He nevertheless deprecates the idea which appears to have been suggested of a free intercourse with the whites. He says "do not force nature; we are improving, but we are not prepared to live among you, or to receive you among us; time has done a great deal, and may do a great deal more for us, if we are left to ourselves."

I thank both you and the ladies who have written "Entomology" and "Dialogues on Botany" (I know you have their consent) for the favour you confer in disclosing to me who the authors are. I confess that the knowledge of this, whatever the intrinsick merit of the works may be, will give them an additional interest. Is it not a son of Dr. Beddoes and a nephew of yours who has written the Bride's Tragedy?[62] While reading some time since a review of this production, I was pleased in believing that the talents of the Edgeworth family were thus inherited.

Accept my sincere congratulations on the happy marriage of your sister; the terms in which you mention her are so sweet and engaging that I seem to have seen, to know, and to have

62. Thomas Lovell Beddoes (see Appendix A).

learned to love her too. Will she not accept the wishes of a warm hearted stranger, that her marriage may prove as happy as her education has been excellent and as the auspices under which it commences are propitious? After you had mentioned this event *en passant* at the commencement of your letter, I was afraid I should hear no more of it, nor even know the name of the fortunate bridegroom; but you were more kind, and tho' you delayed, did not refuse to indulge me with the little domestick detail. I feel an interest in every member of your family, and to become personally acquainted with you and with them would be one of the highest gratifications that I could enjoy. It is delightful to know that this desire has even for a moment been reciprocal, as when, with a charm of sincerity peculiar to yourself, you ask "Why should you not come to Edgeworth's town to visit us? *Answer this.*" The sound is so agreeable that I dwell upon it and hesitate to begin the answer, which is but too ready to present itself.

Our family, principally daughters whom we educate at home, could not spare us for any length of time, nor would my husband's mercantile concerns admit of his absence—reasons of which you will allow the force. Were it not that duty and prudence thus with-hold me, how joyfully would I accept such an invitation! Ourselves we should present with diffidence, but without relying too much on parental fondness, we might feel confident that you would be pleased with our little son. His ready obedience, and affectionate engaging disposition, render him the delight of his friends and fill the hearts of his parents with sweet anticipations of the future. "Frank" is already a favourite with him, and he comes frequently to ask me to read for him, or to tell him about Frank and his father and mother.

We paid a visit last spring to my dear parents, who received from me with delight my young sister Eliza, with the continued care of whom they had indulged me from the time of my marriage till then. She is an amiable girl and will, I trust, realize in maturity the promise of her early years. On our return I had the gratification of beholding in Raleigh (the capitol of this state) a chef d'oeuvre of art such as is rarely to be found in our youthful country. A statue of Washington, from the Chisel of Canova, and which is said to be worthy of that great Master.[63] Too much of a novice to venture an opinion, I will only say that its execution far surpassed any idea I had formed of the powers of sculpture. Our Hero is represented sitting in an attitude of reflection, a stylus in one hand, the other resting on a tablet, on which he is about to inscribe his farewell address on resigning the presidency.

You ask how I like Rebecca? Hers appears to me the most finished female character that Scott has drawn. Her mind, her principles, her feelings, all highly wrought, are still under the control of reason, of discretion and of true feminine dignity. Placed in circumstances where the ordinary as well as the most powerful feelings are excited, she is always just what she ought to be. Her soul revolts at the meannesses to which oppression or the dread of it has driven her poor father; yet in proving her own superiority, she evinces no disrespect toward him. During the interview with Front-de-Boeuf in the castle she is admirable as a heroine; as a woman her situation is more natural and interesting while exercising the offices of kindness in attendance on the wounded Ivanhoe, and struggling with and conquering her feelings, as his expressions, unintentionally on his part, convince her of his indifference towards herself and his devotion to the more fortunate lady Rowena. The storming of the Castle is I think equal in effect to anything the author has ever written, and his painting it to our senses in Rebecca's agitated yet animated description a masterpiece. The firmness with which she supports her subsequent trials command admiration, which in the closing scene, her visit to the lady Rowena, is mingled with those sentiments of esteem and regret which sympathy ever bestows on merit struggling with misfortune. There is a degree

63. Antonio Canova (1757–1822), Italian sculptor; perhaps his most noted work is the reclining nude of Pauline Bonaparte.

of feminine delicacy in the conduct of both ladies during this interview which is very attractive and we find the heroine supported to the last; she yields not to unavailing despondency but devotes her remaining years to usefulness and piety. The whole character is in keeping with the splendid yet solemn magnificence of the scenes of Chivalry by which it is surrounded. Yet it appears to me that the mind of Rebecca is not one of romance, and that there are women, who, tho' not taught by the highly gifted Scott to discourse eloquence like Rebecca, would, under similar trials, have acted with similar firmness and rectitude. As a *whole*, I have sometimes been tempted to give a preference to Ivanhoe over any of Scott's novels, but "Old Mortality," "the Antiquary," parts of "Waverley," "Guy Mannering," "the Abbot," "Kenilworth" pass in array before one and arrest the half formed sentence. "St. Ronan's Well" reminded me of "the Bride of Lammermoor," to which it appears to me in some respects superior, in others, not equal. May we still anticipate "the Crusades"? "Red Gauntlet"[64] is, I see, in the press in this country; you must have already seen it. The report you mention relative to Mr. Greenfield was very current here, but I never thought it had any influence on Sir W. Scott's popularity. The authorship was afterwards ascribed to Mr. John Scott of Canada, then to his lady, and since, beyond dispute to Mrs. Grant! I am greatly obliged by your extracts from Sir W. Scott's letter; it was the very best reply that could have been made to such a communication. I have often remarked his nice evasions in replying to compliments addressed to him as the author of Waverley and have wondered why he took so much pains to deny what does him so much honour. This disavowal to the king had at that time much weight with me; it is a pity he should have been placed in such a dilemma, or that with his accustomed address he did not extri-

---

64. *Old Mortality* (1816); *The Antiquary* (1816); *Waverley* (1814); *Guy Mannering* (1815); *The Abbot* (1820); *Kenilworth* (1821); *St. Ronan's Well* (1823); *The Bride of Lammermour* (1819); *Tales of the Crusaders* (1825) includes *The Betrothed* and *The Talisman*; *Red Gauntlet* (1824).

cate himself, till a more convenient season for acknowledgment. You have probably seen Mr. Cooper's last work "The Pilot."[65] The author's descriptive talent is happily exercised in the Storm, the pursuit of the Whale, the loss of the Ariel, and some other passages, but in the delineation of most of his characters, especially the females, he has I think been less successful.

I ought to correct an error in my last, relative to the death of Gen. Boon. I was not then aware that the account there given had been contradicted. Accept my thanks for your valued recommendation of several works; we have ordered them from N. York, and in my next I shall be prepared to say how much pleasure and information they have afforded us. The works of Bishop Berkeley I have never met with, and I am sorry for it; your remarks make me desirous to become acquainted with them. I wish my knowledge of valuable literature were more extensive, but conscious that want of inclination has not caused the deficiency, it "does not hurt my pride to say, I do not know."

The continued vein of satire that runs through "Anastasius," tho' perhaps well adapted to the characters and manners the author has chosen to describe, is not agreeable to me, and tho' I believe it to portray with truth the habits, manners, and absence of moral rectitude among the Turks, I cannot read it with that admiration to which, as a celebrated production of a man of genius, it is probably entitled. I like best to dwell on those passages in which there is a triumph of natural feeling over hardened profligacy, and there the author has proved that he knows how to touch and interest. It appears to me that "Anastasius" as to its profligate hero admits fewer arguments in its favour than Zeluco. The moral tendency is there so evident that the book may be placed with safety even in the hands of youth. How often have I felt inclined to recommend it to parents, who viewed with indifference the first ebullitions of childish passion. I recollect remarking with pleasure in "the Good French gov-

65. James Fenimore Cooper, *The Pilot* (1824).

erness"[66] (I believe) that your judgment, my unerring standard, was given in favour of Zeluco.

I cannot close this, tho' perhaps already too full, without a line of regret on the premature fate of Lord Byron.[67] With his amiable friend Sir W. Scott, I would say, "Who will not grieve that such a race has been shortened, tho' not always keeping the straight path; such a light extinguished, tho' sometimes flaming to dazzle and to bewilder?" The 4th canto of "Childe Harold," to me the most beautiful, grand and interesting of his lordship's numerous productions, first allowed me to approach near enough to sympathise with, as well as to admire. Always identifying himself with his heroes, he appeared either more, or less than man, as man is found; but in the poem just mentioned, there is a degree of softened feeling which seems dictated by the heart, conveying a consciousness of error with the regret that ought to accompany it. Tho' several anecdotes related of him since his residence in Greece have placed his character in an amiable light, it must be satisfactory to his friends that his *life* will not be placed before the publick.[68] The conduct of Mr. Moore on that occasion does him honour and in the pleasure of self-approbation he must find an ample recompense for the sacrifice.

I am truly sorry that you introduce one of your family as your "poor invalid sister Lucy"; her disease is, I hope, of a temporary nature. Will you tell me if she is better when you next write? I applied to my father in order to reply with more correctness to her inquiry.[69] He says there has been no regular historian

66. *The Good French Governess* is one of ME's *Moral Tales* (1801).

67. Byron died on the evening of 24 April 1824 at Missolonghi.

68. The destruction of Byron's *Memoirs* took place primarily because of Lady Byron's fears of what they might reveal concerning herself. They were burned 17 May 1824 in the rooms of Byron's friend John Cam Hobhouse. The seven who witnessed their destruction were by no means unanimous in the decision; they were Hobhouse, Thomas Moore, Wilmot Horton, Henry Luttrell, Col. Francis Hastings Doyle, John Murray, and his sixteen-year-old son, John. Doyle, as Lady Byron's agent, prevailed over Moore's strong objections.

69. Of Jacob Mordecai his granddaughter Caroline Cohen wrote: "Commer-

since Josephus, whose works are considered not altogether genuine, there having been some erasures and some interpolations, by the persons who have examined or translated them; he refers you to the Abbé de Languera, Bibliotheque anc: and mod: tome 7th. Basnage and the Marquis d'Argens[70] are resorted to as historians of merit, the latter especially. I have not myself read either of these works.

I reply to the question of Miss Harriet Edgeworth, tho' she has probably recollected before this time, that the letters which excited her attention are the printer's memoranda for the insertion of advertisements, *e o t f*—every other, till forbid—*Th & S, 3—m*—Thursday and Saturday, 3 months, *etc.*

The last papers speak highly of "Redwood,"[71] a new American novel, written by a lady. When I have read, I will say more of it.

Be pleased, my dear Madam, to present me respectfully to the much esteemed members of your family and accept assurances of grateful and affectionate attachment from

Your much obliged friend
R. Lazarus

---

cial life did not greatly interest him. Always studious, and devoted to literary, and especially to Biblical research, he must have soon felt that in spite of his early imperfect education, the work in life for him must be intellectual" (*Records of the Myers, Hays, and Mordecai Families from 1707 to 1913* [Washington, n.d.], p. 32).

70. Jacques Basnage (1653–1725), French Protestant theologian and historian, author of *Histoire des Juifs*, 5 vols. (1706). Marquis d'Argens, Jean Baptiste de Boyer (1704–71), French writer, author of *Lettres Juives* (1736–38). The *Bibliothèque Ancienne et Moderne*, 29 vols. (1714–30) was edited by Jean LeClerc (1657–1736). The editor is unable to identify the Abbe Languera.

71. Catherine Maria Sedgwick (1789–1867), "the Maria Edgeworth of New England," known for her historical novels and as a precursor of the New England novel of manners. *Redwood* (1824) is concerned with the Shakers.

My dear Madam

Direct opportunities from this place to the European ports are unfrequent else I should sooner have sent the promised specimen of moss, which accompanies this. When I had last the pleasure of addressing you, I mentioned "Redwood" an American novel which had then just appeared; ere this you have probably seen the work, perhaps received a copy from the author, yet I cannot deny myself the pleasure of presenting a book which merits the high encomium of being worthy the acceptance of Miss Edgeworth. I have read it with great pleasure and think that for purity of style, lively and accurate description, and correct delineation as well as originality of character, it deserves to be ranked among the first rate novels of the day. The characteristic difference between the manners of the Southern and Eastern states is happily and not too glaringly marked; we are enabled to discern, not compelled to observe it. In justice to Virginia I must however remark that the slave picture is coloured far beyond what reality would authorise. The condition of our slaves both in this and the sister states is far less miserable than that of the poorer classes of white people. They are comfortably maintained and with very few exceptions kindly treated. So long as the benefits of education are denied them, their state must be abject, and the necessity of retaining them is by all admitted to be an evil tho' at present an unavoidable one; but their usually cheerful demeanor argues well for the humanity of their masters.

Since I last wrote I have been severely assailed by domestick affliction; in the prime of life, eminently and extensively useful in his profession, my eldest brother has been snatched away by the hand of death.[72] To cherish the memory of his excellence is all that remains to us and to his infant children.

In a few weeks I hope to send you the long promised seeds

72. Moses Mordecai (see Appendix B).

and plants. I would have delayed this parcel to send with them but was reluctant to lose entirely the ready conveyance.

Adieu my dear Madam; that misfortune may long be averted from you and those you love is the sincere wish of one whom your goodness allows to subscribe herself.

Your friend
R. Lazarus

[Original]   Wilmington, February 9th, 1825

My dear Madam,

By a vessel which sails tomorrow I shall have the pleasure of sending you the long promised parcel of seeds, which I regret should have been thus delayed; we have but just received them, and they will I hope arrive in good time for cultivation in your climate. Many of them are indigenous to our soil, others are probably common with you; the selection however will rest with yourself. I send also a Cassine, a Nondescript, and a Multiflora, which I shall rejoice to hear, have reached you in safety. I can hardly flatter myself to be as fortunate with these as with the Dyonaes, but the risk is small, and the satisfaction to me will be great should they survive the voyage. The Multiflora I send at a venture; be so good as to tell me if you have it in Ireland. I hope you received a box which I sent some time last fall containing the moss which I had promised, and "Redwood," an American novel, written by a lady whose name I have since found is Miss Sedgwick.

I am anxious to know what is said in England of "Lord Byron's Conversations,"[73] and whether they are believed to be

73. Thomas Medwin (1788–1869), *Conversations of Lord Byron* (1824). Medwin was a cousin and schoolfellow of Shelley. In her letter of 6 June 1825, ME sums up an attitude that is held by scholars today regarding the authenticity of his work (see Doris Moore, *The Late Lord Byron* [Philadelphia: Lippincott, 1961]).

authentic. Murray, Lord B's. publisher, brings proof, I observe, that certain passages relative to *his* transactions are not to be relied on. It is a work which amuses and interests, without really giving me pleasure. My curiosity is gratified in being permitted to listen to the familiar conversations of a man of preeminent talents, while at the same time I cannot but consider it a breach of confidence that such disclosures are made, especially as they cannot in any degree increase our respect for the memory of Lord B. whom tho' all must concur in admiring, none could approve.

It has been long, my dear Madam, since I heard from you, never since the letter announcing the happy marriage of your amiable sister. I hope I shall not much longer be denied so great a pleasure; in this respect, let me confide in your indulgence, both to receive and to bestow, assured that your letters are always opened with delight and gratitude

by your sincere and much obliged friend
R. Lazarus

Black Castle, County of Meath, May 2, 1825.
I am here with an aunt Ruxton[74] whose name you may remember in my father's memoirs. She is now in her 80th year, warm of heart, clear of head as at 18. I return home next month.

I am ashamed, my dear Madam, when I see the date of your last most kind and touching letter. But I have waited first for the arrival of the box and the books your letter announced and then have been delayed by many domestic circumstances with the detail of which I need not trouble you. Your kindness of heart

74. Margaret Edgeworth Ruxton (see Appendix A).

will be satisfied when I assure you that my silence has not proceeded from neglect nor from any change in my feelings toward you. Indeed that would be impossible unless I changed my nature and you yours, for our intercourse has consisted of a continued series of kindness[es] on your part and of grateful acknowledgements on mine. Yes indeed something more, and much more; your letters have given me an increasing opinion the more I have seen of them of your understanding, plain uprightness of character and real tenderness of heart which attach me as much to you as can possibly be to one whom I have not seen and actually known. I sympathise in your suffering for the loss you mentioned in your last. I know what it is to lose friends dearly loved and valued. For this there is no remedy upon this earth. Friends can do no more than forbear to torture by obtruding common-place consolations. All must be left to the lenient operation of Time, the efforts of our own minds, and the highest and best of all hopes, for those who are so happy as to have and to deserve them.

I have found even in the fresh air and the flowers and shrubs in my garden and in the mere sight of greenfields a sense of *bodily* relief for my *mind*, if I may say so, in sorrow. The stillness and permanence of the objects of nature have a sort of composing, sublime effect, acting upon the whole creature, we know not how or why, but we feel with submission and gratitude to Providence that this is so, that there is this provision in our nature, physical or metaphysical whichever it may be, both perhaps, against the deadening lethargy, the despair of grief. You see I have felt it.

Your kind present has reached me and just at a time when it was most acceptable and useful. I was finishing the part of Harry and Lucy in which I mention the plant which hangs from your trees in such a curious manner. I wanted to have a specimen growing from the branch, and this box arrived at the right moment. I sent specimens to Botanic gardeners in Dublin and London so that you have enabled me to obtain all the information

I needed. The result you shall have in Harry and Lucy, of which I will send a copy as soon as it shall be published, which will be in a few weeks.

Redwood has entertained us very much. I am so much flattered by the manner in which my writings are alluded to in this book that I can hardly suppose I am [an] unprejudiced judge. But it appears to me a work of superior talent, far greater than even the New England tale gave me reason to expect. The character of Aunt Deborah is first rate, in Scott's best manner yet not an imitation of Scott. It is to America what Scott's characters are to Scotland, valuable as original pictures with enough of individual peculiarity to be interesting and to give the feeling of reality and life as portraits, sufficient also of general characteristics to give them the philosophical merit of pourtraying a class. It is of great consequence to sketch and record such characters in America because in another half century they will have passed away and it would require more than the power of the master genius to raise them from the dead. Because your America is not like Scotland a land of traditions, it has little influence over our minds by early associations, great by actual curiosity. The present not the past must therefore be the American writer's domain. If you have any means of communication with this author I wish you could convey to her this idea if you think it just. There is another bit of advice I should wish to give; tho' it may not be palatable it may be salutary. It is to attempt European character only sparingly. There are a vast host of English critics with eyes and stings sharpened by competition and rivalry and party spirit who will detect the slightest deviation from truth in the drawing or even from fashion in the appearance of such characters. Unfavorable and unjust deductions would thence be drawn even against the truth and merit of the American characters. The shades of fashion in minute particulars which it is almost impossible for a transatlantic writer to catch, evanescent as they are, influence irremediably London opinions. Many an inferior judgment will pass sentence in the higher

London circles, sentence of *vulgarity*, equivalent to sentence of death on Redwood because one female character which aims at being fashionable is open to the criticism of "every prating she."

I have ordered my bookseller to send you "Letters from the Irish Highlands."[75] They are written by different individuals of a family who reside in Connemara in the County of Galway, a part of Ireland little known. In many respects these letters have as much the charm of novelty to me as they will have to you. The name of the family is Blake. *H* I believe is Mr. Blake the husband, *B* Barbara his wife, *A* is Anne, one of the sisters-in-law, *F* another. Mrs. Blake was a Miss Attersall. She and her sisters had the expectation of large fortunes from their father who was a London merchant and banker. The bank in which he and his son were engaged broke and they were ruined. Mrs. Blake and her sisters lost their fortunes. The Miss Attersalls are now going out as governesses I am told. The talents they shew in their letters, the various information, and the excellent principles will ensure them good success I think both with parents and children, success as it regards themselves and others. The letters as you will perceive are of very different merit. Some are affected and say a vast deal too much about the rainbow and the authors' sensibility to the picturesque, *etc*. But these are slight blemishes in a work which is calculated to do so much good to Ireland by making the truth known, by interesting the English for the Irish, and by diffusing with all the force of good writing and good humor liberal and enlightened views. I had intended not to have told you my opinion of this book, merely to have asked yours; mine has slipped out, but you will give me yours I know with your usual frankness. I am not personally acquainted with the authors and have no connexion with them. Even if I had I hope you would trust me that I would not betray you; but you may write quite free from all fear of hurting my feelings.

We hope that we are at this moment on the eve of a great

75. *Letters from the Irish Highlands* (1825). ME gives its multiple authorship in her letter.

national benefit. We hope that what is called Catholic emancipation will be granted this session by the English parliament. If this be done the people will be contented and quiet. English capital now overflowing will flow over here, set industry in motion all over this country, and induce habits of punctuality, order, and economy, virtues and happiness which have been for centuries unknown to the despairing, oppressed Irish population. If this bill do not pass or if we have not reason to hope that it will be passed next session, we shall have reason to fear more than ever from the disappointment of highly raised expectation. I seldom say a word on any political subject, but this comes home to every family, every cabin, every heart.

Vast companies of men of science and commercial enterprise have been formed in England for working our mines, establishing manufactories, making canals, working state quarries, mills, *etc.* in Ireland. One of these companies begin their prospectus with these [*words*]: "Our capital is two millions." From this you may judge of the extent of the pl[*ans*] at stake and of the multitudes whose hopes and fears are set upon the cast.

The establishment of many free empires in South America has opened great room for enterprise and for speculation in the British Empire. No doubt a great deal of the spirit of gambling mixes with all this. It is an evil which can hardly be prevented. But that will cure itself and the good will endure. Pray read Captain Hall's book *Six Months Residence in Chile*.[76] He is altogether the most liberal and enlightened, the most reasonable and the most amiable traveller I ever read, and he has illustrated

76. Basil Hall (1788–1844), British naval officer, traveler, and miscellaneous writer, born in Edinburgh. His works include *An Account of a Voyage of Discovery to the West Coast of Corea and the Great Loo-choo Island* (1818), *Extracts from a Journal Written on the Coasts of Chili, Peru and Mexico in the Years 1820–21–22* (1824), *Fragments of Voyages and Travels*, 9 vols. (1831–34). Although Basil Hall dedicated his account of the Loo-choo Islands to ME, they did not meet until 1823, at Sir Walter Scott's in Edinburgh, where she took a dislike to him and his brother, the future baronet of Dunglass, "that odious Caledonian bore and his wife." ME writes later to RML defending Basil Hall, but she confessed to her family, "It puts me in a fever of irritation to sit near him."

the truths of just legislation and of political economy by the most striking examples and on the largest scale ever exhibited to the world. Moreover he is a very entertaining writer with all the charms [*but*] without any of the airs or deceptions of eloquence.

Sir Walter Scott is going to publish another novel on the Crusades I believe, but it is not out yet. His son has lately married much to his satisfaction, a very amiable £60,000 heiress, as Sir Walter describes her to me "with a real truth of character" which has won his warm affection. Sir Walter promises to come to Ireland and to Edgeworthstown this summer or autumn. Autumn I hope it will be because by that time his favorite, my young married sister Sophy Fox who was last year at Abbotsford with me, will have returned from Italy with another of my sisters, Fanny, my *dear* Fanny! who has never seen and has—as who has not—a great desire to see and become acquainted with this great genius, the most amiable author I ever knew and the happiest, the most completely above his reputation and independent of his fame. Then you know how high and how independent he must be!

I wish that some of your friends or relations may sometime come to our country that we might have an opportunity of shewing them that hospitality does not decrease as civilization increases among us.

Our own family are going on well and happily. My sister Lucy we hope will be able to leave her sofa this autumn; her spine complaint appears to be cured, no pain in her back, but some complaints incident to her long recumbent posture continue, and her physicians recommend great care and patience. Send me a humming-bird stuffed or beetles for her or anything of that kind such as can be put in such a little box as you sent before. If you send to Liverpool direct to the care of Mr. Cropper, Liverpool, or to Mr. Williams, Sackville Street, Dublin, parcel office. If the captain who brings them to Dublin had a note from you of a few lines directed to Robert Hutton, Esquire, Summer Hill, Dublin, begging him to take charge of a small packet for

Miss Edgeworth and if this note were sent by the Captain by putting it into the 2d post when he arrives, Mr. R. Hutton would immediately go on board the ship and receive the packet which would save heavy charges and what [*is important*] much more of delay. If you are fond of needle work, send me a little bit of your own work which I should much value, a border for a turban for instance as I constantly wear turbans. If you draw send me a sketch of your children and yourself.

I am with sincere affection for your character and gratitude for your kindness, your friend

Maria Edgeworth

Edgeworthstown, June 6, 1825

My dear Madam, my dear friend, let me say, as well I may, for you are continually shewing me proofs of friendship. A few weeks ago I wrote to thank you for one kind act and now I have to thank you for another. In my last I acknowledged the receiving [*of*] a large box full of the American tree lichen or moss and the novel of Redwood of which I gave you my opinion. I hope my letter will reach you that I may not appear an ungrateful wretch. I have now received the nicely contrived cage in which you packed the three flower pots containing the Cassine, the nondescript, and the multiflora. I am sorry to tell you that notwithstanding your care to give them all possible advantage of light and air, the nondescript will hardly live. Our gardener has just shewn it to me; he has faint hopes however that it may push out roots. The Cassine is alive, the other dead. No seeds have yet come up in the pots. The multiflora is common here. I have numbers in my garden and on the trellis before our windows. The delightful box of seeds, so nicely packed, so sensibly labelled and noted has arrived. It has already given me the power of obliging two of my friends who are curious in plants and I have sent some of each to the Botanic gardener of Dublin who will I know cherish them and has means of doing so which I have not. If mine fail, his will flourish. I shall send a list of my treasures to the Botanic gardener at Glasgow and to Dr. Hooker[77] whose name as a botanist perhaps you know, who about a month before I received your box had sent me a present of seven and twenty young American shrubs for my garden, and I was considering what I could ever do for him in return. You have helped me out of my difficulty. In dividing the packets and making them up in papers and labelling them myself, I spent full two hours a few days ago; consequently I know how kind you were in taking the trouble of making them up for me. I like to be obliged to you and to shew you that I know how much pains you take for my gratification. You succeed.

You ask me what is said in England of "Lord Byron's Conversations." They are in some points believed to be genuine, that is, where the expressions have internal evidence of Lord B's genius and temper. But wherever there can be any doubt they are disbelieved because no confidence can be placed in the person who published private communications. Public indignation has been very justly strong on this subject. Captain Medway [Medwin] has entirely lost his reputation by this publication; no gentleman will keep company with him. Probably he must have made up his mind on that point before he committed such an act, and in a mercenary view no doubt the speculation has answered to him. If any human creature can be paid for dishonor! The public have stood by Murray the bookseller and admire his calm statement which he must have employed some first rate writer to make for him. I have not heard who. As to Lord Byron's character it stands pretty much as it did before the publication. None can approve his character as you justly say and all who admire his genius must regret this. Good impulses

77. Sir William Jackson Hooker (1785–1865), English botanist. Among his official positions were the professorship of botany at the University of Glasgow and the direction of the Royal Botanical Gardens at Kew.

as well as strong feelings he certainly had and much generosity of which I have heard many instances. But he is only one example more and a most powerful example of the truth that good feeling and good impulses will not carry even the greatest genius through even this life with credit or happiness without good-sense and principle and self-control. A stale moral this at which he would scoff, but truth must be stale because it lasts and will outlast all scoffers. Peace to his ashes, if peace can be to such ashes. If any of their wonted fires breathe in them, there can be no hope of peace for him.

I mentioned his generosity. I know Lady Byron and many of her intimate friends. She desired that they should tell the world that in the settlement of her affairs when Lord Byron became by our laws and her marriage settlement possessor of her whole fortune at her mother's death, he behaved in the most handsome manner to her. He had constantly said, "I will not be bound; leave all to my honor." I do not exactly understand the cause of disagreement between him and Lady Byron;[78] one ought to think it was to be regretted that it ever came before the public—sad gossiping! He gave the copyright of one of his cantos to Childe Harold to a friend in distress,[79] and he bestowed large sums on the Greek cause.

I have just been reading in No. 46 of the North American Review (Jan, 1825)[80] a review of Lord Byron's character and

78. Maidenly modesty doubtless prevented ME from repeating the London rumors. The two most widespread reports for Lady Byron's divorce, circulated in large part by the neurotic Lady Caroline Lamb, were Byron's alleged incest with his half sister, Augusta Leigh, and his homosexual practices.

79. ME here refers to Robert Charles Dallas (1754–1824). The impecunious and sycophantic Dallas claimed a kinship with the younger Byron; Dallas's sister had been married to Byron's uncle. Byron, as a gentleman who could not write for money, gave the first two cantos of "Childe Harold" as well as the copyright to the successful *Corsair* to Dallas. Later, when Byron was in need of money for his multiple causes, he accepted payment for his works, whereupon Dallas would be among those who accused Byron of greed.

80. *The North American Review*, published from 1815 to 1911, stressed literature and political thought. The leading American writers of the nineteenth century were among its contributors.

writings. The general tenor I think very just. But I cannot agree with the reviewer in blaming him for engaging in the Greek cause. It was the best thing he ever did. I am glad it was the last. Perhaps it was a special mercy to him that he died when he did; he left *this* good impression at least on men's minds, and it is always advantageous to the cause of virtue and genius that the belief in their connexion should be preserved. If he had lived and pursued his object I fear he would have failed in Greece. The Greeks like the Spaniards have been so long degraded by slavery that they cannot exert themselves sufficiently to regain or deserve liberty. This is the greatest evil and injury done by tyranny. It induces the vices of falsehood and cunning the miserable, the only arms of the weak against the strong. In the Greeks, the West Indian slaves, the Irish "poor slave" as he often calls himself, the same defects of character from the same causes appear. But we must not do the cruel injustice of supposing that these faults of character are *natural* and inherent and incurable, and make this imputation a plea for continuing the wrongs and oppression by which the faults were produced.

You may not feel to what this observation is apropos. It was merely apropos to my own thoughts which started off to the subject of *Catholic emancipation* which has occupied these countries and the English parliament for some months past. I am sorry I mentioned it, for I generally avoid politics, sure that I can do no good by talking of them. I will now only say that the Irish Catholics whose hopes had been much excited by feeling that object almost attained have borne their disappointment with great temper.

Much is attempting now in Ireland by English mercantile companies who have capital and scientific skill. *If* the want of the habits of puctuality in the workmen and lower orders of my but half-educated countrymen do not frustrate these attempts to establish manufactories and keep industry in employment, Ireland will become a flourishing and happy country. I enclose a prospectus of one of the companies I allude to. Mrs. Edgeworth's brother Captain Beaufort[81] is one of the directors. My brother William[82] one of the engineers employed. He is now at Valentia in the County of Kerry, cleaning [*clearing?*] out great slate quarries and examining the capabilities of the harbor, a very fine one. Two steam vessels are ordered for Valentia to trade with America—so that you see we are coming every day closer together. And who would have thought that *Steam* would annihilate both time and space!

I hope you remember Sir Walter Scott's beautiful eulogium on the inventor of the steam engine. No, I hope you do not remember it and that you may never see or hear it till my little Harry and Lucy reaches you, because you will find it there.

I have desired my bookseller to keep this letter till he has "Harry and Lucy Concluded"[83] to send you with it. It will be published I believe in a few days. I do not know whether you have any taste for scientific subjects? If you have not you will not like this little book. It is not nearly so entertaining as Frank or Rosamond, but when you read the preface you will see my reasons for writing it, and I will not tire you with more. If you have any young friends who have a *scientific turn* as it is called, put the book into their hands and you will oblige me by letting me know their remarks, especially where any difficulties occur. If the book should come to a second edition, I can by this means correct errors and supply deficiencies.

I send you a book which I am sure will amuse and please you, "Letters from the Irish Highlands." I think I mentioned in my last that these letters are written by different individuals of a family who reside in Connemara, County of Galway, a part of Ireland little known. Some of the letters are too *fine*, about the

81. Francis Beaufort (1774–1857) was the fourth Mrs. Edgeworth's brother and the brother-in-law of Lestock Wilson who married Fanny Edgeworth. After his first wife's death, he married Honora Edgeworth. He was made a rear admiral in 1846 and was knighted in 1848.
82. William Edgeworth (see Appendix A).
83. *Harry and Lucy Concluded: Being the Last Part of Early Lessons*, 4 vols. (Boston, 1825; London, 1827).

beauties of nature. Your excellent taste will perceive this and your benevolence will pass it over as a slight defect where there is so much good information and such liberal views.

We have been reading Lionel Lincoln.[84] We have made a list of some words and things of which we want to know the meaning or to have a description in that and in the New England tale[85] and in Redwood.

What is the origin and meaning of the *caucus*; what kind of tree is a *ground pine*? What is *musquash*? What is *Freshet*? What are *chores*? Whose lines are these which are in the New England tale?

> He who, from zone to zone,
> Guides through the boundless sky their certain flight,
> In the long way, that you must trace alone
> Will guide your steps aright.[86]

If you have any young friends who have poetical taste I wish you would make them read in the Review in the North American Review of Lord Byron's works a little poem of his and another of Moore's (pages 20, 21, and 22) which appear an amplification of Shenstone's Latin inscription on the death of *Maria*.[87] Let me know which of the two poems they prefer and whether they like either as well as the Latin inscription. Though

---

84. James Fenimore Cooper's *Lionel Lincoln* (New York, 1825) is laid in New England, opening in Boston on the eve of the American Revolution and giving accounts of the battles of Lexington, Concord, and Bunker Hill.

85. Catherine Maria Sedgwick, *A New England Tale* (1822), is concerned with the religious sect of the Friends.

86. Here ME quotes with reasonable accuracy the last verse of William Cullen Bryant's "To a Waterfowl" (1818).

> He who, from zone to zone,
> Guides through the boundless sky thy certain flight,
> In the long way that I must tread alone,
> Will lead my steps aright.

87. William Shenstone (1714–1763), English poet, a precursor of the romantic movement.

I do not understand Latin and have only had a literal translation made to me, I much prefer the terseness and strength of that single line. But do not tell this to those on whom you make the trial.

Have you seen a little poem on the death of General Moore?[88] Be sure you answer this question. Did I send you in my last some lines written by my friend Mrs. Barbauld[89] in her 80th year? Answer this also and you may profit by it.

You have such taste for domestic happiness and [are] so kindly sympathetic in ours that I must tell you we have been from many causes very happy this spring. My sister Lucy, that most patient creature who has been above four years confined to her couch by a spine complaint in the first bloom of life, is now recovering, has no more pain in her back, and can bear to be carried out on her elastic sofa into the lawn and through the shrubberies to enjoy the delights of nature, fresh air, green grass, budding trees, to her great delight. She will yet I trust see some of your American plants blooming.

Honora, another sister whose health had given us last winter great cause of anxiety, is recovering also. My two youngest brothers Francis and Pakenham,[90] fifteen and thirteen years old, who have been for some years at a school in England in London, the Charter House, have been with us for the Whitsuntide holidays and have delighted their mother's heart by their simple characters and cultivated minds. I send you a school prize poem of Francis's for which he obtained a silver medal. You see I consider you as a family friend and am not afraid to trust our little family vanities to you.

88. Charles Wolfe (1791–1823), Irish poet, remembered solely for his verses *Burial of Sir John Moore* (1816). A two-volume biography, *Remains of the Rev. Charles Wolfe*, by John Russell appeared in 1825.

89. Anna Letitia Aikin Barbauld (1743–1825), English poet and writer. She collaborated with her brother, Dr. John Aikin, on several works; her longest poem is *Eighteen Hundred and Eleven* (1811), a pessimistic outlook for the fortunes of Britain. Her niece, Lucy Aikin, published a collected edition of her works with a memoir.

90. Francis and Pakenham Edgeworth (see Appendix A).

Two of my sisters, Sophy (just twenty-one) whose happy marriage to Mr. Barry Fox I announced to you, and Fanny of whom I daresay I have already talked to you too much, are now at Geneva on their way back to us after a delightful tour in Italy. A dear old aunt of ours Mrs. [*Miss*] Mary Sneyd[91] (mentioned in my father's memoirs) is also just returning to us after a year's absence, and Francis and Pakenham are to be with us again in August for six weeks, about the time when Fanny and Sophy will be home. My engineer brother William also will be with us. You may conceive how happy we shall then be all together! Besides, that you may know all, my young brothers have two *new* old ponies, a grey named Bessy, a brown which Pakenham named Grace Nugent.[92] These add not a little to their holiday pleasures. Grace Nugent I am sorry to tell you has a wall-eye. Happy the mother whose sons at fifteen and twelve returning from a public London school are childish and innocent enough to be pleased with such diversions. The fault of our present race of boys is that they set up for men and are neither boys nor men but have the faults of both and virtues of neither.

Sir Walter Scott has promised to come to us this summer. This would complete our happiness. My sisters Sophy and Harriet were with me at Abbotsford and without vanity I may say he liked them much. Fanny is very anxious to see him; she never has had that happiness, and it is a real happiness, for he is as good and kind as he is superior in genius.

Farewell my dear friend. Pray tell me of all your family and of all that interests you, or I shall never more venture upon such family gossip as I have now treated you with. I have had several letters to write to America by this packet and I kept yours for my recreation, because I knew I could let my pen run free with you, free and securely.

Ever your obliged and affectionate friend,
Maria Edgeworth

91. Mary Sneyd (see Appendix A).
92. Named for the heroine of ME's *The Absentee*; Grace Nugent is an orphan of questionable ancestry.

[P.S.] I cannot find the Prospectus of the Hibernian Manufacturing Company which I had intended to enclose, but I enclose one which gives an idea of the plan. Let me know if the postage of my letters is expensive. Pray do, that I may alter the mode of conveyance if they are.

[*Copy*]   Wilmington 4 Oct. 1825

"My Dear Friend"

Let me also say, for who would not grasp with eagerness so valued a title, when bestowed by one whose superiority of mind is only equalled by her benevolence of disposition, and who is equally amiable and sincere. I was in bed and much indisposed when my dear husband entered the chamber with a bright smile on his countenance, and holding up your letter and the accompanying pamphlet said "I have brought something that will cure you" and if real pleasure could have proved a panacea, I should at once have been well, for never was one of these little eloquently silent messengers more welcome. Yet this, like most other human enjoyments had its alloy. It refers to a previous letter and some books, none of which have yet reached me; nor have some others, which as you promised them I am certain have been sent. I allude to "Dialogues on Botany," "Entomology" and "a History of England" for young people. I still hope they may arrive, and only mention them here that you may not deem me both ungrateful and stupid in neither acknowledging them or their contents. Parcels delivered to Mark & Wheatall, London, will be attended to; and from Liverpool I wish them sent to Mr. B. M. Myers, Merchant, New York (by vessels bound to N. York). You, who think of everything, enquire so earnestly respecting the expense of postage that I must tell you for all distances exceeding 400 miles we pay for each sheet 25 cts. or 1/2d Stg.; the expense of pamphlets or printed sheets is trifling provided the envelope is left open at one end, in the manner of newspapers. Your letters we have always deemed a pleasure too cheaply purchased for the postage to cost us a thought, yet as there is a constant water communication between this and New York the above address will obviate even that, and I shall be more secure of receiving them.

I owe many thanks to you and Mr. Francis Edgeworth for the prize poem and may venture to say without fearing to incur the charge of flattery that I read the poem of "Saul" with a mixture of surprise and pleasure, having seen no production equal to it from so youthful a pen. I can readily conceive the satisfaction with which it must have been read by his family and the joy of his mother's heart in welcoming home her good and sensible son.

I am glad the seeds arrived in time for sowing; I feared they would be late. February, March, April, and May are our season for gardening and the daily rose in the open air is not without bloom more than one month in the twelve. I thank you for your gardener's *bulletin* and hope he may have the satisfaction to add "thriving" to the pleasant little monosyllable *up* throughout his American Shrubbery. We have one sort of crocus here, large and double, the petals yellow intermingled with green, not fragrant, but valued because early in February it gives promise to our gardeners of the anticipated cheerfulness of spring. If you have other varieties I should be much pleased to obtain them. The nightingale is a stranger in our woods and we are indebted to poetry for any conception we may form of the sweetness of its notes. The Mocking bird is our best songster, and they frequently sing at night as well as in the day. I wish you could see the beautiful little humming birds flying around and sipping, or rather sucking in through their long slender bills, the sweets of the Woodbine and Convolvulus that grows near our windows; they frequently fly in, but I always regret it, it is so difficult to enable them to escape again without injury by fluttering against the wall or glass.

I have seen no poem on the death of Gen. Moore unless you allude to those noble and beautiful lines commencing "not a drum was heard nor a funeral note" *etc*. You did not send me the lines written by Mrs. Barbauld in her 80th year. I have examined carefully to leave none of your questions unanswered and will now endeavour to reply to your other enquiries. A *caucus* is a political party meeting, for the purpose of selecting one among the number of candidates for an office and supporting him in opposition to the others; the word is said to owe its origin to the circumstance of the first meetings of that kind (held in Boston about the commencement of the revolution) being chiefly attended by ship caulkers and hence denominated Caulkers' meetings; this may be an imaginary derivation but I have heard of none more feasible. I do not know, nor have my enquiries been successful respecting the ground pine, further than by a reference to Rees' Cyclopedia, where I merely find the Botanical name, *etc. Musquash* is the vulgar appellation in the Northern and Eastern states for Muskrat; *Chores*, a term peculiar to the Eastern, or as they are sometimes called New England States; it means little jobs about a house. "I have some chores to do." It may come from the French word chose. *Freshet*, (commonly pronounced *fresh*) the swelling of a river in consequence of great rains. "There is a great fresh in the river." I was not aware of the locality of the term. The lines, "He who from zone to zone, *etc*." occur in some stanzas addressed to a water fowl by William Cullen Bryant, a New England poet. He has written very little, but his poetry has merit; he now edits a new work called the New York Review. I have directed the attention of several of my young friends to Shenstone's inscription and Byron and Moore's amplification; their voice is unanimously given in favor of Moore; they feel the beauty of Shenstone's idea but find an additional charm in Moore's touching illustration, and in deciding between the two poems, they prefer the tenderness of Moore's allusion to character to Byron's energetic expression of personal feeling. One (my sister Ellen) remarks that the struggle between passion and misanthropy on the one hand and good feelings on the other is as evident in this as in Byron's other works. How different for instance the tone of emotion, that dictated the 2nd and 7th stanzas! It has always been my impression that to the want of proper maternal care and judgment in Lord B's early education were in a great measure to be attributed both his errors and his unhappiness; a wayward disposition and uncontrolled passion were throughout his life combating the impulses of a generous and noble heart, vitiating its sensibilities and corroding its enjoyments. What has not a mother to answer for, in training the early years of her son! I am gratified to find that your opinion concurs with my own in relation to Lord B's engaging in the Greek cause. I too have often said "he never could have died at a period more favorable to his character" but he would never, like Lafayette, have witnessed the glorious fruits of his sacrifices in the emancipation, propriety and happiness of a virtuous and grateful nation! I cannot pass your allusion to the Catholic emancipation Bill without a word on the subject of Mr. Brougham's noble and spirited reply to the Duke of York;[93] happy the Country when though birth confers distinction, it shields not prejudice and intolerance from the stroke of honest indignation. It is astonishing to think that the natural advantages of Ireland should so long have remained unimproved, not a single manufactory for pottery in the whole Island and none of its other facilities improved! Sincerely do I hope that your patriotick wishes may be speedily realized and that the attempts now making for the establishment of domestick manufactures may prove as successful, and the benefit as permanent, as similar works have in numberless instances proved, to these States.

My pleasure in reading again Sir W. Scott's beautiful eulogium on Mr. Watt will not be at all diminished by my perfect

93. Henry Peter Brougham, first Baron Brougham and Vaux (1778–1868), lord chancellor of England, 1830–34. Frederick Augustus, duke of York (1763–1827), second son of George III.

recollection of it, or by a renewal of the delightful feelings which its perusal long since inspired. Do not therefore be sorry that I shall not "first see it in your little Harry and Lucy." You say, "I have desired my publisher to keep this letter till he has 'Harry and Lucy Concluded' to send you with it." The letter was forwarded from Liverpool, and as I before mentioned without *any books*. I am not fearful of not liking Harry and Lucy. I delight in scientific subjects when sufficiently simplified to allow one who has no acquaintance with mathematicks, and a very limited knowledge of Natural Philosophy, to understand them. Your work being designed for young persons will doubtless possess this advantage for me, in addition to that charm of style which never forsakes your pen. I hope soon to bid my little instructive friends "Welcome." This last word reminds me that your friend Sir W. Scott has paid you his promised visit;[94] this we learned from the newspapers, and I tried to imagine the enjoyment felt by your assembled happy family in entertaining such a guest. In the bosom of a most amiable family, the friend and companion of talent and intelligence wherever they are found, possessing within yourself inexhaustible resources and in the possession of worldly prosperity, how very happy are you my Dear Miss Edgeworth, and how well do you deserve to be so; what is left for your friend to wish, but that you, like your venerated parent, may through a long life, continue to taste such pure enjoyments. We have been reading the "Crusades." The Betrothed I think in point of interest and various other excellencies ranks next to Ivanhoe. "The Talisman"[95] I find much inferior; the incidents

94. Scott visited Edgeworthstown for a long weekend in August 1825. He was accompanied by his elder son, his well-dowered bride mentioned in ME's last letter, his daughter Anne, and her husband Lockhart. Maria and her sister traveled with the Scotts to Killarney, "agreeably delayed,"Lockhard wrote, "by the hospitalities of Miss Edgeworth's old friends, and several of Sir Walter's new ones, at various mansions on our line of route." At Tralee, William Edgeworth joined them. In Dublin, Sophy and Fanny, just returned from Italy, and Francis and Pakenham joined the party to celebrate Sir Walter's birthday, 15 August, at his son's house.

95. Modern criticism would reverse RML's finding *The Betrothed* superior to *The Talisman*. Richard I of England is the hero of the latter.

appear to want that sort of connexion which denotes a preconceived, though concealed plan, and imparts to fiction a stronger resemblance of reality; in this tale they appear to have been invented as the story progressed. I cannot tolerate Sir Kenneth's breach of faith; if not out of nature, it is out of character in a Valiant Knight, a Scot and above all a Scottish prince, whose nice sense of honor had been a principal motive in inducing him to partake in the Crusade. There is also a want of dignity in his consenting to return to the English Camp disguised as a Nubian; Saladin too is exhibited under too many different garbs. The story is doubtless interesting, but not entirely what I should have anticipated from the subject and the actors, when touched by the magic pen of such a master. The recollection of Madame Cotin's interesting "Matilde"[96] is not perhaps favorable in the comparison it naturally awakens; in the portrait of Richard however, "The Talisman" has a decided superiority. I always wonder at myself after having expressed my ideas on literary subjects so freely to you, but your kindness sets me so much at ease that I do not even fear appearing presumptuous, and am willing to hazard a mistaken opinion in the hope of discovering its defects, in its want of conformity with your more accurate judgments.

We have been much interested in reading Madame Campan's "private journals, and her memoirs of Marie Antoinette;"[97] poor Marie Antoinette, whose life was forfeited to evil counsellors and venial acts of imprudence. What Royal pair were ever less fitted for a Throne! Happy had been their lot to have

96. Marie Risteau Cottin (1770–1807). Called Sophie Cottin, her *Mathilde: ou Mémoires tires de l'Histoire des Croisades* was published in London in 1805. Translated into English it appeared as *The Saracen: or Matilda and Malek Adhel, A Crusade Romance from the French of Madame Cottin* (New York, 1810).

97. Jeanne Louise Henriette Genest Campan (1752–1822), French educator, companion of Marie Antoinette. After the Revolution, she established a school at St. Germain, and later she was appointed head of the academy established by Napoleon for the daughters and sisters of members of the Legion of Honor. She is remembered for her *Mémoires sur la vie privée de Marie Antoinette, suivis de souvenirs et anecdotes historiques sur les règnes de Louis XIV–XV* (Paris, 1823). ME visited her fashionable school for young ladies in November 1802. The visit was made memorable by Madame Récamier's driving there to meet ME.

exchanged royalty for mediocrity, where amid the shades of private life her amiable qualities might have been developed, her levities exchanged for innocent gaiety, and the amicable but weak and vacillating monarch might have enjoyed his favorite pursuits, with the character of a worthy man, a good master, and the kind father of a family. Did you, or did your father in any of his visits to France, become acquainted with Madame Campan's establishment? I am much pleased with her thoughts on education; they present no new systems, but their plainness and good sense evince their practical utility. So much simplicity of character and such a knowledge of domestick occupations and pleasures with a taste for their enjoyment, took me by surprise from the pen of a Court lady and the first woman of a Queen. I have been wishing to ask you something respecting the family of Sir W. Scott; is Mrs. or Lady S. rather, remarkably intelligent? Is their family numerous and do any of them appear to inherit their Father's talents? If any of these questions are at all indiscreet, I know you will pardon and leave them unanswered.

I have not yet told you, that in July last, I gave birth to my second child, a daughter, my little Ellen,[98] who rests on my arm while I write; she was very ill soon after her birth and is still a delicate child, nor has my health since been so good as formerly; I hope much for us both from the bracing season which is fast approaching.

Our son, Marx Edgeworth, is a lively, amiable little fellow, a general favorite. I therefore need not add, not a spoiled child. Mother like, I could relate a score of anecdotes and I believe you will indulge me by listening to one or two. At the table yesterday, some one asked, "Are the Rice birds done?" "Oh," said Edgeworth, "Are the rice birds for dinner?" "Only some for Mother." "Well," replied he, "to be sure I would not be so *cruel* as to want any of *them*, when Mother is sick upstairs." I was

98. See Appendix B.

hearing him his lesson; he spelled and read, "the ink," "my arm," "an egg," and he stopped and said with delighted emphasis, "Oh *thank* you Mother for letting me read so many words that I can understand."

Our summer has been cheered by the presence of my sister Ellen, who had not visited me before for three years, and now I must soon prepare myself for the pain of separation! Tho' I hardly know how to part from her, a pleasure is in reserve for us previously, that of welcoming the return of our third daughter Anna,[99] who has spent the summer with my parents and who will be accompanied by Eliza, the young sister whom I have formerly mentioned to you as being under my special care; their presence will add greatly to the happiness of our domestick circle; a word too of my brother Alfred,[100] who after completing his studies at the U.S. Military Academy, West Point, N. York, paid us last summer a delightful visit. He is enrolled in the Corps of Engineers with the rank of 2nd Lieut. and is at present engaged in superintending some publick works on James River, Virginia; he had been at the academy since 1819 and it is a happiness to his family that he is now stationed near them. I hope it will be in his power at no very distant day to realize his wish to visit Europe; how eager shall I then be to solicit for him your kind attention. You see I am resolved to prove to you the pleasure which your page of domestick occurrences afforded me. I had often thought of her whom you once mentioned as your poor invalid sister Lucy and sincerely congratulate both you and herself upon her improved state of health, as well as that of your sister Honora. I hope you had a happy meeting with Mrs. Fox and your sister Fanny whom you now mention to me for the first time, though you say, "of whom I dare say I have already talked to you too much." Do tell me something of her. I feel quite as if I were acquainted with Mrs. Mary Sneyd to whom as well as to Mrs. Edgeworth I must beg you to offer my

99. Anna, Mr. Lazarus's daughter by his first wife (see Appendix B).
100. Alfred Mordecai (see Appendix B).

best regards. I hope your brothers found their favorites Betsey and Grace Nugent as tractable as ever; if the latter possesses any portion of the tempered spirit of her namesake, I do not wonder at her being thought (the weak eye notwithstanding) a very charming creature.

I send with this two papers, in which you will find a curious proclamation, and an address of Mr. Noah's; they may amuse you by their singularity. The oration affords a concise view of the history of our nation since the captivity. Mr. Noah appears to entertain sanguine hopes of the success of his scheme; by all others it is deemed visionary. His invitation can at any rate do no harm, since none can be injured by emigrating to a country possessing a fertile soil and a free and happy government, tho' they may not incline to submit implicitly to the self-constituted "governor" and judge of Israel. Adieu my dear friend; ere long I hope to be again called upon to assure you how truly I am

Your obliged and affectionate friend
R. L.

Edgeworthstown, January 9, 1826

A happy new year to you and yours my dear kind hearted friend. I hope this will find you in the enjuyment of that great bodily blessing which is of all blessings the only one I know independent of the will—Health. Indeed upon reflexion I should not say independent of the *will* for people ruin their health often by their own will, and though they cannot always preserve it by the best will or conduct yet they can endure with patience and fortitude the want of health, and this often tends to lessen suffering and restore the powers. Of this we have seen a striking example in that sister Lucy I mentioned to you who after five years' confinement (often in agony) to her couch is now in the library again with us every evening and quite free from pain, resuming all those of her occupations and accomplishments which she could not pursue while confined. She is now at the pianoforte again; we can hardly believe our eyes and ears.

I rejoice exceedingly that my letter was a cordial to you when you were indisposed, and you could not gratify me more than by the picture you draw of your husband bringing it to you and saying he was sure he brought something that would do you good.

I enclose a letter I have received from my bookseller in answer to one of the inquiries I wrote concerning books and parcels sent you. You see there is a chance, almost a certainty, of Harry and Lucy and crocus roots being safe with Mr. Carey, Philadelphia, and you must commission some friend to call for them and convey them to Wilmington.

I have desired my bookseller to send Entomology, Dialogues on Botany and Mrs. Kater's[101] little history of England to the person in London whom you mention in your last. I think it appears that I mistook the will for the deed and that no order from me to Hunter to send these books ever reached him. However that may be I hope they will now reach you. Before you plant the crocus roots [*two lines left blank here*] and let me know if they flower next spring. I have been told that you have no crocusses in America. Is that a fable?

Thank you for answering so very exactly all our questions. Lucy thanks you particularly. Pray tell us what kind of birds Rice-birds are. How large? Send me some feathers of a rice-bird, *You dear little boy*, who would not eat one when your mother was ill and wanted it. What are *yellow* violets? We find them in Bryant's poems. Are they found on earth or only in poetical fiction? Send me some seeds of them. Send me also a few more Convolvuli seed, as many of those you sent are new and much

101. ME met Captain Henry Kater (1777–1835) and his wife with some frequency in London. He sold his commission to devote his time to scientific studies, and he published several books in this area. Mrs. Kater was born Mary Frances Reeve.

prized in this country. I gave some to a friend and relative of mine, Lady Pakenham (a near relation to that poor gallant, rash Sir Edward Pakenham[102] who perished at the siege of New Orleans). She was ill and confined to her room when the seeds came up and flowered and her daughters brought her in as she told me a new flower, *quite new* to her, for many successive days. It was a great delight to her in sickness which I owe to you. She had been particularly kind to Lucy and others of my family in sickness.

Lucy asks whether either insects or birds live in the long grey moss which hangs from your trees.

I have read two French books lately which are excessively interesting, written by a father and son in very different styles, both excellent in their way, the one polished and perfect French of *l'ancien régime*, the other less polished in style with many expressions not in the dictionnaire de l'Académie but all strong, expressive, fit for the business of various life, but not for Court. The first work describing the polished yet degenerate Court and times of France before the Revolution and the causes that led to that Revolution, the other work shewing *some* of the consequences during the reign of Napoleon. The two works are by le Comte de Ségur[103] and le Comte Philip, General de Ségur,[104] his son. The title of the first, *Mémoires et Souvenirs par le Comte de Ségur*, the title of the other, *Histoire de Napoléon et de la Grande*

102. Sir Edward Michael Pakenham (1778–1815), British soldier. He was ME's cousin and the brother of the Duchess of Wellington. He distinguished himself under Wellington in Spain. He commanded the British forces that attacked New Orleans on 8 January 1815, and he was killed in that engagement.

103. Comte Louis Philippe Ségur (1753–1830), French diplomat and historian; *Mémoires*, 3 vols. (1824).

104. Comte Philippe Paul Ségur (1780–1873), son of Louis Philippe Ségur, French general and historian. His *Histoire de Napoléon et de la grande armée pendant l'année 1812* (1824) ran through numerous editions and was translated widely. The unfavorable portrait of Napoleon provoked a challenge from General Gourgaud, and Ségur was wounded in the ensuing duel. As a young man he translated ME's *Belinda* into French, and when she visited Paris in 1802, she found everyone reading it and "elderly ladies recommending it to their nieces and granddaughters as a model of what a young woman of the world ought to be" (Elizabeth Inglis-Jones, *The Great Maria*, p. 71).

Armée l'An 1812. The Count de Ségur's book will interest Americans particularly because it gives a history of his travels in America during the American war and of all he and your dear La Fayette and other distinguished French Officers did, said, or thought during that war. It is a curious picture of a French courtier's view of America.

The General Ségur's book is still more interesting to the whole world. It contains a history of the campaign in Russia, of all the heroism, all the horrors of that mad expedition. It confirms all that La Beaume[105] had said and which had been doubted as beyond possibility. Ségur who was an eye and ear witness adds more strong instances of horrible suffering. As a general lesson against Ambition and *Invading* armies, and all the horror of war, it is invaluable, provided mankind would take it.

It is interesting also on another account as recording more of the real history and developing more of the character of Bonaparte at this period of his life and at a most trying crisis than ever before was given to the public. It bears the stamp of truth and is as free from party spirit as we can expect human nature to be. General Gourgaud[106] fought a duel nevertheless with General Ségur for misrepresenting Bonaparte. But the work rises in credit every day in Paris and has gone through many editions as a French correspondent just now informs me.

The Duke of Wellington says it is the best history of a campaign he ever read in modern days and he says it has raised

105. Most likely a member of the family Griffet de la Beaune. Antoine Gilbert Griffet de la Beaune (1756–1805), French writer and translator of English works, wrote for the *Mercure de France*, but his dates do not accord with the events described in ME's letter.
106. Baron Gaspar Gourgaud (1783–1852), French soldier and writer. He entered the French army in 1802 and was closely associated with Napoleon in the Russian Campaign in 1812. He went to St. Helena with Napoleon but later left because of friction with other officers. He lived for awhile in England but returned to active service in the French army in 1830. He was among those sent to St. Helena to return the ashes of Napoleon to Paris. His dispute with Philippe de Ségur resulted in *Napoléon et la grande armée en Russie; Examen critique de l'ouvrage de M. le comte P. de Ségur* (1824). He also took exception to Sir Walter Scott's biography and published *Réfutation de la vie de Napoleon par Sir Walter Scott* (1827).

his opinion of Bonaparte as a general, that he shewed great military talents.

I begin to fear that I have said all this to you before. I am obliged to write in haste, almost illegible haste, as I have many other letters to write and much business to do, having now the receiving of all my brother's rents and much business just at this moment.

Forgive me then for having said too much and too little in this letter and not having proportioned anything as I ought for your amusement. My new married or last-year-married sister and her husband Barry Fox have left us this morning to go and settle in their own house forty miles distant. This has not assisted to clear my intellects, but you Americans with your grand distances will laugh at forty miles separation. I wish some of your steamboats would bring you to us. Whenever your friends come, certain welcome!

Affectionately yours,
Maria Edgeworth

[P.S.] I wish you could send me a mocking bird. If you could get it alive to London, let it be left at Captain Beaufort's, 51 Manchester St. If you can send it to Liverpool, direct it to the care of Mr. Cropper, Paradise Street. But I fear the poor bird would not live in our climate.

Edgeworthstown, January 10, 1826

I must add a postscript to my letter of yesterday which I wrote and sent off in such a hurry that I forgot many questions which I see looking over your letter today I should have answered.

Besides I forgot to fill up a blank I left in my letter where I desired you to steep the crocus roots—in I neglected to say *what*. I now say lukewarm milk and water. I hope some of the crocusses

I have sent may turn out *purple*; they are beautiful and you say you have only the yellow.

In reply to your question about my sister Fanny, I must tell you that you cannot do me a greater pleasure than to set me talking of her, provided you will, as I know you kindly will, permit me to talk as I think of her. She is Mrs. Edgeworth's eldest daughter. I was present at her birth; she was put into my inexperienced, joyful, fearful hands to hold, and so fearful, so foolish, so nervous was I that I did not dare to stir lest her head should come off. I remember I wanted to carry her down to my father to shew the sight, but I could not venture down the stairs. I felt as if I would tumble down with my precious load and tho a servant offered to go down step by step before me and backwards too that he might catch us if we fell, I dared not and actually turned back. I hope this will make you laugh. Fanny is 100,000,000,000,000,000,000—in short incalculably dearer to me *now* than any infant could be to the most unreasonably fond mother. She has a highly cultivated mind both in literature and science. She has a great sensibility, no affectation, highly polished, gentle, soft, and though highly polished perfectly simple manners. Conversation that pleases all the best informed and the least informed, because it has both original thought and select reading to recommend and adorn it. She has a *genius*, yes I must say an hereditary genius for drawing. She is remarkably graceful in her motions, has a sweet voice, a very expressive countenance, beautiful liquid intelligent feeling grey-blue eyes, light brown hair, *was* very pretty till delicate health faded her color and made her person too thin. She has been in London, Paris, Geneva with me for many months and lately with her sister Fox and Barry Fox at Rome, Florence, everywhere abroad, and has had more than her share of admiration, but she is quite unspoiled by this and returned to her own country and own home, preferring them after comparison and all home affections and occupations to all others. Happy the man who shall have such a woman for his wife. But I have not a guess who he may be; that is all I have to complain of.

You ask me about Sir Walter Scott's family. Lady Scott is of French parentage and tho thirty years resident in England still speaks broken English. She is not a literary woman. She makes her house very agreeable to Sir W. Scott's visitors and friends *if* she likes them, but she is too sincere and too vivacious to pretend where she does not like or to disguise dislike where she feels it. She was kind enough to like my sisters and me and was so very obliging to us that I should be most ungrateful if I said any thing derogatory of her. Mrs. Lockhart, Scott's favorite daughter, is most amiable and winning. She did not come with him to Ireland; she stayed at home with her children. Anne his second daughter, unmarried, came. She is as Sir W. Scott says like Shakespear's Beatrice. Mr. Lockhart is very clever and fond of Sir Walter, and tho he is feared as the author of Peter's Letters, I never feared but much like him. He has laid aside his satirical pen. Adam Blair, Reginald Dalton, and Mathew Wald are his.

Sir Walter Scott has two sons, the eldest[107]—an officer, a gentleman, a man of honor and of sense but not with his father's genius and without a taste for literature, just married to a simple hearted Jeannie, a Scotch heiress—travelled with us.

Sir W's youngest son[108] about seventeen promises to have literary talents.

Again much hurried I must break off abruptly.

Ever sincerely yours,
Maria Edgeworth

[P.S.] I think as you do that Lord Byron's mother had much to answer for and his wife more.

How glad we shall be to receive your brother Alfred whenever he comes, the sooner the better.

107. Walter (1801–1847) succeeded to the baronetcy, which had been conferred on Scott in 1820, and the title became extinct on his death.
108. Charles (1805–41).

I am too rich and too joyful to be patient, and must indulge myself by hastening to thank as best I may, my dear, kind, inestimable friend for her several delightful letters and parcels which have just reached me. Two, dated the 16th and 17th of January came by this night's mail, and a line on the envelope tells me that the "Dialogues on Botany" and "Entomology" and "The History of England" are received, and will be forwarded by the first opportunity from Richmond, Va. I have been quite uneasy at the long delay of those sent to Messrs. Carey and Lea; let me give you my husband's account of them. "On my arrival at Philadelphia one of my first objects was to call on Carey and Lea, who informed me that the parcels I enquired for had been lying for three months in the Custom house; this was provoking, for you know I had written to them immediately on the receipt of Mr. Miller's letter, and my friend Mr. Adams assures me he had called on them two or three times, enquiring for these very parcels. I proceeded directly to the Custom house, and there found three parcels. They were of course opened before delivery, and I find they contain "Harry and Lucy Concluded," "Letters from the Irish Highlands," "Friendship's offering for 1825,"[109] (a

109. In a letter to her aunt, Mrs. Ruxton, ME wrote on 6 January 1825: "In a few days I trust—you know I am a great truster—that you will receive a packet franked by Lord Bathurst, containing only a little pocket-book—'Friendships' Offering, for 1825,' dizened out; I fear you will think it too fine for your taste, but there is in it, as you will find, the old 'Mental Thermometer,' which was once a favorite of yours. You will wonder how it came there—simply thus. Last autumn came by the coach a parcel containing just such a book as this for last year, and a letter from Mr. Lupton Relfe—a foreigner settled in London—and he prayed in most polite bookseller strain that I would look over my portfolio for some trifle for this book for 1825. I might have looked over 'my portfolio' till doomsday, as I have not an unpublished scrap, except 'Take for Granted.' But I recollected the 'Mental Thermometer,' and that it had never been *out*, except in the 'Irish Farmer's Journal'—not known in England. So I routed in the garret under pyramids of old newspapers, with my mother's prognostics that I should never find it, and loud prophecies that I should catch my death, which I did not, but dirty and dusty and cobwebby I came forth after two hours' groveling, with my object in my hand! Cut it out, added a few lines of new end to it, and packed it

very beautiful little volume,) and a box of Bulbous roots. All these are safely deposited in my portmanteau, that I may have the pleasure of presenting them myself. But I will not withhold a letter which I found in one of the Vols., and which you will already have seen enclosed."[110] This letter is one which I had long lamented as lost, dated May 2, 1825, and I was so much rejoiced to obtain it at last, that at the moment I could not be vexed even by the delay; feelings of pleasure predominated over every other. A week later, my dear husband returned, and enriched me with the contents of his trunk. Harry and Lucy, charming Harry and Lucy was open before me when these two fresh proofs of your kindness arrived. How can I find words to thank you for the very great pleasure you have already afforded me and I do not yet know the extent of my obligation for I have not finished reading even Harry & Lucy. But I must write now; each moment's delay is treason against gratitude and I love to think that your amiable and ever ready sympathy will make you a participator in the pleasure of which you are yourself the source.

---

off to Lupton Relfe, telling him that it was an old thing written when I was six-teen. Weeks elapsed, and I heard no more, when there came a letter exuberant in gratitude, and sending a parcel containing six copies of the new memorandum book, and a most beautiful twelfth edition of Scott's 'Poetical Works,' bound in the most elegant manner, and with most beautifully engraved frontispieces and vignettes, and a £5 note. I was quite ashamed—but I have done all I could for him by giving the 'Friendship's Offerings' to all the fine people I could think of. The set of Scott's Works made a nice New Year's gift for Harriet; she had seen this edition at Edinburgh and particularly wished for it. The £5 I have sent to Harriet Beaufort to be laid out in books for Fanny Stewart. Little did I think the poor old 'Thermometer' would give me so much pleasure.

"Here comes the carriage rolling round. I feel guilty; what will my mother say to me, so long a letter at this time of night? Yours affectionately in all the haste of guilt, conscience-striken: that is, found out. No—all safe, all innocent—because *not found out. Finis.* By the author of 'Moral Tales' and 'Practical Education' " (Augustus J. C. Hare, *Maria Edgeworth, Life and Letters,* [Boston and New York, 1895], 2:475–76).

110. In Mrs. Lazarus's copy she crossed out a sentence that follows in Mr. Lazarus's letter to his wife: "Should you have been tempted to break the seal [of Maria Edgeworth's letter] before you read this, I will excuse you, or have you like a real epicure reserved the most delicious morsel for the last?"

I ought not yet to speak of Harry & Lucy; having just commenced the 3rd volume of this admirable juvenile encyclopaedia, I cannot do it full justice; but this I must say that I have never read a book in which so much precise and accurate information on so great a variety of subjects has been so pleasingly conveyed. The work stands alone, unrivalled even by those delightful works of the same hand which had preceded it. Dr. Darwin[111] succeeded in adorning science with the fairest flowers and richest gems of poetry, but you have accomplished still more, in forming for it a vehicle simple, elegant, above all eminently useful; a vehicle the mechanism of which demanded equal genius if less of fancy, and which wends its way so smoothly and so easily that those who enter it may with reason declare that they have found "a royal road," if not "to Geometry" at least to many other sciences. How much does the present generation, how much will succeeding ones owe to one who has done so much "to raise the genius and to mend the heart," who has thus without puerility, without deception, combined science with delight. Our daughters are charmed with the part they have read and heard, and what will please you still more, they are anxious to become more thoroughly acquainted with the subjects thus introduced to their notice. Almira,[112] a fine little girl, ten years of age, earnestly enquires how old Harry & Lucy could be, to be so sensible and know so much; she seems to feel an alarming sense of inferiority, which will I am sure prove an incitement to a more eager pursuit of knowledge and more steady habits of attention. "Friendship's Offering" is a precious little volume; its title adds all that a title can to its value. You may be very sure that I have found time to glance at "the Mental

111. Erasmus Darwin (1731–1802), English man of science and poet. He was an intimate friend of Richard Lovell Edgeworth. Among his works are the *Botanic Garden* (1791), a long "botanical" poem; *Zoonomia* (1794–96), a medical treatise; and a paper on *Female Education in Boarding Schools* (1797). He was the grandfather of the famous Charles Darwin.
112. Almira Emma, Mr. Lazarus's youngest daughter by his first wife, born 20 September 1814.

Thermometer."[113] I was in hopes to find the idea which you had started, pursued and illustrated, and it was with surprise and regret that I found I had so soon turned the last page. You only intended to furnish an ingenious idea, for those who please to pursue it to the best of their ability.

It is very, very true that we too often make a false estimate of happiness; yet I have not philosophy enough to agree with you entirely in the sentiment expressed in one of the letters before me, "that health" (and this in a qualified sense) "is the only blessing we enjoy independent of the will." The will, I admit, may mar the choicest blessings and highest enjoyments, but it does not I think depend always on the will to secure them even in a moderate degree. Contentment even cheerfulness may be ours, while suffering under the pressure of care, of poverty, of persecution, of almost all "the nameless ills that flesh is heir to." But that virtue which enables us to endure, to bear up against them, to smile upon the rack, does not still render that endurance easy. Remove the evil, supply the good, an increased sensation of happiness will be the result, and those who have been most capable of exerting equanimity in misfortune will, I believe in most cases, be most susceptible of true enjoyment. Have I mistaken the extent of your assertion and do we agree in this opinion?

But the Mental Thermometer and the ideas that connected itself with it have withdrawn me from the review I was taking of your kind presents. Of the Crocus roots, I was going to say that I fear they have been injured by their long detention; they had sprouted, but the shoot is dry and withered, and the roots as hard as a lump of chalk. I have put them in a cool place, buried in sand, intending to set them out in the fall, but on reflection, it may be better to soak them as you direct and put them in the earth at once, taking care to protect them from the excessive heat of the sun. I hope they may yet retain enough of the

113. "The Mental Thermometer," the rewritten contribution of ME to *Friendship's Offering* (1825).

vegetating principle to be revived. I shall divide them with a friend more skillful than myself and who is exceedingly fond of flowers; perhaps his may succeed if mine do not. I shall try my utmost, if care and attention will avail, to save them and will let you know the result. The purple will indeed be a rarity. I am rejoiced that you found some new flowers among the Convolvulus and that they conveyed even a momentary gratification to your sick friend—how like your own self is it, to turn to me as its cause! You shall have an abundance of fresh seeds as soon as they are ripe. I do not know the *yellow* violet. Bryant may allude to the Viola Tricolor which I have often heard called the Turkey violet, and have remarked in a bed covered thickly with them that the yellow colour is predominant. Have you the Lagerstroemia, the pink and the lilac? Did the Cassine or the nondescript succeed? If not, we must make another trial. My sister Ellen sent me some time since a humming bird's nest for you. I had been waiting till I obtained a bird to send with it, and I am pleased that we had, in part, anticipated your wish. The Mocking Bird I will send when I can place it in charge of some one who will take care of it on the passage; it is a delightful songster.

"If you draw send me a sketch of your children and yourself." How much would it delight me to comply with this request, but Alas! I cannot draw, else my little family group would not probably have staid to await your bidding. But let me shew you just here my berry brown boy, with his oval face, "expressive bluish-grey eyes," and bright animated smile, telling me as he did this morning, "Mother when I give you pleasure, I feel just as much pleasure myself as you have"—or asking sorrowfully as he did yesterday "let me have some other punishment instead of eating my dinner at the side table, because I do not want father and every body that sees me to feel sorry that I have been bad." He does not exactly understand how a lady so very far off can be named his name, and can know that he is here, and want him to send her feathers of a rice bird. "But I will send her some, as soon as I get any." The rice bird—but stay, you must first glance at my little Ellen, who is plump as a rice bird herself, and fair and fresh as a lily or blush rose. She has large clear blue eyes and long silken lashes, coral lips, between which six teeth, like little white grains of rice, display themselves as she laughs and chatters away in a dialect all her own. Now her father enters she claps her hands, and then employing them in aid of her yet unpractised feet, hastens to meet him, and the next moment is happy in his arms!

Now the Rice bird, or Emberiza Oryzivora, so called from its fondness for rice (see Rees' *Cyclo.*); it belongs I find to the "8th order (Passeres) of Linnaeus. The English ortolan belongs to the same genus and has been erroneously described as the same." They visit us annually in their passage from the West Indies (according to Mr. Edwards), arrive early in August while the rice is milky and remain about three weeks committing sad ravages on the rice fields. On their first appearance, they are very poor, but in the course of a few days become a perfect ball of fat, and when shot are said to burst sometimes as they fall. They are not larger than a sparrow, and are esteemed a great delicacy, one with which the planters would gladly dispense, could they be freed from its ravages.

Your sister Lucy inquires whether either birds or insects live among our long moss. She will I know excuse me if before I reply to her question I turn over the leaves in Harry and Lucy to read what you have said of it there. Delightful, delightful! Your pen is surely endowed with all that was enviable in the gift bestowed on Midas! How very interesting do the contents of that tiny box appear, now that it has touched them! My husband sat reading at my side when without a word of preface, I led him into lady Digby's green house and looked up now and then reciprocating the smile of surprise and pleasure that beamed in his eye and animated his whole countenance. While I was reading, Anna, our third daughter entered, caught a familiar sound, and eagerly advanced, "Why Mamma! what is that! do let me see, if you have finished reading it." "Yes, in a moment, when I have seen what follows about the flos aëris." But can this moss be of the genus Tillandsia? It is seldom found on high, dry land, frequently in the vicinity of marshes, and it abounds on trees which grow on the margins of some of our rivers.[114] I have always believed that a moist atmosphere was essential to its production and growth, and so it may be, yet its attaching itself to a tree instead of springing from the earth, which would afford it a greater degree of moisture may obviate the objection. Do you not think so? Bird's nests are found in the trees from which the moss hangs; they evidently do not avoid, but they do not appear to seek it. It is I think free from insects; I have repeatedly examined masses of it and have never seen a single insect on any. Neither have I seen on the trees that *bear* it (if I may say so) such masses of caterpillars' webs as we frequently see in others; nor do their leaves bear the marks of such ravages; I am therefore inclined to believe that it does not form a harbour for insects.

I sympathize with all my heart in your happiness at the restoration of your sweet, amiable sister Lucy. May she continue to improve in health and in the possession of that, and number-less other blessings, find a well earned recompense for her patient, heroic endurance of suffering.

That charming sister Fanny too! Thanks again and again for your animated description of her, and doubt not that you suc-ceeded in amusing me with your essay in the department of nurse. But I must tell you that my pleasures in dwelling on this review of her various attractive and endearing qualities is min-gled with a feeling of restlessness and impatience. Knowing this much how can I forbear wishing to know more of her? To see her, to converse with her, to love her!—and if I could, to make her love me.

It is so easy too to cross the Atlantick now, in our delightfully convenient packets, that if—Ah! that most unaccommodating little word, always obtruding and intruding, and with its auxil-

114. Mrs. Lazarus objected to the description of Spanish moss as essentially a dry-country plant; it absorbs its moisture from the air.

iary host of impediments and obstacles leveling our best built airy edifices prone on the ground. My brother Alfred has not relinquished his hopes of visiting you, tho' not probably within a very short period of time. At present he is occupied in superintending some military works at Old Point Comfort, Virginia. I know how much he will be gratified at your kind cordial invitation and to accept it as soon as he possibly can. I have written to Miss Sedgwick, the author of "Redwood," and copied for her the remarks which you wished should be communicated. When I receive her answer, I will inform you. She is, I am told, a very unassuming woman, an orphan, residing with two brothers at the family mansion in Massachusetts. I have also written to Mr. Miller to acquaint him with the safe arrival of the parcels, having previously informed him that they had not been duly received.

Our citizens are all in mourning, a voluntary national mourning, for our two late ex-Presidents Adams and Jefferson. By one of those extraordinary coincidences, which appears improbable in fictitious narratives but sometimes do occur in real life, they expired on the same day, and that day the *4th of July*, celebrated as a jubilee, being the *50th anniversary* of American Independence! Mr. Adams and Mr. Jefferson had been among the most zealous advocates for the passage of the bill which declared us "free and independent States." Both were on the committee for framing the Declaration, and to the eloquent pen of Mr. Jefferson do we owe that noble production. You have it I am sure, but read it now again for my sake; *I* never can without feeling my heart swell with patriotic emotion, and those less interested than we Americans will admire the energetick, dignified, yet temperate expression which characterizes it from beginning to end. Mr. Adams and Mr. Jefferson with the two surviving ex-Presidents (Madison and Monroe) and Mr. Carrol, now the only survivor of those who signed the declaration, had been invited to attend the celebration of the Jubilee at Washington, and arrangements made for their comfort on the journey. They all declined, pleading infirmity and indisposition, but in language whose warmth and energy indicated the full possession of their mental faculties, and allowed us to indulge the hope that they might yet for years enjoy the comforts of a green old age. On the 3rd of July Mr. Jefferson's indisposition increased; he expressed perfect submission to the Divine Will but hoped that he might survive to breathe the air of the 50th anniversary. He was conscious of doing so and expired about one o'clock, the very hour in which thousands and tens of thousands of his countrymen were assembled, listening to the Declaration penned by his hand. The closing hours of Mr. Adams were not less remarkable; he had dictated a toast to "freedom and independence forever" to be drank in his name, and on the morning of the 4th, hearing the report of cannon he asked the cause; reminded of the time, he replied, "It is a great and glorious day," and spoke no more. Thus was the latest throb of these two great men given to their country and in the heart of that grateful country will their deeds be recorded, their memory enshrined. Mr. Adams had been less popular than his colleague, but all party spirit is laid aside. If the American papers are received in England before you receive this, I may fear to have vexed your ear with a twice told tale, but I cannot forbear touching on a subject which at present forms the theme of every tongue. I perceive by the letter of Mr. Miller which you inclosed to me that you had sent a copy of Harry and Lucy to Mr. Jefferson. I hope it arrived in time for him to receive and acknowledge it; pray tell me if it did. I requested a friend in N.Y. some weeks since to send you Cooper's last novel, The Last of the Mohicans, which I think you will find interesting. I hope you have received it. Your future parcels shall be addressed as you direct in the letters just received; these books were sent to the care of Mr. Evans who had forwarded letters to me some time since. I have so many, many things to say, that I hardly know how to close this, but it will be too unreasonable to trespass on your time and patience with another sheet; besides I shall have this pleasure soon again when I have read "Letters from the Irish Highlands" and all the rest of my delightful volumes. I do not seek to express half the gratitude I feel for all your kindness; I could not without saying both too much and too little, but you my dear, my valued friend, will understand and allow your own heart to dictate that to which I cannot give utterance.

Believe me ever your obliged, affectionate, devoted friend
R. L.

[*Original*]   Wilmington, January 6th, 1827

My dear Madam

I little thought when I last addressed you that six whole months would intervene before I should resume so pleasing an occupation, yet I may say with perfect truth that yourself and the valued proofs of your goodness have never been a day absent from my thoughts, and I am sure you do me the justice to believe that the delay has not been voluntary. Just a twelve month has elapsed since your last date. I trust it has been to you a year of happiness, and that the new one on which we have entered may, like those which have preceded it, find and leave you surrounded with blessings. Happy they, who enjoying every hour, can yet witness without regret the lapse of time, conscious that each moment has borne along with it a record of its usefulness.

I mentioned in my last that I had written to Miss Sedgwick and made an extract from your letter, to which the following is her reply: "The sentiments expressed by Miss Edgeworth, which you have so kindly transmitted to me, are among the best rewards of past exertion, and cherished as they will be, I trust they may give an impulse to future efforts. I need such encouragements, for I often feel depressed by a just sense of vast inferiority, both of natural and acquired power, to a multitude of those who are devoting their talents to the amusement and instruction of the reading world. I am much impressed with the justness of Miss Edgeworth's remarks, in relation to the happiest subjects for American novel-writers. Some of my most intelligent friends oppose this opinion and maintain that there are peculiarities in our early history, which furnish the best materials for the fabric of a romance. There may be, but it requires the touch of a magician to body forth the shadows of the past, while an inferior artist may copy living and visible forms." Miss Sedgwick sent me with this letter "The Deformed Boy," her last publication; it is a pathetick little story, founded on fact, and related with a touching simplicity of style. It was written for the benefit of a Benevolent Society.

I cannot thank you sufficiently for the pleasure I have received from the "Dialogues on Entomology" and "Botany;" both are treasures to me. They class with the works of Mrs. Marcet,[115] conveying the most accurate and precise information, with a perspicuity and elegance of style which are seldom equalled; the scientifick arrangement is admirable, and the selection of facts perfectly adapted to interest the youthful mind and to stimulate it to further research, to which thus assisted and encouraged, it will feel itself not unequal. Both must become standard works. Taste, humanity, the social affections, and genuine piety, are admirably, tho' almost imperceptibly inculcated, and the perusal has left on my mind a most favourable impression of the mental cultivation and active benevolence of their authors. With Mrs. Kater's little history of England I am much pleased and deem it a valuable acquisition to the juvenile library. A mother knows how to feel grateful to those by whom she is thus assisted, especially as such little works assure her how much it is in her

115. Jane Haldimand Marcet (1769–1858). Her *Conversations on Chemistry, Conversations on Natural Philosophy, Conversations on Political Economy*, and other works were widely published in England and America. ME met Mrs. Marcet in 1813, *"plain* and sensible and good natured." Mrs. Marcet entertained Maria and Fanny at a series of breakfasts at her house in Hanover Square in 1819, and she was one of the London literary circle that ME always rejoiced to see. Mrs. Marcet's work is credited with inspiring the young Michael Faraday.

power to assist herself. Your remarks on "Letters from the Irish Highlands" had raised my expectations considerably, but they were not disappointed. Existing evils are pointed out so clearly, with so much earnestness and spirit, yet with so much good humour and so evident a desire to conciliate all parties and to amend the condition of the unfortunate Irish, that it can hardly have failed to attain its object, by interesting the English in their favour. The more I learn of the actual state of Ireland, the more am I inclined to wonder at the mistaken policy of a wise and enlightened government in pursuing a system so glaringly oppressive, and, I should say, injurious to their own interests. Much has been humanely urged in the British Parliament on the subject of Negro slavery; yet is the condition of the Irish poor incomparably worse than that of the slave, either here, or as far as I am informed, in the Islands. I do not mean to defend the Slave System, of which I feel and acknowledge all the evils; but where is the consistency of practising, without even a similar shadow of apology, a system which wants but the name to render it more than equally odious?

You always oblige me by mentioning any current works which you approve; the production, whatever be its merit, acquires from that circumstance an additional value. Even Capt. Hall's delightful books were rendered more interesting, by an imagined participation in your sentiments and opinions, and I perfectly agree with you that "he is the most liberal and enlightened, the most reasonable and amiable traveller I ever met with." His reflections evince a philosophical depth of thought and his reasonings a logical accuracy; yet all is easy and natural, equally calculated to interest the boy and the man. He is very happy too in his descriptive talent. Do you recollect a remarkable appearance of clouds and sunshine formed by the Quebradas along the coast of Peru? The description conveyed in a few plain words is almost poetically picturesque and vivid. The face of the country, the manners of the inhabitants, and the progress and effects of the Revolution are placed before us in full relief, yet with an elegant brevity of style, which leaves us to wonder how we have derived so much information within so small a compass. The volumes of the two Counts Ségur I found each in its peculiar way very interesting and shall be pleased to renew my intercourse with the good old Comte, in a second volume of his "Mémoires and Souvenirs" which has I see been published in Paris. General Ségur's work kept my mind full of solicitude, of astonishment, of horror; after reading this account, what can be called incredible in the blind madness of Ambition, or what too flimsy for the arguments of that sophistry by which it may be led! You say truly, "It conveys an invaluable lesson provided mankind would take it," but unfortunately mankind appears to yield to the control of no teacher but experience. Napoleon had the example of Charles 12th[116] in his eye and in his mind, yet did he plead with himself peculiarity of circumstances, the imagined force of an urgent necessity, and pursued to greater excess, because with greater means, the same headlong career.

"The Life of Napoleon"[117] occupies at present I suppose the time and conversation of the reading world in England, as in a few weeks it will in America. Publick expectation is highly excited and I hope this work may surpass in excellence as it does in importance all that Sir Walter Scott has previously written. Like all really admirable characters, that of your distinguished friend has risen under the pressure of adverse circumstances. His relinquishment of his spendid establishment has obtained for him increased respect and admiration, in the same ratio that probity and justice are more estimable than mental superiority. This superiority will nevertheless, it is to be hoped, speedily reinstate his fortunes. None I think will unkindly envy, but all will rejoice that talent in this enlightened age receives an adequate recompense.

When I last wrote I had not finished reading "Harry and

116. Charles XII (1682–1718), king of Sweden. At the age of twenty, he forced Augustus, elector of Saxony, from the Polish throne and set up his candidate, Stanislaus Leszcynski. Later battles in Russia against Peter the Great proved disastrous.
117. Sir Walter Scott, *Life of Napoleon*, 9 vols. (1827).

Lucy." I could not then, nor can I *now*, express the interest and delight with which I dwelt on every page. Exclusive of the valuable instruction on a variety of subjects, clearly and judiciously conveyed, inculcated as it were by a charm, I found another source of mental fascination. I sympathized in feelings which I knew were yours, in retracing the character, the manners, the expressions of your revered father in his intercourse with his family; I could realize all. I felt with you both pleasure and regret; exalted pleasure, arising from the pure emotions of filial piety; regret—alas! to submit is the duty of man, and it would be selfish to wish to recall to us here the virtuous being, whose ministry performed and race well run, has gone to enjoy the recompense of his good works.

I read the closing conversation again and again, lingered with the volume in my hand, and could not lay it aside without tears or prevail on myself to banish at once by new employment the emotions it had excited. They were such as we feel in parting with friends whom we admire and love. I recurred to Harry and Lucy, to their father and mother, their sweet, sensible, amiable mother; and had I yielded to the guidance of my feelings alone, should instantly have taken the pen to express them freely to you. You have rendered me more than ever desirous to enjoy the happiness of personal intercourse. The wish may be unwise, for whatever the standard at which your impressions have rated me I might justly fear to fall below it and to lose a portion of that esteem which your goodness has bestowed on me. Yet does the wish remain. I feel without fearing your infinite superiority, and in such society could taste the purest intellectual delight.

I sent to Philadelphia a few weeks since a little box containing a hummingbird's nest and the seeds which you requested; I sent also a *Sodom* apple, given to me as a *Soda* apple and marked accordingly;[118] make allowance for the blunder and tell me if you have known the plant. Is there any that you would like me

118. *Solanum aculeatissimum*, known as soda apple, one of the nightshades.

to send you, any I ought to say within the little scope of my ability, for ours are not the favoured regions of Flora? The Humming bird, which I could not have well prepared here, I requested a friend in Pennsylvania to place in the box with the utmost care and hope it may reach you with unruffled wing. Not knowing whether it would be sent to Liverpool or Dublin, I gave the address of your agent in each place. The wings of a rice bird, which my little Edgeworth has been reserving for you, were unluckily forgotten; this we both thought a great pity. Do not despair of your other feathered friend the Mocking bird; I hope it will serenade you next summer. I have been on the watch for a guardian for it, but direct conveyances from Wilmington are unfrequent, and I am fearful of intrusting so delicate a little creature to the casualities incident to passing through several different hands. Our winter here has been remarkably severe; for several days the Thermometer (Farenheit) was as low as 6° below 0, and we are told there was a frost in the island of Cuba, a circumstance never before known there. But in this genial clime, winter does not long reign triumphant; the latter end of February ushers in the spring, the foliage expands itself, and by the middle of March, our gardens wear almost their summer livery. My poor Crocus bulbs were as I feared quite dead; not one has put forth a shoot.

I observed a remark, I think in "Dialogues on Botany," that every well educated person is expected to know the Botanical names of plants; this brings to mind that I have been wishing to ask you whether you think that Latin ought to form a part of female education; can sufficient time be devoted to its acquisition without interfering with other more essential branches?

I hope it will not be very long before I again have the pleasure of hearing from you; your goodness does not I trust render me presumptuous, but experience of past cherishes the anticipation of future indulgence to the earnest wishes of

my dearest Madam, your friend
most truly
R. Lazarus

Your delightful, warm-hearted letter of July 10, 1826, reached me three months ago and gave me as much pleasure as you could desire. I am glad you have at last received my letters and books and crocus roots; little worth as they were I rejoice that they have reached you since they give your kind nature so much pleasure. I only wonder how you can be so enthusiastically grateful. It is a great blessing bestowed by Providence on the good, this power of feeling that most pleasurable of all benevolent sensations. Your picture of domestic life and of the sympathy your husband and children have in all your pleasures is felt in this family and recognized immediately to be all true.

I reproach myself for not having sooner written to tell you how much delighted we all in this house were by your letter. But in fact I waited on from day to day, expecting still expecting, like a greedy creature as I was, another letter from you because you imprudently hinted that you intended writing again when you should have finished reading the 3rd and 4th volumes of Harry and Lucy and Letters from the Irish Highlands. Do not imagine, pray! that I am craving for more praise for my Harry and Lucy, for expecting creature as I have allowed myself to be of letters from you, believe me I am more than satisfied with the full, overflowing approbation bestowed by you on that book. I rejoice that you like it. You certainly seize completely the object I had in writing it, and give back to my mind in your praises the very ideas I had in view. All that I wished but in my most sanguine vanity could not flatter myself I had accomplished. I shall be very truly obligated to you if you will note for me any remarks which your young people or you have made on the 3rd and 4th volumes, because we are preparing a new edition and any parts which have been found difficult we are endeavoring to improve. When I say *we* I mean my sisters Fanny and Honora and my brother William who have been indefatigable in going over this work again and again to correct it. I kept a little portfolio into which we put all remarks from letters or conversation and upon revising with them before us we have profited much. Yesterday I sent to my French translator in Paris many pages of corrections for a new French edition. For instance:

Daniel's hygrometer was described so ill that it was incomprehensible by young readers, and even those who have seen the instrument observed that the principle was not clearly explained. I am so much ashamed of this that I cannot wait till printed reparation reaches you. I send a manuscript page for you.

In the description of the improvement in the Potters wheel, 2nd vol. page 21, there was also a mistake which made it impossible that a child or any body could understand the description. This page I also send you.

These are I believe the only absolute blunders in Volume 2nd. There are other parts which I have rewritten, many pages from 230 to 244 of the sugar-bakery at Bristol, but with these I will not trouble you till they are printed, because there the facts are all correct and there is no danger of leading your young people into error. They would only probably feel the whole *tiresome*. Those pages were in the 1st Edition rewritten by a learned chemist and friend for me who saw the manuscript as it was going to press in England. He found several errors of fact, set them all to rights, but not being used to writing for children he did not put the whole into *children's style*, and all my young readers have complained of that part as too long. "Mechanical impurities," for instance; a child cannot understand what is meant by *cleansing from mechanical impurities, etc*.

I will not weary you with more of our improvements but I only give you proof that I am aware of many faults and most desirous to correct them. My little brother Pakenham has made for me an index which was much wanted. You shall have it as soon as it is printed.

I am at this moment preparing for the press a little volume, a seventh volume of Parents Assistant which will contain three *tiny* Dramas, about the sort of those 2 which your young people may have read in Parents Assistant, Old Poz and Eton Montem. The names of the new ones are "The Grinding Organ," "Dumb Andy," and "The Dame School." They will be published in June I believe and as I send a copy of the manuscript to Philadelphia for an American edition to come out at the same time, I hope that a copy will soon reach you. I will desire my friend Mr. Gerard Ralston[119] to have it sent to you. The direction I shall give him shall be to Mrs. Lazarus, Wilmington, North Carolina. Is this right, or can you send me any address you prefer?

You ask me to send you Mrs. Barbauld's verses written in her 80th year. I would willingly copy them for you, but I can do better. I can send them to you in print. I have desired my bookseller to send for you to your own direction (Messrs. Gowan and Marx, 46 Lime Street, London) Miss Aikin's[120] Memoirs of Mrs. Barbauld and new edition of her works, two volumes. The whole of this publication will I am almost sure suit your taste. The letter *to a friend* written in her 80th year was addressed to me, but I requested that my name should not be mentioned and indeed made this a condition before I gave it to her niece for publication.

And why do you think I did so? Assuredly not because I did not approve of the letter for I think it was beautiful. Assuredly not because I did not wish to see my name joined with Mrs. Barbauld's in print, for I think it most honorable to me to be her friend, and to have my name go down to posterity with hers would gratify me in every way.

But I do not approve of the practice now so common of publishing private letters; among the numerous reasons which I could give that which is least weighty perhaps but which is of itself of sufficient weight to decide me against it is that it would

119. Gerald Ralston of Philadelphia, the son of philanthropic parents, traveled widely in Europe meeting the noted people of his day. He was a nephew of Mrs. Mary Griffith referred to earlier.
120. Lucy Aikin (1781–1864), English historical writer. See notes 89 and 132.

necessarily lead people to write private letters *for* the public, either with the hope or the fear of publication before their eyes. In either case the truth and freedom and peculiar value and charm of private letters would be destroyed. Everybody would be trying to appear well to the world or to hide defects from the world, and at best all would be given to the public and nothing reserved for friends and private confidence. I detest the practice. I have constantly refused to give up any letters that have been written to me by private friends for publication and unless I were positively assured the writer desired it no entreaties would prevail upon me to do it. Miss Aikin "urged me sore" and pleaded her aunt's permission. To that I yielded and gave this one letter. But I desired that my name should not appear because others of my correspondents and I hope many of my particular friends who are quite of my opinion and feeling upon this point would perhaps feel alarmed by seeing a *letter to Miss Edgeworth* in print and might naturally say to themselves it will be my turn next; my letters to Miss Edgeworth or hers to me may figure in the same manner some time or other. Never say I.

I hope you approve? It is said that all virtue is sacrifice; to this I don't agree. But in all virtue or in most virtue there may be some degree of sacrifice required, and in this instance I own it is a sacrifice to give up the chance of reading some admirable private letters. But why is this reading so delightful? Because we flatter ourselves we get behind the scenes into the private life and character and inmost souls of the writers. Had they thought we should read, how differently would they have written. *So* I have no objection to treating myself to reading very old letters which come out from old receptacles, heaven knows how, and when I can wash my hands at all events of any share in the treachery.

Now having finished this prosing, I have to add a fresh supply of crocusses, and purple crocusses, to the things I mean to send you. But these cannot go by the parcel I order to be sent to Gowan and Marx. I must send them by another conveyance from Dublin or Liverpool and the crocusses cannot set out for some little time, because they are all now in full blow, beautiful bright orange and purple circles of waving lines of them in the lawn before these library windows at this instant. They must have time to live and die and dry. I will send you purple roots from my own garden and mark them while in flower that I may be sure of them. Of those roots I sent you from London obtained from a seedsman I could not be sure as they are often inaccurate. I will add some other seeds of cowslips, polyanthus, larkspur, *etc.* which though perhaps may be common with you, you may like to have from our lawn and from my little garden to give to your children for theirs. This exchange of seeds, *etc.* seems to me very agreeable between friends in distant countries.

And now my dear Madam it is high time having got through all parcel details of my own to come to the pleasure of telling you that your nicely packed and pink-lined box has arrived. The joy and surprise of opening it I wish you had witnessed. The humming bird is in perfect preservation. But oh its nest! Its delicate nest is far more valuable, more uncommon than the bird itself. And here it is in its nice case as safe, as snug as when placed there by your own nice hands. Did not you make the case? And did not you make it on purpose for the nest and for me? I say you did. But there are spiteful and envious relations of mine who maintain that I herein flatter myself too much and that it is evident you took a netting case that was ready made. Pray settle this point in your next; that is, if I am right, say so. If I am wrong you need say nothing about it.

I ought to tell you some sense in a letter that is to go so far instead of so much nonsense.

The most sensible book I have read for some time past is a small octavo volume "On the Formation of Opinions," author unknown. Next to this an interesting American book of travels sent me by Professor Norton of Philadelphia,[121] "Flint's Letters

121. Though ME writes Philadelphia, she would appear to mean Andrews Norton (1786–1853), American theologian and a professor at Harvard 1819–30.

Written During Residences and Progress Down Mississippi-Missouri Rivers,"[122] and another American book *Tudor's Letters on the Eastern States*,[123] remarkably sensible, but not remarkably entertaining.

The most entertaining book and by far the most *new* which has appeared in London for some time is Captain Head's *Rough Sketches*[124] (as he calls them) of his passage across the Pampas and over the Cordilleras. He is in a gallop at the rate of about 120 miles per day, but he sees more and points more and better than any other traveller who goes at the slowest rate, with all conveniences and appliances to boot. Besides the great amusement of the living figures in his masterly magic lantern there are two or three chapters of solid sense at the end of his work on the state of the mines and prudence or rather imprudence of speculations in Chile, *etc.*, which will do infinite good in England. People are recovered completely from the Speculation fever and are recover*ing* from the debilitating effects—slowly. I daresay you have seen Captain Head's book; if so, pray tell me how you like it. Then I will send you a copy of a letter which the author

---

He was co-editor of *The Select Journal of Foreign Periodical Literature*, 4 vols. (1833–34).

122. Timothy Flint (1780–1840), American clergyman and writer. His *Recollections of the Last Ten Years Passed in the Valley of the Mississippi* (1826) was reprinted in England and translated into French; it has been termed the first account of the Western states which revealed the real life and character of the people. He edited the *Western Review* in Cincinnati (where he met Mrs. Trollope) from 1825 to 1828 and *Knickerbocker's Magazine* (New York) in 1833. He wrote histories and novels. The *Letters* in ME's title may indicate that she confused Timothy Flint's account of life in the Mississippi Valley with James Flint's *Letters from America, 1818–1820* (Edinburgh, 1822).

123. Henry Tudor, *Narrative of a Town in North America; Comprising Mexico, the Mines of Real del Monte, the United States, and the British Colonies; with an Excursion to the Island of Cuba. In a Series of Letters, Written in the Years 1831–2* (London, 1834).

124. Sir Francis Bond Head, Bart. (1793–1875), English soldier, traveler, and author. His *Rough Notes* (1826) of his rapid journey across the Pampas and the Andes earned him the name of "Galloping Head." The following year he published *Reports of the La Plata Mining Association*. He wrote a considerable number of other works, chiefly travel, highly popular in their day.

has just written to me in reply to one which I addressed to him to tell him how much we liked his book. Captain Head is quite a stranger to me.

Another very interesting book we have been reading in the evenings is "The Voyage of the Blonde,"[125] the frigate which carried home the remains of the King and Queen of the Sandwich Islands. It gives also an entertaining account of all their Majesties said or did in London previous to their illness and a most touching picture of their affection for each other. This King was really a man of a great mind and it would be well for the subjects of many an European state if their rulers desired their happiness and the diffusion of knowledge among them as did this poor King of the Sandwich Islands. He really threw himself with magnanimous confidence into the hands of the English for this sole purpose, and I admire the freedom from suspicion afterwards in all his people. They never suspected any thing wrong of the English though the sudden death of so many and at such a distance might have almost justified suspicion.

Sir Walter Scott's life of Bonaparte is to appear immediately. As his friend I look to it with great anxiety. How he will represent the conduct of the English Government in sending him prisoner to St. Helena and their treatment of him there I know not. Very sorry should I be to have it to do. It is curious that when I was at Abbotsford I told him so, and without guessing that he had any thought of writing Napoleon's life in discussing with him this Elba affair on which we widely differed. I said, "Consider *how* it will appear in history. Even you, I do not think you could make it appear well for England if you were to state it. How could you?"

He answered, "I think I could. Very well, I think I could," and he drew himself up as if bracing himself for the feat. Perhaps

125. [Maria Graham], *Voyage of H.M.S. Blonde to the Sandwich Islands, in the Years 1824–25. Captain the Right Hon. Lord Byron Commander* (London, 1826). This Lord Byron was the seventh, the writer's heir to that title, George Byron. He allowed no native nobles to dine at his table on this voyage.

this put it into his head. It was not till a year afterwards that I first heard he was writing a life of Bonaparte.

If he was engaged in it at the time I spoke, he must have been surprised and must have thought I guessed. The book has already reached nine volumes Mr. Lockhart his son-in-law tells me.

Mr. Lockhart is now editor you know of the Quarterly Review,[126] which brings him in a handsome income. He has 3,000 pounds per annum. I believe some place under Government tho' is added to the Editorship. The Review has regained its credit under his administration considerably.

There was an excellent article in the last Edinburgh Review (Dec. 1826) on the society for the *Diffusion of Knowledge* written by Sidney Smith.[127] Mr. Brougham who has the chief merit of promoting that institution has just published an admirable "Preliminary Treatise" to the intended library of the institution. There is a learned and entertaining article on Hieroglyfics in [*this*] December, 1826, edition. The opening of a mummy within these last few days at Paris, who proves to be one of the priestesses, a person of great consideration with a papyrus manuscript clasped to her breast and another to her head and a scarabaeus fast plastered on her breast bone, will throw much new light upon this wonderful subject and will help us to find out some more Egyptian riddles.

The riddles in Harry and Lucy (apropos) have been some of them beautifully translated into French by my excellent and amiable translator Madame Belloc.[128] Some which it was impos-

126. *The Quarterly Review* (first issue, Feb. 1809) was largely instigated by Scott's urging John Murray, his London publisher, to set up a Tory competitor to the Whig *Edinburgh Review*. Scott reviewed himself in *The Quarterly Review*.

127. Sidney Smith (1771–1845), English writer and clergyman. He was one of the founders of the *Edinburgh Review* and edited the first number (October 1802). ME professed to be afraid of his satirical tongue but they proved good foils in conversation. He wrote of her, "She does not say witty things, but there is such a perfume of wit runs through all of her conversation as makes it very brilliant."

128. Anne Louise Swanton Belloc (1796–1881). ME met Mademoiselle

sible to translate literally she has most ingeniously translated by equivalents; for instance: Ma-jest-y—what is Majesty without its externals, by the word R-o-i, a cipher, zero. If you have a mind to see the French Harry and Lucy I will send it to you. There are some good notes, one about dolls' eyes—delightful. It would perhaps be a good way of improving, in learning French to read these French and English copies in schools, the translation is so accurate, and for boys, Engineers, *etc.* it would be an easy way of learning many technical terms.

We have had deep snow here in Ireland and in Scotland within this last month, unusual at this time of year, so deep as to stop the mail coaches and for two days to stop all travelling. We have heard of several persons being lost who had unawares set out in the snow. In this country a young lady was found standing straight beside her pony, both dead, under the snow, and perhaps you may have seen in the newspapers, a post boy in the highlands was found standing upright with the letter bag in his hand. But *why* all of them standing upright! Poor little boy, faithful to his trust to the last.

Bid your little boy not [*to*] forget the rice bird feathers for Lucy. She is delightfully well. She is now on a visit to one of her married sisters, Sophy Fox. She [*Mrs. Fox*] has a charming little boy, who is the delight and pride of course of Mamma, papa, grandpapa, and all of us doating aunts. Another of my sisters, Harriet, has married most happily, Mr. Butler, a clergyman of highly cultivated mind and benevolent character, suited to her in literary tastes, sincerity, and uprightness of character and passionately attached to her for the qualities which he knows she possesses, not for fancied charms, those which the illusions of love sometimes create and which marriage dissipates. Most happily for us Mr. Butler's living (and his very good but not large private estate) are both within thirty miles of us—so that

---

Swanton, of Irish descent, in Paris in 1821. She married Hilaire Belloc and became the grandmother of two distinguished English writers.

Mrs. Edgeworth has both her daughters settled within reach of a *dinner visit*. Never were happier creatures than we were last Christmas when we were all assembled, Mr. and Mrs. Butler, Captain and Mrs. Fox and their little boy Maxwell, my brother William at home too! Oh I wish you could have seen Mrs. E. herself blooming with health in the midst of her children and her grandchild in her arms; never woman deserved her happiness more. My own dearest Fanny still remains to us. My brother William is now laying out a railroad between Manchester and Bolton. Francis is at Trinity College, Cambridge, studying hard, and as simple as a child with all his abilities. Pakenham the youngest boy, fourteen, has left the Charter House and is now at home for a year *reading*, previous to his going to a college in England to prepare him for India; a friend has given him a writer-ship.

Now my dear madam you see I have taken your request that I would give you all our family history *literally*. Pray tell me more anecdotes of your children; they interest me much. I forgot to mention the alligators' eggs which are to us great curiosities and all the seeds. Oh thank you for them. I sent a *pinch* of each yesterday to Paris to the children of a French friend whom I love. The scarlet berries are beautiful. Pakenham assures me they belong to a great thistle. He knows best, but I can scarcely believe it. Mrs. Edgeworth will sow the seed immediately *et nous verrons*. The Glycene died alas. So did the nondescript. Send me some more anemonies.

My brother's school continues to prosper, and the young men who have gone out of it have succeeded each in his own way in life.

I hope your brother Alfred will come to see us. *I wish you could.*

Ever affectionately yours,

Maria Edgeworth

[P.S.] I am afraid I never thanked you for your brother's copy of The Last of the Mohicans of which you robbed him to please me and you *did* please me. The book is admirable, quite new and *original* in the best sense of the word, a picture of manners new to us, characters extinct and nowhere else preserved—or so well portrayed. It is astonishing how interesting he has made the lives and characters of these Indians, and how real his personages appear. I am sure I *have seen* Long Carabine and Hawk-Eye and Cerf Agile.

The history of the Nowlan's in the 2nd series of letters by the O'Hara family[129] is a work of great genius. [*An illegible sentence follows.*]

Edgeworthstown, April 9, 1827

My dear Mrs. Lazarus,

I wrote to you so long a letter March the 21st that I will only trouble you with a short note now to tell you that last week I received your very kind letter dated Jan. 1827.

In my long epistle I have assured you of the safe arrival of your nice little box and of the pleasure all its contents have given me and many of my friends. I regret that your dear boy's wings of his rice bird which he had intended for me were forgotten. I hope you will find some other opportunity for I must not have his kindness lost.

We have no such plant as the Sodom apple—by that name. Is it the Solanum tomentosum which is described as having scarlet berries as large as a gooseberry with a purple or lilac flower, a few prickles on the stalk?

Our crocus roots are not yet dry enough to send you, but they shall go in due time.

I have had the Deformed Boy sent to me by Mr. Ralston of Philadelphia. I like it much.

129. The O'Hara Family, pseudonym for John (1798–1842) and Michael (1796–1874) Banim. *Tales by the O'Hara Family* appeared in London, 1825–27. *The Nowlands* is attributed to John Banim and *Peter of the Castle* to John and Michael Banim.

I send you a copy of a letter which I have lately received from Capt. Head in reply to one I wrote him expressing how much pleasure we had received from his book. I think you will like his letter.

I have this morning written a note of introduction to you for a gentleman whom I am sure you will be very glad to see, Captain Basil Hall. He sails from Liverpool the 16th of this month. He and Mrs. Hall intend to spend two years in America and to make extensive tours. His object is to make himself acquainted with the country and the people and to dissipate prejudices in both countries by representing America in a true light to England, to Europe. No man [*is*] better qualified so to do. *When* he may reach your part of the world I do not know, but you will of course hear from him. Is Wilmington a seaport?

I am honestly and frankly delighted that you like Harry and Lucy so well and *Botany* and *Entomology*.

Yours affectionately,
Maria Edgeworth

[P.S.] Read the lives of the three Norths written by Roger North[130] in the reigns of Charles 2nd and James 2nd, a new edition republished by young Roscoe with good notes.

Have you seen Roscoe Senior's[131] pamphlet on prison discipline and on American prisons? Well worth reading. There is in it a curious letter of LaFayette's on the effect of solitary confinement. I do not go the length that Mr. Roscoe does in recommending solitary confinement. I am much of LaFayette's opinion; besides want of space would render it impracticable to the extent Roscoe wishes. Solitary confinement by night I should think indispensible; by day it should be punishment only for the

130. Roger North (1653–1734), English lawyer and biographer. His *Lives of the Norths* was published after his death. ME probably refers to a new and revised edition (London, 1826).
131. William Roscoe (1753–1831), English historian and writer. He wrote tracts on penal jurisprudence and other subjects, but is best known for his *Life of Lorenzo de' Medici* (1796). ME and her father visited William Roscoe in 1813 at his home near Liverpool.

refractory or corrupt, for those who would corrupt others. It should not be for life except in the case of murder or irreclaimable offenders, and who can decide as to *irreclaimable*, except in the case of murder which is at least irretrievable, irreparable. I am almost inclined to prefer capital punishment for murder. Solitary confinement in other cases should be for a limited time, always with a view to reformation to let the offender redeem himself if he can by good conduct and industry upon trial, and then recommit to solitary confinement for a longer period if necessary. In the Milbank Prison in England, conducted on this plan, the effects are excellent. The governors of that prison told me that experience proved to them that solitary confinement has little effect upon very young persons and has great effect upon those more advanced in life and capable of reflection. Boys or girls thirteen or fourteen sang themselves to sleep in the solitary cell and never became melancholy. But men of thirty or forty became wretched, thinking over the past and present and considering the loss of liberty and character, and all their families must suffer. If you know any facts on this subject tell them to me. Direct your letters as follows:

> To Miss Edgeworth
> Edgeworthstown
> Ireland
> To the care of R. W. Horton, Esq.

And then enclose that in a cover of strong white paper directed

> To Earl Bathurst
> Foreign Office
> London

These packets will bear any weight and reach me free. You might send the rice bird's wings between pasteboard in a packet so directed.

[Copy]

Wilmington, June 24th, 1827

My dear Madam

The spell of detention which has been so frequently cast over our mutual communications is I trust broken; my last letter appears to have reached you in due time and I have the happiness of acknowledging yours of the 21st March and 6th April, and also the works of Mrs. Barbauld, which arrived within a week of each other. Many thanks for each and all of them.

Highly as my expectations had been raised by the encomium passed on the writings of Mrs. Barbauld in your Harry and Lucy, they have been more than equalled by the perusal of these volumes. Sound sense, fervent piety, and strong argumentative powers, aided by an irresistible eloquence, with genius to create, taste to modify, and fancy to adorn; [*all*] form so rare a combination of excellencies that we scarcely expect to find all united in any one writer; yet are all these, and even more, the attributes of Mrs. Barbauld. When she rises to the sublime it is with dignity; she descends to the playful with grace, is always easy, always consistent. I could not but regret that her beautiful poem "Eighteen Hundred and Eleven" should have been productive to her of any other than the pleasant feelings, attendant on well merited distinction and praise. The "lines to Mrs. P." with some drawings of birds and insects are charming; her "Character" of Dr. Aikin[132] speaks to the heart. "Lines on the first fire" and "on a Caterpillar" take one by surprise and are very beautiful and ingenious; and the "Fragment," Octogenary reflections and the "Elegy" are solemn and touching in the extreme. But of all her poems, those which I prefer are "An Address to the Deity" and "A Summer Evening's Meditation"; with these I have been long acquainted, and now recur to them with renewed admiration. It is a pity that Miss Aikin did not omit her remark relative to

132. John Aikin (1747–1822), English physician and writer. He collaborated with his sister Mrs. Barbauld on a popular series entitled *Evenings at Home*, 6 vols. (1792–95), which were widely translated.

[128] The Correspondence, 1827

Goldsmith. Mrs. B's beautiful lines required no such testimonial of their merit; and we have been so long accustomed to think of Goldsmith as a favourite of nature, rather than of fortune, our feelings of admiration have become so blinded with those of pity, that his faults and his foibles are cast into the shade whence benevolence would dictate, that the impartiality incumbent on a biographer should alone withdraw them. I have said so much on the first volume that I ought hardly to indulge in any remarks on the 2nd; let me just say, that the piece against "Inconsistency in our Expectations," "The Cure on the Banks of the Rhone," "On Education," "On Prejudice" and remarks on "Mr. Wakefield's Enquiry, *etc*." pleased me particularly. Mrs. B's frequent allusions to America, her approbation of our system of government, her warm eulogiums on our beloved Washington, and her benevolent wishes that we may improve in all that is worthy and truly great, must fill the mind of every true American with sentiments of honest pride and gratitude. You will not wonder at my wish to know something of her adopted son;[133] he is amiable I daresay. Is he a man of talents? Just this question and then I turn to your letter to say how entirely I coincide with you the score of publishing private correspondence; few circumstances can justify it, and yet it is not in nature to regret that similar scruples have not withheld from us such a moral and intellectual feast as the letters of Lady Russell,[134] of Cowper,[135] and of Mrs. Barbauld.

133. The Barbaulds had no children of their own. They adopted her nephew Charles Rochemont Aikin (1775–1847).

134. Lady Rachel Wriothesley (1636–1723), second daughter of Thomas earl of Southampton, who married (1) Francis Lord Vaughan; (2) William Lord Russell. *The Life and Letters of Lady Russell*, edited by Mary Berry, appeared in 1819. (ME knew and liked Miss Berry and her sister Agnes.) A *Life* of Lord William Russell (1639–1683) by Lord John Russell appeared in 1820. When her husband was being tried for treason against Charles II, Lady Russell assisted him in his defense. The night before he was beheaded, 21 July 1683, he supped with his wife, and his parting from her was his one great trial in an otherwise calm acceptance of death. His attainder was reversed six years later by William and Mary.

135. William Cowper (1731–1800), English poet, ranks as one of the great letter writers in the English language. His *Private Correspondence*, edited by John Johnson, appeared in two volumes in 1824 and again in 1835.

You probably know that Mr. Sparks,[136] late editor of the North American Review, is employed in arranging and preparing for the press a voluminous collection of letters and papers left by General Washington to his nephew and heir, Judge Washington.[137] This will be to the world a most interesting work, to the United States invaluable. You have probably read his letters to Congress in the course of the Revolutionary War; it is wonderful to observe, how amidst the fatigue and bustle of the camp, his counsels (always combining a dignified firmness with the highest respect) were capable of directing their most important resolves. I have seen a letter in his own hand writing addressed during this period to one of the Managers of his estate; it was interesting as a proof that his mind could turn with facility from the great and perplexing concerns by which it appeared engrossed to the minute details of farming economy. Order and regularity he insists on, and many little directions relative to his slaves evince his humanity and interest in their welfare. I wished much to obtain this letter but it was in the possession of a distant relation of General W's who very rightly would not part with it. Let me ask, before I forget, if you have any lately published map of the U.S., if not, may I send you one?

Carey and Lea[138] have commenced publishing the "American Quarterly Review";[139] the first two numbers promise well.

136. Jared Sparks (1789–1866), American historian and educator. After extensive research at home and abroad, he published the *Life and Writings of George Washington*, 12 vols. (1834–37), later abridged (1842). ME met Jared Sparks when they were both the guests of Gerald Ralston at Croydon (13 March 1841); she liked him personally and wrote that his was "the only life of Washington I ever saw that was not too long and too tiresome to read to the end."

137. Bushrod Washington (1762–1829), American jurist, nephew of George Washington. He was his uncle's literary executor and supervised the preparation of John Marshall's *Life of Washington*, 5 vols. (1804–7). He inherited Mount Vernon in 1802 upon the death of Martha Washington.

138. Henry Charles Carey (1793–1879), economist and publisher. Isaac Lea (1792–1886), malacologist and publisher. The publishing house of Carey and Lea in Philadelphia was one of the largest of the period and was the American publisher of Sir Walter Scott.

139. The *American Quarterly Review* (1827–37) was established in Philadelphia by Robert Walsh but came to an end when he departed for Europe.

An article on Sir Walter Scott's preliminary view of the French Revolution has served at once to gratify and to excite curiosity. We expect the work itself in a few days. Your conversation with Sir W. was indeed in the event singular; do tell me, daughter of Eve as I am, if you ever discover whether this did in fact turn his thoughts to writing his life of Napoleon?

We are far behind you in the reading world, and your recommendation of new works is always acceptable. I have seen none that you mention, except those of native growth, with which I am glad you were pleased. We are expecting from Philadelphia such of them as can be obtained there. Shall I presume again on your indulgence and beg you to send me the little work "On the Formation of Opinions"? It is among those not to be had, and as Rosamond says, "I like the name." Head's Sketches I shall have and am impatient to see it; fortunately among some extracts which have appeared is that passage to which his lively, unique letter alludes. Incredulity on such an occasion might pass as a venial offense, but I, like your sister, felt disposed to receive the *fact*, miraculous as it is, without hesitation. His letter is thrown off in a wonderfully easy and happy style; feeling, compliment, and point, all in perfection; it must be characteristick. Many thanks for it, my dear Madam, and very many more for the introductory one you have been so good as to give Capt. Hall for me. Can it be possible that I may see and know Capt. Hall! When I saw in a newspaper his intended visit announced, I exclaimed, "Do my dear husband let us go to New York and see Capt. Hall!" The expression was jest, but the desire was real; yet little did I dream of its probable fulfilment. I read yesterday a short but interesting biographical sketch of him from the New York Albion, which also alluded to his intended visit; his mother I find was the daughter of Lord Selkirk,[140] and an eye witness to the incursion of Paul Jones's

140. Thomas Douglas, fifth earl of Selkirk (1771–1820). He encouraged the dispossessed Scottish peasants to emigrate to Canada.

crew into her paternal mansion.[141] But shall I tell you that my delight in this anticipation is not unmixed with alarm? Shall I leave you to guess, or have you already done so, that I dread to appear totally insipid, to a man, unquestionably superior in many respects, to any I have ever known? This feeling extends yet further. You too will know me better, through the medium of a mutual acquaintance, and tho' your indulgence bears with me on paper, how can I be sure that it could be equally extended to my real self? In truth we labour under many disadvantages; our society is composed of kind, amiable, benevolent people, but with very rare exceptions, Gray would say again that "Knowledge to their eyes her ample page, rich with the spoils of time did ne'er unroll"; nor can they plead "chill penury" in palliation of this want of improvement. Few read with any view to mental cultivation; the turn of conversation is consequently frivolous, and tho' we associate with and cordially esteem many, yet "the feast of reason" is denied us. There exists not that interchange of opinion and reciprocity of sentiment which awaken the faculties, exercise the mind and improve it. When you read this, I dare say you will unite with us in regretting that circumstances render a change of residence for the present unadvisable, and I am yet more secure of your acquiescence in our maxim, that it is wisdom to submit to an unavoidable evil with the best possible grace.

Wilmington (in reply to your inquiry) is situated thirty miles up the Cape Fear river, which is navigable to this town, its principal commerce with the West Indies, direct communication with Europe unfrequent. My letters *etc.* I generally send to be forwarded to you from New York; you have the address of my friend Mr. B. M. Myers of that city for parcels, and for letters my own address is sufficient, as it will also be for the books you

141. John Paul Jones (1747–92), naval officer. While commander of *The Ranger* in British waters (1778), he went ashore on St. Mary's Isle and sent a squad to the house of the earl of Selkirk, ostensibly to seize the earl as a hostage. Only the countess was home, and Jones's men seized the plate that he later returned.

have kindly requested Mr. Ralston to send me. We are all delighted to hear of a continuation of the "Parent's Assistant"—even my little Edgeworth when I told him exclaimed with a countenance full of animation, "Do Mother, tell Miss Edgeworth that I am *very* much obliged to her!" "I will my dear, but why!" "Oh Mother, because I know you will read some of the stories to me, so that I can understand them, and if Miss Edgeworth had not written the book, and then sent it to you, you could not do that you know." He loves to read "The Cherry Orchard," "The Orphans," and some other "easy" ones for himself, and he dwells upon any little circumstance related as *true*; indeed he appears uncommonly interested in historical facts, and his wee books of history are among his chief favourites. I find the wooden cubes recommended in Practical Education an admirable auxiliary in the first steps of Arithmetick; he had always been inquisitive about numbers, and almost insensibly learned the multiplication table, before he knew a single figure, and with the aid of his dear cubes has learned in a few weeks to add and enumerate with ease. I must tell you all this, because it gives me pleasure, and I owe it all to you. Could I but reap half the benefits you have placed within my reach in the education of my children, I should rejoice indeed; but I am often dissatisfied with my own endeavours and wish that you were near, to confirm or to advise me. But I must not indulge myself on this subject or it will lead me too far. You say "a 7th vol. of Parents Assistant"; do you include "Moral Tales" under this number? I have but 3 Vols. of Parents Assistant;[142] they contain, "Lazy Laurence," "Tarlton," "The False Key," "Birthday Present," "Simple Susan," "Bracelets," "Little Merchants," "Old Poz," "Mimic," "Mademoiselle Panache," "Basket Woman," "White Pigeon," "Orphans," "Waste Not Want Not," "Forgive and Forget," "Barring Out," and "Eton Montem." Tell me if there are

142. The London editions of *Parent's Assistant* (1800, 1817, 1822, 1824) were in six volumes. Most foreign editions (Boston, Philadelphia, New York, 1814) were in three volumes.

more than these. I hardly think there can be three volumes which I have not seen. You ask for remarks on "Harry and Lucy." To say the truth, I read but to admire, and if any description appeared at all obscure, I imputed the error rather to my own dullness than to any fault in the detail. In the account of the sugar refinery, the change of style struck me and I remarked to one of my daughters that I did not think those expressions were yours. A sensible child thirteen years of age did not understand the construction of Harry's kite and enquired how it was to be made of use; both my sister and myself were of opinion that this was rather implied than expressly stated. Observe in the story of Tamerlane and Bajazet, is not Bajazet represented as the Conqueror? I regret that I cannot refer to the volumes at present; they are at my father's in Virginia. A letter from my sister Ellen some time since says: "I think I never read a book with so much pleasure; I felt sorry as I finished each volume, and when I came to the 6th was disposed to linger by the way. When I had read the last word, I looked on it with a lingering farewell, and closed the book slowly as if I were shutting the door after the departure of a beloved and intelligent friend. Laura (our youngest sister, nine years of age) was not allowed to read the whole, but she followed the book; as each of us read it, you would see her reading over the shoulder with the greatest avidity, and when told she could not understand the coming part, would beg us to call her as soon as she might read again." In the corrected page on the potter's wheel (copied in whose beautiful writing?) Almira asks *how* the motion is communicated from one of the cones to the potter's wheel, and when the man pushes down the band to the largest part of that one whether it *continues* round the largest part of the other, so as to draw it tighter; otherwise she does not see the use of the two cones, or how they can affect the wheel; but you say, it is *always* at the thicker part of the one, while it is at the thinner part of the other. The 2nd sentence on Daniel's Hygrometer, might I think by a little change in the arrangement be rendered more perspicuous; "By observing, *etc.* . . . You obtain" seem too distant from each other; suppose it thus: "Now you may obtain the measure of the quantity of water supported in the air, by observing how many degrees cooler than the atmosphere any substance must be made before dew will be formed upon it." Why will you invite me to be so presumptuous? And why will you throw temptation in my way by asking whether I should like to see the french translation of "Harry and Lucy"? Surely it would please me to ascertain whether they converse as delightfully in a foreign language as in their own. There is a steam mill here for cleaning rice which your Harry would I think be pleased to see, and which I should like to hear him describe. I am glad you have an index; I found one requisite and intended making it as soon as the books were returned.

Alfred's Mohicans have obtained their high preferment neither through merit, nor through fault of mine. A gentleman whom I had requested to send the work to you took *mine* to read on his passage to New York, and inadvertently put that up for you, and sent the new set to me. I ought sooner to have apologised for the oversight, but you, my dear madam, like the bee who extracts its honey from weeds, see commendable motives even for the seeming indiscretion of your friend. The safe arrival of the bird and nest rejoiced us greatly; as to the box, I reply with the less hesitation as I can do so without fear of widening the breach between those "spiteful relations" and yourself. I did make it (for I could not find one of the right dimensions) in great haste, and of the only materials at hand; and made it for the *nest*, but surely not for *you*. Of the manufacture of one which will accompany this, I can with better grace plead not guilty, tho' every imperfection in its contents must be laid at my door. Some time since you gratified me by expressing a wish for some piece of work done by me. A border of a turban you mentioned, and I shall have just cause to be proud if this be deemed worthy of encircling a brow, already bound with many a lovely amaranthine chaplet. I have been most pleasantly employed in this work, for my thoughts have been almost constantly with you, and many a pleasing reverie has beguiled the hour's occupation. It is not what my wishes would have made it, but your acceptance will supply every deficiency in intrinsick value. I shall address this packet as directed in your last; tho' Lord Bathurst has retired it will no doubt reach you in safety; tell me how to direct hereafter. The seeds you wish for I have not at present but will send them soon; those which you intend sending me will acquire much added value from being the production "of your own little garden." I have not seen Mr. Roscoe's pamphlet, to which you allude, but have read some letters of Mr. Vaux,[143] a quaker gentleman of Pennsylvania addressed to him in reply, which I found very interesting. Have you seen them? I do not know any original facts on the subject, but should yield to the arguments of Mr. Vaux; in favour of solitary confinement for adults, I like your ideas on the subject.

Your family details are always agreeable and interesting, and I rejoice that with each succeeding year, your sources of domestick felicity appear to increase; many blessings are graciously bestowed on you, nor is it the least that you are so capable of appreciating and enjoying them. Beetles in abundance but not this time for your sister Lucy whose health I am glad to hear continues improving.

Adieu My dear Madam—ever truly yours
R.L.

Edgeworthstown, August 19, 1827

My dear Madam,

I rejoice that Mrs. Barbauld's works have reached you and that you have enjoyed from them all the pleasure which you so

---

143. Roberts Vaux (1786–1836), American philanthropist. Among his many public interests, prison reform held a high place. He advocated separate confinement for prisoners and the establishment of a house of refuge for

well describe and which they are so well calculated to inspire in an amiable, enlarged, and judicious mind. I quite agree with you that it would have been better if the editor had omitted the disparaging remarks on Goldsmith. It is unworthy of a great genius to be praised at the *expense* of another and shews poverty of resource in whoever offers such incense stolen from another shrine. I like your spirit of justice.

But I will tell what I do *not* like, that you should have wasted your precious time and eyes in working for me the most beautiful imitation of lace I ever beheld. All who have seen it, and some professed fine needle-women have examined it with the closest scrutiny, aver that they never before saw such ex-quisite work, and in truth they could not believe it was done by the needle until upon minute inspection two leaves which had been left undone by happy accident proved that the whole was really needle work. Still we think it was not the work of mortal hands but of some little fairies whom you must have in your service with hands that never knew the dew of human kind. *Fairly-fair* of far-famed hands would certainly look upon this piece of work with envy. As to wearing it for a turban, I never could do such a thing, to hide its beautiful texture by rolling it in thick folds! Impossible. I will if I can ever persuade myself to wear it throw it over a colored bonnet or hat as a veil and let the spectators admire it, or I will now and then when I want to display it to advantage throw it over the pretty heads of some of my young sisters. But unluckily they have none of them dark hair or dark eyes which are essential for shewing a veil to advantage. I have a niece here, Anna Beddoes (the daughter of the celebrated Doctor Beddoes), over whose head I threw it last night and it was the admiration of all beholders for she has eyes of a true Juno size and lustre; ten of our degenerate eyes would hardly make a pair of hers in size. But my dear lady, nonsense

---

juvenile delinquents in Pennsylvania which was done in 1826. RML refers to his *Reply to Two Letters of William Roscoe, Esquire, of Liverpool, on the Penitentiary System of Pennsylvania* (1827).

apart, I am seriously ashamed and sorry, and yet proud and grateful to see that you could think it worth while to do such a quantity of work for me. I assure you that by my request I meant only a little border of this breadth [*indicates 1¼" width on the paper*] and of about ¾ of a yard long to be worked on a slip of muslin as a bandeau to pin around my head when I wear, as I almost constantly do, a muslin turban. How very shamefully ill I must have expressed myself. But thank you! Thank you! I will not pain your kind mind with telling you more of my sense of shame when I opened the packet and saw what you had done— and what I had led you to do for me. The work shall be left when I die to my most loved sister—Fanny.

I should tell you that it came perfectly safe and as fresh as when you folded it up and pinned it with the delicate little pins. The rice bird's wings lay light upon it, and they are much prized by our young people. I send you this day a few crocus roots from my own garden in your own little box which brought the veil, directed to B. M. Meyers, New York, which I hope will be more fortunate in reaching you than the last. I will send another parcel of them next month; there will be purple ones among them I hope. I have also desired my bookseller to send you from London the little book "On the Formation of Opinions." I am told by some of my American correspondents that they like to have packets sent separately from letters, that they inquire for the packets when they receive the letters and that this insures their receiving the packets. Let me know if this be your wish in future.

You may (if ever you wish it) send packets of the size of your last or of the size of an Edinburgh Review directed thus: inside cover to Miss Edgeworth, Edgeworth's Town, Ireland, outside cover to

The Right Honorable
R. Wilmot Horton,[144] Downing Street, London,

144. Sir Robert John Wilmot Horton, third baronet (1784–1841), politician, assumed the name of Horton upon the death of his father-in-law in 1823; governor of Ceylon 1831–37. ME met him in London in April 1831.

or if you prefer Liverpool, direct the out side cover to

      Messrs. Brown and Co., inside to The Earl of Rosse[145]

      Parsons Town, Ireland

within that another cover to Miss E., Edgeworths Town.

You have all the stories in the Parents Assistant. Your edition is one in three volumes, but published in London there are several in six volumes. The seventh volume for which you thank me so much contains only three little plays. I fear they will disappoint you.

Many thanks for your corrections for Harry and Lucy; they are quite in time for the new edition which will not come out till Xmas.

I am much interested in the life of Napoleon. It is wonderful that even Sir W. Scott can keep up such a strong interest through nine volumes of realities, where all the facts are well known. The interest too is of the most useful and moral kind. This history contrary to the effect of most histories of conquerors operates as the finest lesson against ambition that ever was given by man to man. Macbeth is the finest moral tragedy I ever read on the same moral, but Macbeth is on a small scale compared with Napoleon and he was of *woman governed* if not of woman born. He could not compare in talents or daring to Bonaparte, the individual who as Scott describes him has possessed the most power that any individual ever possessed in this world! And how little did it contribute to his own happiness and how little to the happiness or benefit of mankind. After all, the author who writes Napoleon's life has had probably more influence on the happiness of the present generation and altogether has and will have more influence, more power over the *mind* of the world than Bonaparte ever possessed. Assuredly Scott has made himself and others happier by the use of his powers. Bonaparte was right to fear the Press. It is an over match for his cannon.

145. Sir Lawrence Parsons, second earl of Rosse (1758–1841). He was appointed joint postmaster general for Ireland in 1809.

I have hardly left room to tell you that we are all well and happy. Lucy continues quite well.

Believe me my dear Madam your obliged and affectionate friend.

Maria Edgeworth

[P.S.] Yes I have seen Mr. Vaux's letters. My friend Mr. Ralston sent them to me. He also sends me regularly the American Quarterly and North American Reviews.

[Copy]

Wilmington, August 20, 1827

To Miss Edgeworth

Permit me my dear Madam to recommend to your kind attention a little pensioner, who will I trust repay in grateful warbling all solicitude for his welfare. A vessel sent by my husband with the Capt. of which I am well acquainted affords the opportunity so long desired of transporting it—under good guardianship, and with a reasonable prospect of safety. I regret to add that this is the survivor of four which we have been endeavouring to rear for you; the little fellow is now full of life and spirits. I have arranged all things necessary for his health and comfort and shall be truly rejoiced to hear that he survives the voyage and assures you in his own sweet notes of the cordial attachment of his late mistress. I was unwilling to wait till the season became so far advanced and endeavoured but without success to send you a pair from Charleston; they are so delicate that without the greatest care they hardly survive during a sea voyage. Mr. L. will request his correspondent at Hull, to which port our little mariner is bound, to send it to Mr. Hutton as some time since directed.

I sent a letter and small folded parcel some time in June addressed to Lord Bathurst which you have no doubt received. Since then I have read with much pleasure Head's Journal and the Nowlans. My expectations were fully gratified in the former. No man could have been better gratified for the execution of such an enterprize and none I think ever described so concisely, so vividly and so well. Who is the author of the Nowlans? You say an obscure young man; he evinces great fertility of invention, writes well, and will no doubt write better; the Nowlans is I think rather overcharged with incident, and are not some of the characters and scenes in Aby Nowlans' family somewhat over-wrought? We were much amused with the picture of Shrovetide. Is it known who is the author of Vivian Gray, Tremain and De Vere?[146] They have all been attributed to the same hand but I must think erroneously. Neither the life of Napoleon nor your Volume of Tales is yet published; if much longer delayed they will at least furnish a delightful occupation for our winter evenings. By a paragraph in today's paper I find that you have read and approve the first number of the American Quarterly Review mentioned in my last. It is with equal wonder and delight that I view the advancement which a period not exceeding ten years has made in the still infant literature of our Country; in many instances it evinces a vigor and stamina which promise at maturity all that is desirable in its several departments. It is not fair that I should trouble you now with a long letter; mine I am always conscious are little worthy [of] the indulgence and ever kind attention you bestow on them. In the pleasing anticipation of being furnished with a sufficient apology for again resuming the pen, it shall now only express with what truth and sincerity

I am dear Madam
Your friend
R. L.

146. Robert Plumer Ward (1765–1846), British novelist and politician. *Tremaine: or the Man of Refinement* (1825); *DeVere: or the Man of Independence* (1827). ME liked *Tremaine,* and a contemporary reviewer compared it with her work for its social realism. When ME came to write *Helen*, the character Horace Churchill, a master of anecdote, was partially modeled on Ward's personality. For *Vivian Grey,* see note 156.

Edgeworthstown, October 1, 1827

This worthless note is merely to tell you my dear kind friend that I have by the same post which carries this letter dispatched a parcel containing two very small pasteboard boxes containing purple and other crocus roots and a very few seeds from flowers in our own garden. At the bottom of one of these little boxes is a little drawing of a bud of Pyrus Japonica which Pakenham Edgeworth sends to that kind little boy of yours who sent him the rice bird's wings. The parcel is directed to the care of Mr. B. M. Myers, New York, for you. I had intended to have sent letter and parcel together but I think you tell me to send *letters* separately from parcels in order to give you notice of the probable arrival of parcels, and perhaps because if parcels were sent as letters are by post they might cost *terribly*. Let me know if I understand that matter rightly or whether I take a useless precaution in this separation.

Before I quit the letter and parcel subject I should warn you that Secretaries of State having all been changed in the late change of ministry in London, you must no longer follow my late instructions [*to*] direct to Wilmot Horton. When you send to London, *letters* or *small parcels without string* with *white* paper outside, size of two reviews, may be directed thus: To Edward G. Smith Stanley, Esq.,[147] Treasury, Downing Street, London. The inner cover direct For Miss Edgeworth, Edgeworthstown, Ireland.

When you send either letters or parcels of the above size or of the size of that which I now send you (to Messrs. Myers) to Liverpool or Dublin, direct them thus on the *white paper stringless* cover To The Earl of Rosse, Parson's Town, Ireland, directed on the inner cover to Miss Edgeworth, Edgeworthstown. The parcels sent by vessels bound for Liverpool may have a brown paper *outside* directed to Messrs. Brown and Co. They will forward the parcels by post to Lord Rosse after taking off the

147. Edward George Geoffrey Smith Stanley, fourteenth earl of Derby, (1799–1869), secretary for Ireland under Earl Grey.

brown outside. The parcels for vessels bound for Dublin may be in like manner consigned by the direction on an outer cover to Mr. G. McBride, Abbey St., Dublin.

I hope I have made the affair of these triple covers clear to you and I hope you will excuse my being so tiresome. It is to secure the pleasure of hearing from you with certainty and to prevent the hazard of losing any marks of your kindness.

I hope you have received long ere this my letter of thanks for that beautiful piece of work which has been the admiration of all my female acquaintance who are connoisseurs in needle-work. How human hands *could* do it and do it so astonishingly clean none of our "Fairly-fairs" can comprehend.

I answered your questions about Moral Tales and Parents Assistant. You have them all, except the little Plays, 7th Vol. Parents Assistant, which are new and which I hope have before this time reached your young people as I desired my bookseller to send them. Let me know.

We have just had a visit of a day from one of the first scientific men, in my opinion, of this age. I mean Herschel,[148] the first in scientific invention and perseverance, the first in candor and desire to improve science independently of all motives of personal vanity or interest. His conversation is delightful, full of information on all subjects—not a mere astronomer, or mere geometrician, geologist, or chemist. He is as amiable in private life as great in science, the best son, the kindest friend!

He came over to Ireland with a friend who was travelling to refit his mind after deep affliction from the loss of a beloved wife and two children. Of this gentleman you may perhaps know the name as accounts of his inventions in mechanism have appeared in journals and reviews—Babbage.[149] He has brought to perfec-

148. Sir John Frederick William Herschel, baronet (1792–1871), English astronomer, a man of broad culture and talents. While an undergraduate at Cambridge he made a pact with Charles Babbage and Dean Peacock that they would "do their best to leave the world wiser than they found it," an agreement that all three fulfilled.
149. Charles Babbage (1792–1871), English mathematician and scientific

tion a machine for calculating tables of logarithms, the most perfect arithmetical machine by far that has ever been made, carrying in itself a principle of rectifying its own errors or rather the errors of the person using it. That is to say it *stops* if an error be committed in addition, multiplication, *etc*. I wish there were any moral mechanism by which governments or individuals could be so checked in the act of committing error and the evil prevented before proceeding to consequences.

We have had visits this summer from several agreeable and celebrated people, among others from Doctor Brewster of Edinburgh,[150] and from a most amiable and intelligent young Russian, a nephew of Count Orlof's,[151] Monsieur Davidoff.[152] When shall we have the pleasure of seeing some of your friends? Whenever you send us any one be assured that a line from you will ensure them a kind reception.

I have nothing new to tell you of ourselves, but that my sister Sophy Fox's little boy is now able and willing to fight a turkey-cock; "stick in hand and stamping at the cowardly creature" as Sophy pictured him in her last letter, [he] drives him fairly off the field of battle. Both my married sisters are as happy as possible in their own homes, happily near enough to us to insure our frequent intercourse, inestimable blessing, for the small *feltings* [*softenings*] of sympathy cannot be extended to great distance, tho' there are strong chains of esteem and regard resting on the solid qualities which will reach from one world's end to another, oceans between.

---

mechanician. While the computer commissioned by the government was never completed, it contributed to the advancement of manufacturing machinery.

150. Sir David Brewster (1781–1868), Scottish physicist and writer. His popular fame was due to his rediscovery of the kaleidoscope.

151. One cannot be certain which Count Orlov ME had in mind: Count Grigori Grigorievich Orlov (1734–83), officer in the guards, favorite of Catherine II, and chief organizer of the palace revolution of 1762; or his brother Count Aleksei Grigorievich Orlov (1737–1808), officer in the guards, who also rose to prominence under Catherine. The latter was entertained in London at Dr. Burney's, father of Fanny, who recorded his visits in her *Memoirs*.

152. Vladimir Davidoff (d. 1882), traveler and enlightened Russian landlord.

My sister Lucy continues in excellent health. She has just now been folding up some seeds for you from her own flower beds and has written upon the papers in her own *upright-old-lady-of-the-last-century's-prim-hand* [*here ME writes like her sister*].

I have not time to say any thing of books except that I have read Scott's life of Napoleon, nine volumes, with unabated interest from the first volume to the last. There are in this work many faults of style, but there is a life and spirit and candor throughout the whole and a moral adherence to principle which distinguish it above most, I had almost said *all*, the histories I have ever read. It is to be compressed from nine to six volumes I hear and it will be the better for it.

I hope you will have the pleasure of seeing Captain Hall. I receive the North American and American Quarterly Reviews from my friend Mr. Ralston regularly and find in them many interesting and instructive articles. There is a French review called "Revue Encylopédique" of which I send you a notice which I think you and Mr. Lazarus might like to bespeak. It contains a great deal in small compass. It is not on the plan of our Quarterly or Edinburgh Reviews but gives an analysis and extracts from works both of literature and science all over the world. It must be useful in keeping those who live remote from cities up to the current of the times, though it is not amusing like other reviews.

We thought the Prairie interesting 'tho it does not display as strong power as the previous work. The scene between Tachechana and her faithless husband is one of the most pathetic I ever read in novel or tragedy. Tears *only* could give it due applause. You know the epigram on Garrick and his rival actor Barry to which I allude. I forget the first line but the sense of [*it*] is that the different opinion[*s*] the public hold of the two actors

"in this appears

To Barry we give loud applause, to Garrick only tears."

Cannot you get somebody to make a sketch of your house and send it to me? Tell me who, or rather what kind of people are your neighbors. Have you any or no agreeable society out of your own family?

I am ever yours affectionately,
Maria Edgeworth

[P.S.] I have ordered Hunter to send the Essay on Opinions and the French Harry and Lucy to Mr. Myers, New York, for you. Tell me if they reach you.

[Copy]

Wilmington, November 28th, 1827

Many thanks my dearest Madam for your welcome letter of the 19th August and for the accompanying Crocus bulbs, which arrived in good order and in good time to occupy their station in my little flower beds. I trust they will find their new soil and clime not ungenial, but will grow and bloom and flourish and look lovely and charm my eyes, by the pleasures of association even more than they of late charmed yours.

I am glad the handkerchief arrived safely and shall be rejoiced to hear that a sweet little Mocking bird which I sent some time in August has been equally fortunate. As to the aforesaid handkerchief, I believe I cannot plead guilty, much less can I bear that you should accuse yourself with having imposed the task on me. In the first place the lace work is much more quickly done than embroidery on muslin and is not more injurious to the sight, and though you are pleased to compliment the execution, it is I assure you far inferior in delicacy and beauty to several specimens that I have seen from the hands of our young fair ones. In the second place tho' I have not in some years devoted any part of my time in that way, yet when *you* kindly expressed a wish to receive a piece of work done by *me*, could I be reconciled but in accomplishing it in my very best manner? I would more willingly have presented some offering better worthy of your acceptance, but the aid of the pencil or the pen being hopeless, I was fain to compromise with the needle. Pray wear it sometimes for my sake.

Accept my thanks for another volume of friendships offerings just received and for having directed the little work on the formation of opinions to be sent; it will I dare say soon arrive. I am reading and exceedingly interested in Scott's Napoleon, anticipating indefinitely, I know not what, but every excellence from that master hand; I must say, in spite of the palpable defects of style, I am not in the least disappointed; as to the charge of imperfection from having omitted to avail himself of valuable documents to which access was allowed him, I cannot decide as to its justness. I find the detail clear, well connected, and equal in interest to one of his own unrivalled romances, the reflections judicious. And so far as I can judge, the Historian, tho' sometimes tempted to extenuate, has not set down aught in malice. In the case of Gen. Gourgoud, Sir Walter's reference to public documents brings such proof of the authenticity of his statements, as it would seem unpolitic in Gen. G. to have urged him to produce. The gradual rise of Napoleon through the adaption of his talents to the exigencies of the times, his mighty grasp at sovereign power, his soaring and insatiable ambition and its disastrous downfall, afford as you remark, the finest of moral lessons, but is man so constituted as to take warning even from this? The bold, ambitious, enterprising adventurer will not see in his own a parallel case. He seeks another path up the steep ascent, vainly imagining that he shall escape such pitfalls as have entombed his predecessors; and he too sinks, leaving behind him only another proof that since the Building of Babel, the aspiring Visionary has been still the same. I send you with this, a pamphlet written in consequence of the publication of Napoleon's life, by Dr. Channing,[153] a Unitarian Minister of

153. William Ellery Channing (1780–1842), American clergyman. After graduation from Harvard in 1798, he lived in Richmond, Virginia, for two years as a tutor in the home of David Meade Randolph, an experience that made him take a moderate attitude toward the South although he declared against slavery.

Boston, with which though you may not accede to the correctness of all his views you will I think be pleased. It is serving mankind to strip so dazzling a character as Napoleon of all meretricious ornament and present it simply as that of man, preeminent in talents, but distorted by failings and crimes. As to the circumstances attending the close of Bonaparte's career, I can admit the justness of Dr. Channing's reasoning, but my feelings are at variance with his conclusions. Tell me what you think of the essay. Tell me too how you are pleased with "Hope Leslie" (Miss Sedgwick's). I hope you find it as charming as I do, and though I thus seem to beg a favorable sentence, I am sure you will give me your candid opinion. Nothing yet of Capt. Hall, but I still hope to see him. You make a transition from Napoleon to his Biographer, in reference to the power possessed by each over the human mind. If greatness (and true greatness it indeed is) be measured by its beneficial influence upon the mind and character of man, there *are* [*those*] who possess higher claims than either the mighty Napoleon or the talented Scott, there *are* [*those*] who content to enlist genius in the cause of usefulness, have aided the parent, informed and delighted the child, instructed even the sage, and in inculcating the lessons of virtue and truth have traced the path and led the way to as much happiness, "our beings end and aim," as in this sublunary state we are capable of enjoying.

Do you recollect my sister Eliza, my *child* of whom I have sometimes spoken to you? Ten days since she became a wife; she has married Mr. Samuel Myers, an amiable, well educated, intelligent young man, sufficiently her senior to be her friend and guide as well as her chosen companion for life. Her path thus far has been a flowery one; her sweetness of temper and innocent gaiety of heart have rendered her a favorite with the many, while other qualities of sterling value have bound her still more closely to the hearts of her friends and of her family. You

---

As early as 1810 he warned against the ambitions of Bonaparte, and his *Remarks on the Life and Character of Napoleon Bonaparte* (1827–28) appeared in the *Christian Examiner.*

know for you have felt how deeply I am interested in this event, and you will listen with indulgence to the little eulogiums to which a more than sisterly affection, prompted by the occasion, has given utterance.

The newly married pair are to reside in Petersburg, Virginia, about twenty-five miles from my Father's residence. I rejoice that she will be so near our parents; yet I could almost find it in my heart to envy her, so anxiously do I desire that intercourse with my family which at near 300 miles distance is in a great measure denied us. But happy as I am in my own domestic circle, I ought not to complain, nor do I. Our children are improving daily, our son is a sensible, reflective boy and evinces an integrity of mind, which we delight in cherishing. I am half tempted to give you some anecdotes but will be discreet this time and not inflict much more of my tediousness upon you; I send with this a small collection of insects, which I think you wished for your sister Lucy. My sister Ellen who has been chiefly instrumental in forming it sends with it the habitation of a large spider of which a little note from herself will give the history. You enquire respecting the sending of parcels. I greatly prefer that the letters should come separately, because I then receive them certainly and with more expedition; the parcel last sent containing your letter and the roots you mention intending to send to the care of Mr. Myers, but this was forgotten in the address, and the Gentleman, Mr. Morton, who had charge of it deposited it in the post office which rendered it expensive. I mention this only because you are so particular in your enquiries on this score that I believe you would rather be informed of it. The letter notwithstanding was most welcome. In truth I can merit your great kindness, in granting to me a portion of your time and thoughts, only by the estimation in which I hold them and by the gratitude and affection with which I am and shall ever be My Dear Madam

Most truly
Yours
R.L.

Edgeworthstown, Jan. 20, 1828

Alas my dear kind lady all your efforts have been unavailing; the little pensioner you intended for me and whom I should have loved and valued for his own sake and yours never will, never can "repay me in grateful warblings all solicitude for his welfare." On the outside of your letter was written in black letters

Hull the 10th Dec. received and forwarded by
Richard Totten
The bird died on the voyage.

You cannot feel more pain on reading these words than I did. I cannot console you in any way except by the assurance that your letter and all the proofs of your goodness and I may say affection for me touch me sensibly.

I am so exceedingly sorry that this happy little bird perished and so many of his predecessors in the attempt to reach this country that I cannot bear you should ever try to rear any more for me. Let them be happy with you and in their own country and climate and live out their little lives in song and joy as Nature intended. It would be selfishness and barbarous selfishness for me to sacrifice any more of them to an idle wish. Probably the mocking bird would not live through the first winter in this climate even [if] it could accomplish the voyage.

I wrote immediately after I heard of the death of my destined bird to Mr. Bullock,[154] author of the travels to Mexico, and a person who has had the care in his museum of all manner of foreign birds. I asked him whether he had ever brought over a mocking bird to England and whether any have lived under his care.

I have waited some weeks in expectation of his answer, but

154. William Bullock (fl. 1827), English traveler, naturalist, and antiquarian. His museums in Liverpool and London attracted wide attention for their many curiosities brought back from the South Seas by Captain Cook. His writings include *Six Months' Residence and Travels in Mexico, Containing Remarks on the Present State of New Spain* (1824) and *Sketch of a Journey Through the Western States of North America* (1827).

now conclude that he has left London and perhaps England; therefore I no longer delay writing to you lest I should give you just reason to believe me very ungrateful, a belief which I am sure nothing less than incontrovertible evidence could ever impress upon your gentle and kind nature.

I hope you have long before this time received a letter of thanks from me for the beautiful piece of needlework which you sent me. I cannot prevail upon myself to soil it by wearing that veil. It is the wonder of all who see it. We think that none but fairy fingers could have worked it so delicately—and so white.

Long ago I ordered my bookseller to send you "Little Plays," though I was ashamed to send you any thing so trifling, and I fear they must doubly disappoint you as I see by one of your letters that you expected from the advertisement of a seventh volume of Parents Assistant new stories. However it cannot be helped and you will make the best of it. I enclose for any of your young people who may be musical, for him who sent me the bird's wings if he wishes it, the setting of the kite flying song in "Dumb Andy." A gentleman who is now between seventy and eighty who is a stranger to me but a friend of one of my married sisters set it for me, unasked by me, and sent it to me. This gentleman set the beautiful popular ballad of "Auld Robin Grey" with which perhaps you are acquainted, or if not, let me know and I will send you both the words and music.

For many years this ballad was believed both by the English and Scotch to be an ancient Scottish ballad. It was quoted by Sir Walter Scott in one of his books. In consequence the authoress, a lady who is now living, wrote to thank him and to claim the ballad as her own. When I was at Abbotsford Sir Walter Scott shewed me this lady's letter. She said that she wrote the ballad when she was a young girl in imitation of the auld Scotch ballad style and was much surprised and amused by finding that even Scotch people took it for a real old ballad. She often heard people talk of it before her. One gentleman said in her presence that he suspected, indeed he felt sure, it was not Scotch from this circumstance. Auld Robin Gray begins thus:

Young Jamie loo'd me weel and asked me for his bride,
But saving a crown he had nothing else beside.
To make the crown a pound my Jamie went to sea
And the crown and the pound were baith for me.

But in the olden times in Scotland, in the days when the song was supposed to have been written, *a crown* was worth a great deal more than a pound. Therefore Jamie's going to sea to make a crown a pound was a manifest anachronism or absurdity, proving him at least not to have been a true born Scotsman of the aulden times. Some pretty drawings have been made from this ballad and engravings have been taken from them, one in particular I recollect, by Mr. now Sir George Robinson,[155] brother to a friend of mine. If the ballad interests you and you should wish for one of the prints, tell me and I will try to get and send you one. I wish I could think of anything that you would better like to have. I hope the crocus roots reached you; I sent them.

You are quite right in judging that Vivian Grey and Tremaine and de Vere are not written by the same persons. Tremaine is written by Mr. Ward, a friend of ours; he was for many years in parliament and one of the Secretaries of the ordinance department. He has now retired from public business and amuses himself with writing works of fiction. De Vere though much too long is I think superior in talent and design to Tremaine. Mr. Ward's experience in office has given him the power of drawing some of the characters in official life with great truth and spirit. I do not mean that they are or that he intended them as portraits, which he positively disclaims, but they are true to nature.

Vivian Grey is said to be written by a son of D'Israeli[156] (author of Curiosities of Literature, *etc.*)[157] Whoever he may be

155. Sir George Robinson, sixth baronet (1765–1833), member of Parliament for Northampton, 1820–32.
156. Benjamin Disraeli, first earl of Beaconsfield (1804–81), author and English prime minister under Victoria. His novel *Vivian Grey* (1826) created something of a sensation because of its eccentric and worldly hero.
157. Isaac D'Israeli (1766–1848), English writer, father of Benjamin. His

he is a man of great talent and great assurance. The public however seem to like to be braved and to be treated with this insolence of genius, for his books sell well.

DeLisle[158] or the sensitive or the mistrustful man is one of the last novels that we have read, parts of it very good, but much too long and too many people and stories crowded into it so as to confuse the interest and destroy the effect.

Flirtation[159] is amusing and amiable and written by a well bred person, who has seen the life she describes.

In the last Edinburgh Review there is an excellent article by Jeffrey on O'Driscol's History of Ireland.[160] In the Quarterly for October 1827, No. 72, there is a most useful essay by Sir Walter Scott, *On planting waste lands*, which cannot be of the least interest to you in America but which is highly interesting to us in Europe. Some of your American reviewers ought to match it if they can by an "Essay on Clearing Wooded Lands." There has lately appeared in London a *Foreign* Quarterly Review in which there are two excellent articles, one on the introduction of supernatural characters in works of fiction, the other on the history of the Moors and Spaniards.

The passage you copied for me about models and patents is excellent. I have sent it to Mr. Rotch,[161] the inventor of the patent fid (mentioned in Harry and Lucy to which I ought to be ashamed to refer). Mr. Rotch is at this moment doing his utmost to have the patent laws of England improved.

Curiosities of Literature (1791, 1793, 1817, 1823, 1834) is a miscellany of literary and historical anecdotes, critical remarks, curious information.

158. Elizabeth C. Grey, *De Lisle; or the Sensitive Man* (New York, 1828); *De Lisle; or the Distrustful Man* (London, 1828).

159. Lady Charlotte Bury, *Flirtation*, 3 vols. (1827–28). Besides being a novelist, Lady Charlotte Bury (1775–1861) was a lady in waiting to Queen Caroline. ME met Lady Bury in London at the Lockharts in 1830.

160. John O'Driscol, *The History of Ireland*, 2 vols. (1827). The reviewer was Francis Jeffrey, Lord Jeffrey (1773–1850), Scottish judge and literary critic. He was one of the founders and a long-time editor of the *Edinburgh Review*. He later became a member of Parliament and still later a judge.

161. ME possibly refers to William Rotch (1734–1828), American whaling merchant, or possibly to his son William Rotch, Jr.

Whatever you do for me or send me is always marked by your characteristic good sense and good taste as well as kindness. All my family agree in wishing that they could become personally acquainted with you as they think that they should like you above any of my American correspondents. What has become of the brother you promised us should visit Edgeworths Town?

I forgot to tell you that we have read the Red Rover[162] with delight, notwithstanding the tedious minuteness of the first half of the first volume. It has powerful interest, wonderful considering the few characters and contracted scene of the whole, but a master hand can be shewn in a few strong touches and with a few colors. The Negro does more for the Negro race than any English act of Parliament can do. The one affects opinion, far above law in its range of power.

I have given Capt. Basil Hall a letter of introduction to you. I hope he will present it and that you may be pleased with his visit. He is a man of great talent and great candor and liberality, eager for information and indefatigable in his desire to obtain information respecting America. He takes the means to obtain it by giving himself time enough to see, hear, and understand, instead of galloping or steaming through a vast country and giving a vue d'oiseau of the whole in the shortest time possible. He has been one year and will remain another year in your world.

We have lately had a visit at Edgeworthstown from a Miss Douglas of New York, originally of a Scotch family, rich and benevolent. She left with me fifty pounds to be applied in any way I choose for the advantage of the poor of Ireland; she also gave considerable sums to charitable institutions in Dublin.

Mrs. Edgeworth and I have determined to employ the £50 in small loans to the poor upon condition of punctual returns of the money at stated times. This will, as we hope, preserve the fund unimpaired *and* improve at once their circumstances and

162. James Fenimore Cooper's *Red Rover* (1827) has as its hero a "gentleman pirate more sinned against than sinning."

their moral habits. On a small scale Mrs. Edgeworth has tried this lending scheme for years and has found the people grateful and improved by it, in that habit which they need *most*, or at least *much*—punctuality.

I must now finish this letter, for I have many others to write and must not indulge myself longer with you.

Believe me my dear Madam, with sincerely grateful and kind feelings, your affectionate friend

Maria Edgeworth

Edgeworthstown, March 26th, 1828

Dear Kind lady,

All you have done this time for my pleasure has perfectly succeeded. Your nicely packed box in its twofold case arrived safely and nothing that it contained was injured by voyage or journey. The collection of beetles has very much pleased Lucy and she thanks you and your dear Ellen for them. She wishes that a list of their names, numbered and referring to their histories or anecdotes of their lives and habits, could have been sent with them. She wishes to know whether you or your sister would like that she should collect for you any of the beetles or spiders of this country. And I wish to know whether there are any seeds or roots that you would particularly like. You sent Lucy a caterpillar's nest fastened to a twig of a tree. The leaves of the tree seem to be wound round the nest. On what tree was this found? The spider is the largest I ever beheld, and its nest or house is the most curious I ever saw. I have read descriptions of this sort of nest but that only increased my desire to see the reality. It is more wonderful than I had expected. This spider's den is so curious that I wonder the possessor of it could bear to give it up. I beg you will assure her that I know the value of what she has given to me and this spider and house I keep for *my own*. I will not part with it even to Lucy. I think this monstrous spider must be of the same sort as that which you may remember sending me, in the year 1824, an anecdote, copied by you from the Georgetown Metropolitan, an account of a battle which Mr. John Logan witnessed between a black spider and a frog. The battle lasted twenty minutes. The spider was victorious and having strangled his frog, dragged the body four times his own size up a precipice five inches high and almost perpendicular and began to feast upon him. This anecdote in your handwriting has been pasted by my brother Pakenham to whom you sent it into one of the volumes of his Kirby and Spence's Entomology— a delightful book.

Mr. Prince,[163] proprietor of the Linneau [*Linnaean*] Botanical Garden at New York, sent me, in the outer box which covered your insects, nicely packed in wet moss some anemonies rooted—now all alive! One of them, the Spotless Anemone[164] with a beautiful star-shaped white flower rising from green leaves trefoil shaped, is now standing beside me on our library table and is the admiration of all beholders. It is called in Rees' Encyclopedia the rue-leaved anemony and I see is accounted a hardy plant; so I shall take care not to kill it with too much care.

The next thing Mr. Prince sent me, Clematis Virginia, is now coming into flower. The flowering Hypericum prolific[165] I dare say will be very pretty when it flowers. It is now well and looks happy and pleased with its present situation in Mrs. Edgeworth's greenhouse.

Mr. Prince also sent me a number of small packets of flower seeds which I am now going to divide among various of my friends. I will write a note of thanks to Mr. Prince by this packet; but I enumerate to you all he was so kind to send as I know it

163. William Prince (1766–1842), American horticulturist. He was a member of horticultural societies in London and Paris as well as this country. His *A Treatise on Horticulture* (1828) was the first comprehensive treatment of the subject published in the United States.

164. Probably *Anemone quinquefolia*, known as nightcaps, snowboys, wood anemone.

165. *Hypericum prolificum*, known as broom brush, shrubby St. John's wort.

was all done at your kind instigation. I found in your box a little bag, sewed up I am sure by you and written upon by your own hand *Variegated pride of China*.[166] My sisters, who saw the China Tree or Pride of China abroad, not in flower but in seed, admired it and say it is reputed beautiful in flower. It is called the *bead tree* in some countries because the pilgrims gather the seeds for *beads;* there is a natural hole through each. Flint's Travels made me very much wish to see this China Tree. Thank you for these seeds—even if I should never live to see the tree.

My brother Pakenham who will be sixteen next May left us last week to go to Edinburgh where he must study two years and acquire oriental languages to prepare him for being a writer in India. We have the greatest confidence in his principles, steadiness, and manly wish to acquire knowledge and the means of independence, but still it is an anxious, awful event for us to part with him, even to Scotland. What will it be at eighteen when he must go to India! I had lately the pleasure of giving him a beautiful book which was sent to me from a bookseller in Philadelphia in acknowledgment for Little Dramas of which I sent him the manuscript. The book is *Bonaparte's American Ornithology*.[167] The colored engravings are most beautiful. I know of none superior to them of the sort in England.

I have never yet seen Hope Leslie which I hope I shall like for I like the author and her previous works.

We have been much pleased with the Reviews in No. 70 and 73 of the Quarterly on Heber's Life and Diary in India.[168]

166. *Melia azedarach* (mahogany family), a favorite shade tree, once used for cabinet work; known as chinaberry, China tree, pride of India, still common in the South.

167. Charles Lucien Jules Laurent Bonaparte, prince of Canino and of Musignano (1803–57), French ornithologist. He lived with his uncle and father-in-law, Joseph Bonaparte, during his residence in America and studied the ornithology of this country. He published widely in this field; the book alluded to here is his supplement to Wilson's *Ornithology* entitled *American Ornithology, or History of the Birds of the United States*, 4 vols. (1825–33).

168. Reginald Heber (1783–1826), English bishop and hymn writer. He became bishop of Calcutta in 1823. His widow, Amelia Heber, published *The Life of Reginald Heber, D.D.* (1830) which contained a number of his miscellaneous writings.

The book itself I have not yet seen but have sent for it. I daresay it will be republished at one third of the expense in America. But we do not grudge the price as it is to make a fund for this amiable and valuable man's widow. Would to Heaven that we had such men ruling in this our Ireland, spreading by example and precept the spirit of toleration and virtue.

Another book which has lately much interested me is Jan Van Halen's escape from the Inquisition and his travels.[169] He is much more interesting in my opinion than Trenck[170] because a better man, perfectly honorable, and thoroughly a *gentleman* in all his conduct. I hope this is not too aristocratic an expression for you, my dear American.

I forgot to tell you we were exceedingly interested by the *Red Rover* and wondered how from such limited materials and such a few characters such breathless interest could be sustained through three volumes. One really sees the vessels in motion and in fight before one's eyes. And I am sure I know the Red Rover himself and Dick, Fred, and Casey the Black. I am afraid it makes us all immoral admirers of pirates. Certainly the Red Rover is a far nobler character than the Englishman Wilder or Cork or whatever he is.

I think I mentioned to you Cunningham's Two Years in New South Wales.[171] It contains many new and curious facts but certainly is not written by a man of much delicacy. It is indeed inconsistent to expect delicacy from the surgeon of a

169. [J. Llanos], *Juan van Halen, count de Perecamps. Narrative of Don J. van H.'s Imprisonment in the Dungeons of the Inquisition at Madrid, and his Escape in 1817 and 1818: . . . His Journey to Russia, His Campaign with the Army of the Caucasus, and His Return to Spain in 1821. Edited from the Original Spanish ms. by the Author of "Don Estaban" and "Sandoval,"* 2 vols. (1827); *Memoirs of Don J. van H.,* 2nd ed., 2 vols. (1830).

170. Friedrich, Freiherr von der Trenck (1726–94), a Prussian soldier who served in the Austrian army. His autobiography enjoyed a wide success, being translated into several languages. It first appeared in German in Berlin and Vienna (13 vols., 1787) and shortly afterward in a French version by his own hand (Strasburg). He was guillotined as an Austrian spy on 25 July 1794.

171. Allan Cunningham (1791–1839), English botanist. His account of his travels in New South Wales appeared in the *Journal of the Royal Geographical Society.*

convict ship. The value of the work arises from the facts which prove that the most depraved rogues can be reformed and which show the circumstances on which this reformation depends and by which it is accelerated or retarded, a fine lesson for lawgivers and for all the rulers of the land and for all moralists. There is a sermon in the novel of The Vicar of Wakefield supposed to be preached to men in prison which anticipates these results. Pray read it.

Did I mention in my last Cyril Thornton, a novel in which there is an account of the peninsular war? Extremely interesting, so much so that I could not resist writing to the author who was then unknown to me even by name. I directed to the Author of Cyril Thornton at his publisher's in Edinburgh. He turned out to be the nephew of a family of our friends. Mr. Hamilton.[172] We hope to see him here this summer. And when shall we see your Brother, my dear Mrs. Lazarus? I congratulate you most cordially on the marriage of your sister Eliza—your child. Believe me most truly your affectionate friend

Maria Edgeworth

[P.S.] Tell Lucy something about the spotted snake in the bottle.

[*Mrs. Lazarus next received by post the letter of introduction Maria Edgeworth had written for Basil Hall the previous year.*]

Edgeworthstown, April 9, 1827

My dear friend,

When this note may reach you I cannot even guess, but in writing it I have the agreeable certainty that whenever it does it will give you great pleasure.

---

172. Thomas Hamilton (1789–1842), Scottish writer. His novel *Cyril Thornton* (1827) was based on his military service. He also published *Annals of the Peninsular Campaigns 1808–14* (1829) and *Men and Manners in America* (1833). The British prejudice of the latter offended RML's American sensibilities.

For it is to present to you the Traveller whom you think the most "liberal, enlightened, the most reasonable and amiable" of all whose works you have ever met with.

I have it under your own hand in a letter received from you last week, received at the very moment when I learned that Captain Hall was preparing to visit America and to spend two years there accompanied by Mrs. Hall.

I am sure you will write to me soon after you receive this, and I leave you now to enjoy the pleasure of Captain Hall's conversation.

I am your sincere friend,
Maria Edgeworth

[*Written on back in another hand*]

Captain and Mrs. Hall regret very much that their route to Charleston will not carry them through Wilmington which would have given them the pleasure of making Mrs. Lazarus's acquaintance.

They are now on their way to Charleston, via Columbia, and hope to reach that place in time for the races, after which they proceed to New Orleans by land.

Fayetteville, 16th Feby. 1828

[*Copy*]

Wilmington, April 13th, 1828

Two days since my dearest Madam I had the happiness to receive your letter of the 10th of Jan., and am the more obliged by your indulgence as I had been apparently tho' not really remiss in suffering a previous one to remain unacknowledged. It is that in which you mention having sent two small boxes containing bulbs and seeds, and also having directed Mr. Hunter to send the French Harry and Lucy and the Essay on Opinions. Inquiry was immediately made at the Custom House in New

York whence the letter was post marked and has been more than once repeated but without success; no parcel for me had been either deposited there, or left with Mr. Myers. Some weeks after, a packet much larger than that which you describe, probably containing the book, arrived through the medium of the post; the direction to Mr. Myers had been forgotten and being charged by weight at letter price rendered the amount so large, $22, that we thought it most prudent to curb our impatience and suffer it to pass through the General Post Office, where it will be opened and returned to us in safety as printed sheets. I cannot tell you how I have been tantalized by this delay, and I have waited from week to week in the hope of being enabled to tell you that they had arrived at last. I will write immediately when they do, for I know my dear friend that you will feel pleasure in the certainty that my mind is relieved and that I am enjoying the benefits of your kindness. In future, be so good as to direct parcels of any kind for me *under cover* to Messrs. Alley and Trimble, Merchants, New York, and letters to their care. I shall then I trust receive them safely and without delay. Why can I not balance this catalogue of regrets by the information that my flower beds have been gaily arrayed in purple and yellow Hibernian Crocuses, but though soaked and planted, and watered and watched, they have failed to realize our hopes. Shall we persevere and renew the attempt this season? I think you will not say *nay*, and the association will be so agreeable to me that I must beg you to grant me one more trial.

Let me now tell you of Capt. Hall, and again thank you for your kind attention in giving him a letter to me, which procured me the pleasure of hearing from, tho' not seeing him. His route lay within 90 miles of Wilmington, but in retracing his steps (for our town is not on the post road) the distance would have been doubled, and he mentions being desirous to reach Charleston by a particular day. I wished very much to become acquainted with him, but knowing the probable inconvenience to which he would be subjected, and feeling that unless he had some other object in view, the inducement of a visit to us would not counter-balance it; I had sought to "hope humbly" and the event proved it fortunate that I had not been more sanguine. A lady of our acquaintance who travelled in a steam boat with Capt. Hall and his lady from Pennsylvania to Norfolk was delighted with his affability and intelligence, and the little domestick sketches of this philosophic and enlightened traveller, pacing the Cabin floor lulling his little girl to sleep in his arms, formed no un-pleasing addition to the picture. While at Norfolk Capt. Hall visited the military works at Fort Comfort where my brother Alfred is stationed. Unfortunately Alfred was absent, a circum-stance which both he and I regretted extremely, though we could not regret that he was on a visit to me. He feels much obliged and flattered by your wish to see him, and though his engagements forbid his idea of leaving the U.S. at present, he has not entirely relinquished the hope of visiting Europe, and Ireland and Edgeworth's Town, whence many of his earliest and most delightful recollections are drawn. While with us, Alfred made a drawing of our house and grounds, but being better initiated in topographical than in perspective sketches, he was dissatisfied with the *tout ensemble* and declined sending it as unworthy [*of*] your acceptance. I endeavoured to overcome his scruples, my opinion though probably less correct being more favourable, but without success. A friend of mine has since promised to do it and I hope to send it in my next. You have several times mentioned the handkerchief I sent some time since, bestowing on the needlework encominums far beyond its merits. I feel ashamed that so trifling a performance should have elicited so much of your notice; let me however undeceive you in one important particular, that, I mean, in which the delicate hand of fairly fair is concerned, for certain it is that tho' the work when finished was not more yellow, as my friends assured me, than the lace should be, I preferred employing the agency of soap and water, to which it is indebted for the pure whiteness which you so much admire. Within the last two years a lace school, as it is called, has been established in Newport, Rhode Island, where a great number of young ladies are instructed in the art of working on lace; it is executed with ease and rapidity in a style far superior to my poor specimen, and affords amusing occupation to the leisure hours of the wealthy, and a ready means of support to those in inferior circumstances.

You inquire what kind of people our neighbours are. Very pious, charitable, kind and good, but with one or two exceptions, indifferently educated, and little improved either by reading or conversation. I esteem many, but assimilate with few, and when intelligent and improving society is occasionally within our reach, we enjoy the luxury with additional zest. Ours is the only family of Israelites in the town. All Mr. L's children have been born here and though some have been educated from home yet their early attachments and intimacies are all local, and formed as mine were, among Christians. There is such a spirit of unity and benevolence among us as ought to exist between virtuous members of the same community, and tho' many feel and even express regret at the difference of religious sentiment which exists between us, it proves no barrier to mutual kind offices and sincere regard.

When I reply to your letters, I scan them from beginning to end lest I should leave any enquiry unanswered, and now having examined the previous letter I turn to that just received to deplore with you the fate of the sweet little Mocking bird. I had often thought of and longed to hear of its safety. We knew that the vessel in which it was sent had suffered severely from a storm soon after leaving here, and had been forced to put in to New York for repairs, but its passage must afterwards have been uncommonly tedious; it sailed from here in August and did not I find from your copied memorandum reach Hull till December. The poor little warbler could hardly have been expected to survive such a series of hardships as it must have had to encounter especially so late in the season. I will obey you in making no similar attempt at least until season and circumstances offer a rational prospect of success. Should you hear from Mr.

Bullock be so good as to tell me what he says on the subject. I would not attempt what he may have found impracticable.

Your "Little Plays" I found very pleasing and am not disappointed in them. They *are* perfectly innocent and if you will take the word of all the young persons in our family, they pronounce them also "very entertaining." Dumb Andy is the general favourite and I have many thanks to return you for the kite flying song. The music is well adapted and very sweet. My son does not sing but is very much obliged to you "because he knows that Sister Almira and Aunt Laura who are at his grandfather's in Virginia will like to play and sing it very much and he can send it to them." I sometimes think how happy I should be to show you my children; maternal partiality does not mislead me so far as to make me imagine my son a second little Frank or Harry. Yet his good sense and candour frequently remind me of both. I commended him the other day for having learned a rather difficult lesson in my absence; he replied, "I don't think I should have done it Mother if Sister Anna had not helped me a little." "Well, my son," I replied, "I am glad you are an honest boy and do not like to receive praise which does not entirely belong to you." The next day after standing by me some moments silent, he said, "Mother, what makes you praise me sometimes for such things as that about Sister Anna and my lesson yesterday?" "Because you did right, and I thought it would make you feel happy to know that I was pleased with you." "Yes, Mother, but wouldn't it have been wrong, if I had not told you so; it seemed like praising me for only telling the truth, and I like it better when you praise me for some good thing that you do not expect me to do and that it would not be wrong for me not to do." I readily gave my promise to oblige him in this respect; but now let me ask you my Dear Madam (that is, if you are not tired of both me and my son) whether in your opinion the commendation was in the first instance injudiciously bestowed? In this case it was evidently superfluous either as a gratification or an incitement, but in a general way is it not useful in education to evince our approbation of even what the young moralist may feel to be negative virtues?

Sir Walter Scott's "tales of a Grandfather"[173] form a valuable addition to our stock of juvenile literature. The style is not always adapted to the capacity of children, even should they, as he advises, stand on tiptoe; still, in combination with the subject, it is perhaps sufficiently simplified; parts which do not interest a child of six or seven years will possess sufficient attraction two or three years later and the youth of fifteen who opens Dr. Robertson's delightful Volumes[174] will not regret having obtained a little previous insight into the times and actors through the pleasant medium of "Tales of a Grandfather." Has Mrs. Kater changed her intention and continued her admirable History of England? I wish she could prevail on herself or be prevailed upon to do so. No other work of the kind that I have seen bears any comparison with it, and children who have read her little Volume with delight and understood every word of it, turn in melancholy perplexity from every other abridgement and would fain beg Mrs. Kater to write more for them.

The facts you relate of the beautiful Ballad of Auld Robin Gray are very curious and interesting. It is not long since a conversation occurred here relative to the authorship. Some from having met with the song in an edition of Burns' were of opinion that it was written by him. I did not think it in his style and imagined it of much more ancient date than any production of his, having neither the knowledge nor the acuteness of the Gentleman who discovered the Anachronism from the erroneous valuation of the crown and the pound. Are you not at liberty to tell the author's name? Can it be possible that one who could write so well, so true to nature, with so much simplicity,

173. *Tales of a Grandfather* (four series, 1828, 1829, 1830, 1831), inscribed to "Hugh Littlejohn," Scott's grandson John Hugh Lockhart, who is mentioned with some frequency in this correspondence.
174. RML probably refers here to William Robertson (1721–93), Scottish historian. His *History of Scotland*, begun in 1753 and published in 1759, went through fourteen editions in his lifetime.

feeling, and pathos has suffered her talents to be dormant, or has produced nothing else for publication? I should be much pleased to possess one of the prints you mention, if you can obtain it without difficulty, but shall I tell you, since you so kindly "wish to think of something that I should better like," shall I tell you that which above all things I most desire? To behold a resemblance of my kindest of friends and of her revered Father! Do I ask too much or can you indulge me? You see how unwise it is to throw temptation in my way. This request has been long at my heart and I cannot resist the occasion for expressing it. I am glad you are pleased with the Red Rover; Cooper excels in describing nautical scenes and most of our criticks agree in preferring this work to the Pilot. I know not why, however, but it has been more highly commended in the English and French than in the American reviews. You will see in the last North American Review remarks on "Hope Leslie" which I believe I mentioned to you. I rejoice to see it so highly commended, but shall be still better pleased to know that you have found it equally attractive. I wish I could return equally interesting information on literary subjects for that with which you enrich me. In this, however, as in all things relative to our correspondence, you consent to be the generous donor, and I, feeling the delight without being oppressed by the weight of obligation, am the willing receiver and thus the matter ever rests between us. I hope the articles you mention as being particularly interesting in a late foreign Review will be transferred, as they sometimes are, to our literary journals. I shall be on the watch for them. A Southern and a Western Review have lately appeared, both containing some well-written articles, and though the increasing number of such publications may not perhaps add greatly to the stock of general information, they are useful within certain limits and interesting as evincing the gradual development, if I may so speak, of national talent and national industry.

I hope my last letter and a box containing some shrubs with

a smaller one enclosed, in which were the long promised insects for your amiable sister Lucy, has reached you in safety. They were sent according to your directions to Messrs. Brown and Co., Liverpool, and left New York some time in January. Mr. Prince, who has an extensive garden on Long Island, mentions that he added some plants with a note from himself, to those I had requested him to put up for you. We neither had nor could obtain the seeds you wished at that time and if the plants arrive in good order you will not I think regret the exchange.

It is time for me to close this too long letter but not before I have thanked your sisters for forming so favorable, so much too favorable an opinion of me. They and you tempt me to be almost unwise enough to wish that I could test your approbation by placing myself in the midst of your family circle, just as I often represent it to myself, seated around a cheerful fire in the Library; a *fire*, for though it is April and our trees were in full leaf in February, a return of frost renders the evening fire quite desirable and we are fain to invest our friends with the comforts it may fall within our lot to enjoy. Unfortunately, or, as it might be, fortunately, Prince Houssain's tapestry is not within my reach and I must e'en confide to this little messenger all that it can convey of the truth and affection with which I am my Dear Madam

Yours
R. Lazarus

[*Original*]

Wilmington, May 22nd, 1828

Your good gifts, my dear Madam, seldom come single; by the last mail I had the pleasure of receiving your letter of the 2nd of March, and this morning came the long expected boxes of seeds, in good order and not I hope too late, with care, for the present season. They proved to be the contents of the parcel mentioned in my last as being sent to the P. M. General for inspection. Tho' small, the weight and consequent mail charges would have been considerable, but they were returned to me through the medium of a friend free of expense. The books have not arrived. Will you be so good as to enquire of Mr. Hunter if they were sent, and how addressed, or if not sent, let them and all future parcels be addressed to the care of Messrs. Alley and Trimble, Merchants, New York.

Yourself and your kind sister Lucy have greatly obliged me, nor will my sisters and friends be less gratified to behold flowers from the seeds of *your gardens* blooming in our own. We have already sown them, and I trust to give in a few months favourable accounts of our successful cultivation. They will be more highly prized by us than the rarest plants of a foreign soil, unaccompanied by so many pleasant associations.

Our little son begs you to thank your brother Pakenham for the pretty drawing and for the Grape Hyacinth seeds. With these, the Lychnis, Lavatera and some few others, we are unacquainted, at least by those names. I should very much like some seeds of the Laburnum; I have only once seen it growing, and I think it would mingle beautifully with our weeping Syringa and be as great a favourite with us as it was with your own Rosamond. The Crocus bulbs had sprouted in the box and have I fear lost their vegetative powers, but they shall have a fair trial; I begged in my last for a few more, but am fearful of robbing you after this large contribution. Half a dozen bulbs will be quite sufficient; if they thrive, we will propagate from them. Your sister Lucy's offer of collecting some insects for us is very acceptable, especially as we hope they would receive from her the advantage which ours had not, of remarks and references. My sister would have annexed the *common* names of many had she known they would be desirable. For instance, there is in the box if I recollect aright, a very large long black beetle, speckled with white, probably the "Beating Ptinus, or Death Watch," but whose popular name with us is the "Hommony Beater." And what you will ask is Hommony? Indian corn beaten in a large wooden mortar in such a manner as to remove the outer husky covering and leave the grain entire. This after several hours boiling forms a favourite article on our winter's breakfast table. The insect above alluded to frequents the wainscots of old wooden buildings, and makes a noise by striking with the nether part of its body, against the wall or floor, hence the name. If I recollect the caterpillar's nest, to which you allude, was taken from a cedar tree. The snake was killed in a field by a little black boy. It is deemed harmless and is I think the *"painted snake"* described as residing in woods and feeding on various insects, especially the Scolopendrae or Centipede, which are common here, tho' not exceeding two inches in length. See Naturalists Miscellany, Vol 1st, Plate 7th.[175] We were remiss in not noting such little particulars as were in our power and will do better in future.

At the time I read the anecdote of the Georgetown spider, I thought it was probably one of the kind lately sent you by Ellen, but I hardly supposed you would recall the circumstance after so long an interval. How is it my dear Madam, that while constantly increasing your store of information, you possess in such perfection the faculty of retaining even the minutest incident? By habits of attention you reply. But how difficult at all times to control the attention. My thoughts *are* vagabonds. I rejoice that the Anemonies and other plants reached you in thriving condition. The Hypericum and snowy virgin's Bower were voluntarily added by Mr. Prince to those I had requested him to send you. The pride of China is a beautiful tree of rapid growth. It flowers I think the third or fourth year; a light sandy and rather dry soil is most congenial. In our warm climate it is very valuable; it puts out early and continues till late in the fall, and I was remarking this evening, several which two years ago were so completely shattered by a storm as to leave only the bare trunk remaining [are] now rich in boughs and branches

175. *Naturalist's Miscellany*, 24 vols (1789–1813).

rustling their deep green, thickset foliage, as if an age had witnessed their growth and expansion. I shall enclose a little sprig of the variegated kind which is not common; the lighter part of the leaf when fresh is quite white, like the edges of the silver leaved geranium.

But I must not fill my letter with remarks on plants and insects unless indeed I had the power possessed by some of your friends of rendering these subjects truly instructive and interesting. I have not seen "Bonapartes American Ornithology." Wilson's American Ornithology,[176] a very pleasing work, was published in Pennsylvania some years ago, with very beautiful and tastefully arranged coloured engravings such as you describe. Proposals have been lately issued for a new edition. Knowing that Miss Sedgwick's little tract "The deformed boy" has been sent you from Pennsylvania, I had not ventured to flatter myself that the pleasure of placing "Hope Leslie" in your hands was reserved for me or it should have been yours long ago; I shall direct it to be sent with this from New York and hope it will still be new to you. I am glad you are so much pleased with the "Red Rover." It is I think among Cooper's very best. Do you not think he had Lord Byron's Corsair[177] in mind in delineating his Pirate? He has a Gulnare too, but a sweet interesting "Medora"[178] he has not. I have just read "Sketches of Persia," an amusing little work which you have probably seen. It would be more agreeable had Sir John Malcomb,[179] by whom I suppose it is written, either attempted no incognito, or been able to

176. Alexander Wilson (1766–1813), Scottish-American ornithologist. He traveled extensively along the American frontier collecting birds in the employ of Ree's *Cyclopaedia Ornithology*. The first volume of his *American Ornithology* appeared in 1808, and the ninth volume appeared after his death in 1813. An edition in three volumes with a life by Sir William Jardine appeared in 1832.

177. *The Corsair, a Tale* (1814).

178. Medora is a character in Byron's *Corsair*. It was also the name of Byron's niece, Medora Leigh, who claimed she was his natural daughter by his half sister, Augusta Leigh.

179. Sir John Malcolm (1769–1833), British soldier, administrator, and writer. His *Sketches of Persia* appeared anonymously in 1827.

support it better. So thin a veil gives an imperfect and confusing impression of the object it seeks to conceal and in a light work of the kind, containing no personalities, it was superfluous. We have, it seems, been erroneously informed with respect to the condition of Mahometan females. Their state is indeed far from enviable yet they enjoy greater privileges and are more on an equality with their lords than we have been generally taught to believe. I have not seen "Cyril Thornton." Your discovery of the author in the person of a connection of your friends was an agreeable little incident. I wonder if a novel "Sandoval or the Freemason,"[180] containing an account of Van Hulin's escape from the Inquisition, can be the book to which you allude? *"Thoroughly honourable and perfectly a gentleman"* is not at all too aristocratick an expression for your "dear American" who feels the force of and can on occasion indulge in a similar one. It is only the value of *empty titles* that we deny; that dignity of mind and force of character which constitute true nobility are acknowledged and honoured by us as by you. Indeed I could almost venture to assert that on this subject, there exists very slight difference of opinion between us.

I sympathize very truly with you and your family on your separation from your brother Pakenham. Sixteen is an early age for the possession of those just views and that steadiness of character which he evinces, and these offer the best grounds of hope and consolation under this trial and under that, incomparably more severe, which will in all human probability succeed it. It is astonishing how much of trial the well-governed mind can bear! And is it not improved by them? Not as ascertaining and glorying in its own powers of endurance, but in being taught humility from an increased sense of dependence on the Mercy and Providence of the most High, to whose care alone we confide the beings most dear to us on earth. Even now the anticipated tho' still distant period, at which, unless we change

180. [V. Llanos Gutierrez], *Sandoval, or the Freemason. A Spanish Tale. By the Author of "Don Esteban,"* 3 vols. (1826).

our place of residence, I shall be under the necessity of sending my dear little son from me, occasions many an anxious thought, and our constant endeavour is to form his infant mind to the exercise of probity, stability, and to habits of regularity and order his conduct and employments.

We labour under great disadvantage in the Southern States. Schools abound, but there are few, very few at which a solicitous well-informed parent could be satisfied to place a child. How have I been led to trouble you with these observations? It is not half fair. Will it be more so to acquaint you with a little domestick occurrence which has lately given me pleasure: the advancement of my brother Alfred to the place of Assistant to the Chief U.S. Engineer. I have so often spoken to you of Alfred that I cannot forbear informing you of this, his unsolicited good fortune. You will retaliate very agreeably by continuing to tell me of such family occurrences as interest you. How are Mrs. Fox and her little son, and how and where is your sister Fanny? You have not mentioned her in a long time. Adieu my dear Madam, believe me, ever truly yours.

R. Lazarus

[*Undated, but Maria Edgeworth was at Bloomfield near Dublin in July 1828*]

My dear friend, as I may well call you who have been proving your regard for me by continued acts of kindness for upwards of twelve years.

I perhaps may not have time to write a long letter, but I must write a few lines with a small parcel, a book with the leaves cut out into a receptacle for a few crocus roots. This is the right time of year, and I have them well put up by a gardener and nursery man at whose house I am at this moment. The roots are of the purple crocus. I do hope they will spread their purple beauty in your garden early next spring. When once they have taken root you may divide their bulbs in autumn and have a great number of offsets. You need not take up the roots but leave them always in the ground, planting the offsets where you please. Mice love them too well. Guard against mice by sawdust or lime round the roots or furze branches if you have them. Some put their trust only in traps, of bricks held up at one end by a slight stick, which the mouse disturbing brings the weight of brick vengeance down on his little smooth devoted head. Your boys I daresay know more about this matter than I do and would sacrifice [a] 100 head of mice while I am going thro' the description of ways and means.

The laburnum seeds of this year cannot be had till autumn; last years' would not be good.

There is in the County of Cork a gentleman who has made an establishment of silkworms with mulberry trees planted for their use. The trees and the worms have done well. His object is to make silk for sale and to establish the silk manufacture in Ireland. But I should think that the dampness and variations of our climate would be an invincible objection, and even if he could overcome it I am not clear that it would be useful to establish the silk manufacture here. Why not purchase in France and Italy what they can make so much cheaper and better than we can, and not force a manufacture unsuited to the habits of our people as well as to our climate?

But pray send me a cocoon and skein of your daughter Anna's silk. My brother Francis when he was a schoolboy at the Charter House used to amuse himself in rearing silkworms; many of his schoolfellows had this taste. As Fanny observes to me at this instant when I said it was an odd taste for schools, "They had the silkworms completely in their power and these were the only *pets* they had room for." They require as Frances told me nice management, as they are ravenous gluttons and will eat till they burst if allowed as much as they can eat. Perhaps with good education they might be less disgusting and shew more *self-control*. Has your daughter succeeded in teaching them better manners?

I congratulate you most sincerely on your brother Alfred's having obtained such an honorable situation as a reward for his talents, knowledge, and perseverance. It must be more satisfactory to himself and more gratifying to you thus to see him recompensed than it can be to any individual to obtain the titles or places which in these countries are often *bought*, sometimes bargained for and exchanged for parliamentary votes and often the price of talents sold to corruption or party. My own brother William can peculiarly sympathise with your brother as he has the same principles of independence and is pursuing without patronage the same useful profession, enjoying at every step the pleasures of science practically applied and the sense of integrity and utility. Even considering the matter independently of public good, professions ought not to be estimated merely by the money they bring but by the happiness which they confer on those who follow them, and in this view I do not know any profession except perhaps medicine which I should prefer for a young man of scientific taste to this of civil engineering. My brother William is enthusiastically fond of it.

Lucy will I am sure be glad to have an opportunity of obliging you by making the collection of insects you desire. I am not with her at present. I am at sixty miles distance from home (nothing to you, *no* distance in your American eyes). I am staying with a dear old Aunt, my father's only [*living*] sister, Mrs. Ruxton, eighty-two, and as young in heart and head as you are. I have my dear Fanny with me. We are in a beautiful place, near the Bay of Dublin. This bay is equalled only in Europe by the Bay of Naples. Fanny, about whom you inquire so kindly, is in much better health than she was on her return from Italy two years ago. But she is not strong and we hope sea bathing will strengthen her; she enjoys it much.

I am very sorry you did not see Captain Basil Hall and still more sorry that he did not see you. He is a very superior and liberal man.

I have read and liked the novel of Sandoval in which Van

Halen's story of escape from the Inquisition is introduced but the book of which I spoke to you is quite another thing. The title is exactly as follows:

"Narrative of Don Juan Van Halen's imprisonment in the dungeons of the Inquisition at Madrid and his escape in 1817 and 1818, to which is added his Journey to Russia, his campaign with the army of the Caucasus and his return to Spain in 1821," 2 vols. oct.

I shall stay here till the 1st of August. Direct letters to me, Miss Edgeworth, Edgeworthstown, under cover to the Earl of Rosse, Parson's Town, Ireland.

Ever affectionately yours
Maria Edgeworth

[P.S.] I will send you an engraving of my father's portrait soon. There is no picture of me. I never gave any even to my own nearest relations. My face has nothing remarkable in it of any kind nor has it any expression such as you would expect; therefore I would rather you took your idea of me from my writings. I send the crocus roots by Brown of Liverpool directed to the care of Messrs. Alley and Trimble, Merchants, New York. The engraving I do not send by this opportunity.

[*Original*]

Wilmington, Nov. 3, 1828

Just released from the sick chamber, it is one of my first and most pleasing occupations, my dear Madam, to acknowledge the receipt of your letters from Dublin and the highly prized portrait of your respected father which I last week received in perfect safety. I cannot express my feelings as I beheld for the first time the countenance of one so long loved and venerated, that countenance which I had so much wished to see, and need I say that my anticipations relative to it were fully realized? The eye so mild, yet beaming with intelligence, the benevolent smile, the whole expression so bland and engaging—just what I should have fancied and could have wished.

In a letter long since received you say "how you would have loved my father had you known him." I am sure I should, and how gratifying to my best feelings is your assurance that I was deemed worthy a place in his regard. Thus it is, my dearest Madam, that your benevolence finds means to enhance the value even of a gift so precious. Such esteem as his and yours is to me a source of heart-felt satisfaction, of honest pride I might say, did you know me otherwise than on paper.

I regret your determination not to sit for your portrait but must console myself with the very engaging image with which the medium preferred by yourself has constantly presented me; honoured too as I am with familiar intercourse, I should be unreasonable not to be satisfied.

You do not yet know that my illness was subsequent to the birth of another daughter (my 3rd child).[181] I was for some days at the point of death, and my infant was also despaired of; but through the goodness of the Almighty, it has nearly recovered, and I find myself, too, happy in being restored to my beloved husband and family. We call our daughter Mary Catherine, after two of my friends, to whose kind attentions during this trying period, I feel particularly indebted. But for my confinement I should long since have thanked you for indulging me with a fresh supply of bulbs, which having arrived in good time will I trust succeed. We admired the ingenuity of your *packing case*, which answered the purpose extremely well. With respect to the plants for which you apply to me, your friend will not I fear, find them exactly what he wishes. The Pitcher plant is not found in our Savannas but in those of South America. There is a species of it here, much smaller and formed like a trumpet, from which it derives its familiar name; within the pipe a small quan-

181. Mary Catherine, born 12 September 1828 (see Appendix B).

tity of water is always to be found, generally filled with insects. I am uncertain whether they are to be procured at this season; if not they shall be sent in the spring. We have not I believe the white bog moss which Mr. Mackay[182] recommends for packing, but they shall be put up carefully, and I hope, but cannot flatter myself, they will bear transportation. Mr. Mackay is misinformed with respect to the Acasia Julibrissin;[183] it is not that but the common white flowering locust which shades the side walks in Charleston. The Julibrissin or Sensitive tree is rare, but I can obtain the seed and will send some as soon as possible.

I hope you received "Hope Leslie." It accompanied a letter which reached you some time since. With this I send the long promised view of our dwelling, drawn by a friend of mine. That of Edgeworthstown house, taken for me eight years ago by your sister Mrs. Fox, I often look at with pleasure and prize it very highly as one of the many proofs of your kindness and regard. When you last wrote you were passing your time happily with Mrs. Ruxton. How lovely is such a green old age, combining the wisdom and experience of years with the cheerfulness and kindly feelings of youth. One excellent friend I have whose character till of late vied with that of Mrs. Ruxton—but alas! sorrow has of late made sad inroads on her heart—the death of a beloved and only daughter with other domestick afflictions has robbed her of all but equanimity, and the unfailing comfort of pious resignation. Thank you for recommending Van Halen's memoirs; I do not know when I have been more pleased and interested. Tho' so much a man of the world, he evinces a sort of plainness, I might in a certain sense almost call it a simplicity of character, which has many attractions for me. What he often terms his "Castillian pride," I am inclined to call true dignity, and I agree with you in approving him as a "perfect gentleman." Have you

182. James Townsend Mackay (1775?–1862), British botanist, curator of the botanical garden at Trinity College, Dublin ,from 1806 to 1862.
183. *Albizza julibrissin*, also known as acacia or silk tree, a native of India. The locust tree (black or common) is also called false acacia (*Robinia pseudo-acacia*).

seen Savary's memoirs?[184] Mr. L. read to me last evening some very interesting extracts from them, relative to the great, the unfortunate Napoleon. It will form a valuable addition to the accounts already before the publick, of the eventful period in which he swayed the sceptre of France.

My reading hours are now very limited. The care and education of my children, with domestick duties, engross almost my whole time—not unprofitably, nor undelightfully; yet do I often wish that my hours could be lengthened, or that some of those which hang heavily on the idle could be transferred to me. Sir. W. Scott said to you, "We may find time for every thing, if we will only employ all that we have." I am not so happy as to realize this.

I am impatient for the appearance of Capt. Hall's travels in the U.S. If the opinions he has formed of us be as liberal and as favourable as what he has published of the South Americans generally, we shall be well satisfied. How is it that Capt. Back of the Blossom[185] contradicts the account given by him of the Loochoo Islanders? I am too partial to Capt. Hall to entertain a doubt of his veracity, without powerful evidence to the contrary.

Some Winebago Indians, now in New York, have excited a good deal of attention and curiosity. They have been taken to many places of publick amusement. At the theatre they listened with attention to the musick; the play was Pizarro.[186] When the

184. Anne Jean Marie René Savary, duke of Rovigo (1774–1833), French general and diplomat. The *Mémores du duc de Rovigo* appeared in both French and English (1828).

185. Sir George Back (1796–1878), English admiral and navigator, *Narrative of the Arctic Land Expedition to the Mouth of the Great Fish River, and along the Shores of the Arctic Ocean, in 1833, 1834, and 1835* (London, Paris, Philadelphia, 1836). The *Blossom* was engaged in polar exploration, having passed through the Bering Strait in August 1826. Basil Hall visited Luchu in 1816–17 and recorded that the natives evinced a curious mixture of courtesy and shyness. His visit is recorded in his *Account of a Voyage of Discovery to the West Coast of Corea and the Great Loo-choo Island* (1818).

186. Most likely Richard Brinsley Sheridan (1751–1816), *Pizarro*, an adaptation from the German of August Friedrich von Kotzebue. *Pizzaro*, was first performed at Drury Lane on 24 May 1799. The character Rolla mentioned by RML plays a heroic role in the drama.

curtain rose their gestures indicated surprise and delight, and on the entrance of Rolla, they stood up and by signs testified their approbation. At Peals's Museum[187] they were entertained by an exhibition of phantasmagoria, but after witnessing some experiments upon the air pump, atmospherick pressure, *etc.*, the old chief said, "these things were too great for them to understand, they must come from the Great Spirit." On witnessing the ascent of an air balloon, one on being questioned through the interpreter replied, "Americans fools," another with more sense than taste, "No Use." I did not intend to give so much space to these Indians. It is quite time that I should think of relieving your eyes and your patience by closing with an assurance that I am my dear Madam

Yours sincerely
R. Lazarus

[*An introductory note to the following letter would help the reader to understand Maria Edgeworth's outpouring of emotion to Mrs. Lazarus. When the third Mrs. Richard Lovell Edgeworth died, speculation in the family centered on Frances Anne Beaufort, daughter of the Rev. Dr. Daniel Beaufort, to become the fourth Mrs. Edgeworth. The fifty-four-year-old Mr. Edgeworth found the twenty-nine-year-old Fanny Beaufort attractive and intelligent, but Maria, now thirty, had seen her only once and had not liked her. She feared that such a stepmother would imperil her close relationship with her father. She wrote her cousin Sophy Ruxton, "I have told my father in much stronger terms than ever I used in speaking to you* the exact state of my mind." *When Miss Beaufort came to Edgeworthstown for a visit Mr. Edgeworth proposed, but she was daunted by the size of the*

187. Rubens Peale (1784–1865), a son of Charles Willson Peale, relinquished his interests in the Baltimore Museum and opened Peale's New York Museum in the "Parthenon," a specially constructed building on Broadway opposite City Hall on 26 October 1825. It closed in the economic panic of 1837.

Edgeworth family as well as by Maria's ill-concealed disapproval. She asked for time, and Mr. Edgeworth sought to win over Maria. Maria was swayed by her father's confidences and agreed to visit the Beauforts where her prejudices were overcome. Miss Beaufort wrote Maria, "Say that you give me your friendship as I give you mine; that instead of lessening your dear father's love to you by taking part of it myself I have awakened in his heart another equal portion of affection, only made the third side of an equilateral triangle–all equal all necessary to each other." Maria pledged that she would be a grateful stepdaughter. The first child of this fourth marriage was named Frances Maria to symbolize the joining in friendship of the two women, and Maria's letter of 10 January 1826 to Mrs. Lazarus tells of how this child, Fanny, was presented at birth to Maria as her own.

Maria's affection for this half sister exceeded all her other affections and became truly maternal. Fanny Edgeworth developed into a charming young lady and at eighteen attracted the admiration of Lestock Peach Wilson, the son of a wealthy merchant-captain who had made his fortune in the India trade. He was twenty-eight, plain, shy, unambitious. Despite his heart of gold, Maria Edgeworth decided he was not for her talented and beautiful Fanny. Her child should see something of the fashionable world; the following year a tour of visits was undertaken. Maria took her sisters Honora and Fanny to stay with Lord and Lady Stafford at Trentham, a great place built to resemble Buckingham House. She wrote that the magnificence did not interfere with their comfort. On St. Patrick's Day they called on their cousin the duchess of Wellington at Apsley House, now a museum. Lady Elizabeth Whitbread, Lord Grey's daughter and widow of a rich brewer, was asked to look over Lestock Wilson for whom Fanny confessed a fondness; her ladyship disapproved. They stayed with the Thomas Hopes in their great mansion that housed their collection of sculpture, furniture, and paintings; they stayed ten days with the Hopes at Deepdene in a house that was too Egyptian for Maria. Back at Grove House as the guests of Lady Elizabeth Whitbread, Fanny seemed to have attracted a young man to Maria's taste–young Samuel Whitbread, tall and handsome. They cantered in Hyde Park; Maria wrote, "Mr. Whitbread has become Fanny's gentleman *in waiting." In 1820 it was Paris with Fanny riding with Lady de Ros in the King's Riding-House. The best dressmaker and best hairdressers were employed; Bourbon and Bonapartist royalty as well as nobility were hosts. The years passed. Fanny entered her thirtieth year, and her graces, universally admired, had not yet attracted the quality in a suitor that Maria continued to hope for. Fanny confessed to an uncle that she still cherished an affection for the awkward, unprepossessing former suitor. Lestock Wilson, now forty, too was unmarried. He appeared again in Edgeworthstown and within three days he and Fanny were engaged. All Maria's fond hopes gave way to the uncomfortable realization that she had kept the lovers apart for ten years. She expressed herself as "perfectly satisfied" to her family, but her anguish is expressed in part to her distant friend in the following letter.*]

Edgeworthstown, December 2, 1828

I write now to claim from you, my dear kind lady, sympathy—which I am sure you have to give, and which I am equally sure you will give me, as I would give you where your feelings were as intimately concerned.

My sister Fanny, that dear young pretty sister, who has been more a daughter than a sister to me from infancy to childhood and who ever since she ceased to be a child has been my most beloved companion and friend is going to be married.

Happily? you will ask. Oh yes, happily, most happily, or else my heart and her mother's and the heart of all the brothers and sisters who adore her, to say nothing of uncles and aunts and troops of friends, would break at once. And as for my being in a condition to write to you or anyone else if it were not a happy marriage that she is going to make, that would be an utter impossibility.

I firmly believe that it will be as happy a union as can be. The man to whom she gives her heart has been devotedly attached to her for nine long years, ever since she was quite a child. His affection has been proof against all trials and will now be rewarded as such constancy of affection deserved. She has seen all that England, France, and Italy could produce of elegant, cultivated, witty, and fashionable. With me in London and Paris she was in the highest and most polished society and had much admiration and great means of deciding upon perfect experience and comparison as to what constitutes the real permanent happiness of life and as to what is essential to her own.

She has made her choice and will be a happy woman and make her husband happy as man can be. They will neither be rich nor grand, but will have a moderate income such as will make them to live comfortably in London. They will have excellent scientific and literary society, and will never look to the paradise of fools, the land of *Exquisites* and *Exclusives* and *Elégantes* and *Ennuyés* for that happiness which let fools think what they may they have it not in their power to bestow. "Felicity is painted in your countenance" will not do. It must be natural color that will stand; all the painting that ever was put upon face will fade and leave an ugly stain beneath.

Mr. Lestock Wilson is the name of Fanny's "happy man." He is of the firm of Palmer Wilson and Co. in London. His person and countenance are pleasing; he is suited to her in age, that is about nine years older than she is. He has an excellent temper, excellent sense, a taste for science, great strength and courage and tenderness of mind with timid, gentle, shy, reserved manners, little powers of conversation himself, but great power of being amused and pleased by the talents of others, whether amusing, shining, or solid. Fanny will supply all that he wants of conversational powers in a feminine, ladylike, most agreeable manner so that people will, as she will manage it, always give him credit for thinking what she says. When I say as *she will manage it* I don't mean to imply that she will manage with any artifice—that word *manage* was wrong—but that her manner and conduct will be so proper and graceful as to produce this effect.

They are to be married on New Years Day which is my birthday. You may imagine how entirely her mother's head and all our heads are filled with her, and therefore you will forgive me for not entering upon any other subject. Lucy continues well. She and Honora are now my only unmarried sisters. They will have a great loss of Fanny.

I am ashamed of sending you this letter, completely filled with ourselves.

Shall I send you some more crocus roots? I sent some a few months ago; I am not certain whether you received them.

Believe me very affectionately yours
Maria Edgeworth

[P.S.] Mr. Gerard [Gerald] Ralston of Philadelphia, in his last letter to me, suggests that perhaps he could be of service to you in transmitting any parcels you might have at any time to send. You may he says forward parcels to him thro' one of the half dozen lines of packets which sail between Philadelphia and the different parts of North Carolina and will forward these to Liverpool.

[Original]

Wilmington, March 14th, 1829

Accept dearest Madam my sincere congratulations on the marriage of your sweet and amiable sister. May every anticipation you have formed for her happiness be realized, and in contemplating her enjoyments in the station she is so eminently qualified to fill and to adorn, may you experience the best and only compensation for the loss of her beloved society. I know full well the struggle it costs to banish self, and to relinquish without repining some sweet solace which has long been identified with all our enjoyments, but happily we are so constituted that the very sensibility which renders us most alive to the endearing intercourse of friendship awakens that generous disinterestedness which finds its own enjoyment increased by sympathy with that of the object beloved. Then come new claimants on our best affections, which expand, and receive, and embrace them all. In reading your letter I looked forward with some degree of impatience for a description of the happy man who has obtained so high a prize, and you failed not to anticipate my wish. Your sister's selection reminds me of that of one of my favourites, your own Rosamond in "Patronage." In both instances a slight tincture of romance would have led me to desire somewhat of the beau ideal in the partner elect, but a little reflection suggests that it is from solid rather than brilliant qualifications that we are to derive that happiness which is "our being's end and aim." I hope you will continue to speak to me occasionally of this favourite sister. I love domestick scenes and occurrences, and all that relates to the members of the Edgeworth family possesses a high degree of interest with me.

I have just been superintending the packing of a box of the plants I promised to procure for your friend in Dublin; they are imbedded in their native soil and securely packed in wet moss. I trust they will reach their destination in safety. I send also two young trees of the Mimosa Julibrissan.[188] Your request came too late for the seeds of the last year. A very few were accidentally found, and these, as I have not addressed a line to Mr. Mackay, I prefer inclosing to you. I have requested that some may be saved for me this summer and will send them to you. Be so kind as to inform me if either the plants or the trees arrive in such order as to give promise of doing well. We have had a remarkably cold winter and a late spring for our southern climate. I have for a month past been watching for the appearance of the crocuses and cannot tell you how joyfully I welcomed not only their green leaves peeping through the soil, but also three days ago a number of their delicate purple flowers! Thus am I constantly

188. This is the acacia referred to earlier. The *Albizzia julibrissin* is a member of the mimosa family.

reminded of the kindness so repeatedly exercised for my gratification.

What do you think of "Pelham?"[189] I consider it a work of genius. The author has read much and perhaps thought more, yet he is not always fortunate in holding the mirror up to nature. His characters appear to me too artificial; and no delineation of a heroine, charming as his Ellen is intended to be, ever struck me as more laboured or less defined. There is wit, brilliancy, and grace, but then there is, in the 1st volume especially, too much flippancy and conceit, and what I conceive to be a perversion of taste, to oppose to them. From the "Disowned,"[190] which we are expecting, I anticipate greater satisfaction; a review which I saw of it has impressed me favourably, but it appears to me that the generality of novelists of the present day succeed rather in presenting the publick with something *new*, than with any thing really valuable or excellent.

A few weeks since we had the pleasure of becoming acquainted with a French nobleman, the Count de St. Ildegonde,[191] quite an event in our plain republican annals. This gentleman was late Commandant at Martinique and has now accepted an appointment in the service of the Emperor of Russia. I have termed our short acquaintance a *pleasure*, and indeed it was one. In the manners of the Count dignity and affability are happily blended; he is polite and unassuming, and his conversation highly interesting. He speaks the English language very well and has a general acquaintance with English literature. Thus has our first specimen of nobility been very favourable. I am told he married the widow of Marshal Soult.

Our Presidential Election has just closed and General Jack-

189. Edward George Earle Lytton Bulwer-Lytton, *Pelham, or The Adventures of a Gentleman* (1828).

190. Edward George Earle Lytton Bulwer-Lytton, *The Disowned* (1829).

191. The editor cannot identify this gentleman. His name was possibly Aldegonde. He could not have married the widow of Marshal Soult as RML was informed as Soult did not die until 1851, some twenty-two years after the date of her letter.

son, the Hero (as he is termed) of New Orleans, is appointed the first magistrate of the United States. There has been great excitement for many months past, and a strong opposition to the General, both on the score of his private character, and from an opinion that the election of a successful military chief might form a dangerous precedent; but since the will of the majority has been declared, party feeling appears to be subsiding into a calm. My brother Alfred mentions to me the General's entrance into Washington, in a plain carriage drawn by two horses and attended by a single servant, and continues, "As the carriage passed my window, I could not but reflect that there is little danger to the republick from Military enthusiasm, when such an event, can, after the recent excitement, take place in so quiet and unpretending a manner. At the ceremony of inauguration an immense crowd, probably 12,000 persons were present and of course a great number of the Political friends of the President Elect, but not an expression escaped that was indicative of slavish adulation towards him, or of any desire to wound the feelings of the fallen." This extract cannot, I am aware, possess the interest for you that it has for me; yet viewing it with the eye of calm Philosophy, does it not convey a picture of moral sublimity on which the mind may be gratified to dwell? If I mistake individual for general impressions and have fatigued you by this political sketch, pardon me, and I will engage to sin in this guise no more.

I send this, and the plants, by a vessel which sails direct to Liverpool, and on some other occasion I may be happy to accept the obliging offer of Mr. Ralston. Adieu my dear Madam, accept assurances

of unalterable regard from,
yours most truly,
R. Lazarus

Edgeworthstown, July 28th, 1829

You have often I daresay wondered at not having heard from me my kind and dear Mrs. Lazarus. And you have had good reason to think me ungrateful tho' I know you have not thought so, for it is not in your nature to think so without strong proof—as little I hope as it is in mine to be so.

We have had a great family misfortune. We have lost a very dear brother, my brother William,[192] a young man of great talents and of high principle, esteemed by all who knew him for a strictness of integrity and a love of public good, pure from the spirit or habit of jobbing which I must say are uncommon in Ireland. He had been much harrassed some months before his death by some jobbing work and mean underhand proceedings in the laying out of a public road in the North of Ireland in which he was employed as Engineer. He worked too hard mind and body, he was out in all weather eager to get the public work done and in weather in which the workmen employed would hardly stand out. He was of a delicate constitution, I should say of a consumptive constitution by the mother's side; her lungs were diseased. He might with care have lasted longer for our happiness, but perhaps it would have been for his own misery in the protracted sufferings of decline. It is best as it is, as every thing ordered by divine wisdom must be. He came home to us with only the appearance of a common cold, on the 7th of April last. He took to his bed three days afterwards, inflammation on his lungs came on, he died on the 7th of May.

During his illness he repeatedly said to his family and to those who sat up with him at night that he never was happier in his life than he then was, in the intervals of bodily pain. He was surrounded by the friends who loved him best and whom he best loved. How we rejoiced that at least we had him at home, that he was not taken ill at a distance from us in the North

192. William Edgeworth (see Appendix A). Later medical opinion suggests that he may have died of pneumonia rather than consumption as his family supposed.

among those unworthy people, or at best with cold strangers perhaps at an inn. Thank Heaven that misery was not added. He enjoyed to the last moment the soothing kindness of his friends and his own deep manly warm affection for them. He had the delightful reflection that in his whole past life he had done as much good as he possibly could to his fellow creatures and done injury to no human being, that to use his own dear words, "he never injured man or deceived woman." He had in the course of his profession forwarded in life many young men, many who succeeded, many who were grateful, who felt anguish in losing him, some who outstripped him in the course of wealth and honor. He never rose to what in wealth and worldly honor his scientific knowledge and talents merited; his health, four years loss of health early in life, retarded him. But what is wealth, what is any honor this world can give compared with the love and esteem which he possessed of the best and wisest of his own country, and of all who knew him in foreign countries? Wollaston[193] was his great friend and many others I could name. But above all the testimony of his own conscience, how far above all worldly praise! He is gone, but never can he die in our hearts. You will I know forgive me my dear Madam for having thus claimed your sympathy. His sister Honora who was his favourite friend from childhood is the greatest sufferer; for her it is impossible to find any thing in this world that can be called consolation. She finds in the sense of duty and piety the best support; with a delicate frame of body, too like her brother's, she has the most steady, enduring, feeling sympathy that I ever saw.

Thank Heaven Fanny was married and she was settled at a distance with new duties, new affections and new love before this calamity came upon her old home. She was extremely fond of William and sympathised in his highmindedness and in his scientific pursuits; but she has new objects, thank God.

193. William Hyde Wollaston (1766–1828), English experimental scientist.

I have not told you my dear Madam that your kind present of American plants [*arrived safely*]. Mr. Mackay is extremely obliged to you for the Cypress Julytressens[194] which had been the great object of his wishes. The plants were in capital condition, fourteen plants all in good health at this time and now in the College Botanic Garden [*Dublin*] where I hope I shall see them this autumn, when I go to that neighbourhood to visit my dearest Aunt Ruxton.

Adieu dear kind Lady. I know you will pardon my stupidity.

Ever affectionately
M.E.

[P.S.] I am very glad that your purple crocusses blew well.

[*Before Mrs. Lazarus received the above letter, she read of the death of William Edgeworth in a newspaper.*]

[*Original*]

Wilmington, August 30, 1829

My dearest Madam

It was but yesterday that I learned the afflictive dispensation with which it has pleased the All Wise Disposer of events to visit you. Deeply, sincerely, do I sympathise with you and yours in this sore bereavement. A beloved brother cut off in the flower of manhood, in the full exercise of talent and usefulness, and endeared to his family and to society, by every amiable and estimable quality of the mind and heart. Ah, my friend, for such a one you mourn, for such have I too mourned, and the deep wound now bleeds afresh, as in thy sorrows I recall my own. To the office of consolation, I feel my incompetency; in the sadly pleasing retrospect of departed worth, honoured by the friend, the acquaintance, the stranger, the lacerated heart finds solace.

194. ME seems to refer to the *Mimosa julibrissin* mentioned in the previous letter.

Yet is there a Higher, a surer resource, that confidence in unerring wisdom, which enables us, when nature has claimed her tribute, to bow in humble resignation to the Divine Will.

I had been long expecting some of your accustomed proofs of kindness; your latest date received, was of December last. I had begun to fear that some indisposition of your own might cause the delay and I had resolved to write and inquire whether my anxiety were well founded, when this sad intelligence received through the publick prints too surely accounted for your silence. I know that when you feel adequate to the effort, you will write to me, and if the recurrence be not too painful, I would ask if this melancholy event took place at Edgeworth's Town. I trust it did and that the last sad offices of affection were not denied to maternal tenderness. Does your own inestimable health continue unimpaired? I shall feel anxious till I hear it is so. I have long ceased to feel towards you my dear friend as a stranger, and you need not the assurance that my heart is interested in every inquiry.

I hope that two letters of mine, the first written early in the winter, the other in the following March, have reached you. The first contained the long promised drawing, the latter accompanied some roots and young trees for Mr. McKay of Dublin. I only mention them here, because in case of failure, I would not incur in your mind the charge of negligence. Adieu my dearest Madam, you will I know excuse my not entering on other subjects at present, and believe me with the utmost truth and affection

Your friend
R. Lazarus

[*Copied in Mrs. Lazarus's hand*]
Died on Thursday Inst. at Edgeworths Town after a short but severe [*illness*] William Edgeworth, Esqr., C. E., son of the late celebrated Richard Lovell Edgeworth, Esqr. Mr. E. was in the prime of life, possessed of a powerful and highly cultivated

mind guided by the purest principle; and whether as a man of science or as an amiable and highly enlightened private friend, those who had the pleasure of his acquaintance must always respect his memory and regret his premature death. Mr. E. was employed by the Port [*Post?*] Office as an Engineer; and among his projects is that new line of road from Belfast to Antrim, skirting the base of the Cave-Hill which when finished will be one of the most useful as well as the most beautiful in this country. Belfast Com. Chronicle of Monday, May 11th.

Edgeworthstown, January 10, 1830

My dear kind friend, Your affectionate sympathising letter must have crossed one of mine on its way to you, one which I wrote to you some time after our loss of my dear brother William. Depending on your sympathy and general kindness of heart I entered into details which to any one uninterested I could not have done.

Time and the sense of its being our duty to the living and the best respect for the dead to exert ourselves to make what remain of friends and life happy certainly have acted upon us all in different degrees, and most upon that sister of William's who was most his companion and constant friend and who has had the most irreparable loss. But she never makes us feel this; her equable, kind temper keeps her sufferings from any apprehension that can pain others. Her health has not suffered.

I have been for six weeks absent from home with a certain dear Aunt Ruxton (now 83) to whom I pay a yearly visit and from whom I am just returned, brought back by my curly headed sister Harriet Butler and her husband, their house lying most conveniently half a day's journey from near Dublin where my aunt lives and my sister Sophy Fox's half a day's journey (say thirty miles) from thence so that a course of family visits can be pleasantly accomplished with no fatigue and less expense. You

Americans will smile I daresay at our ridiculously short distances and half-days journies, you who have every thing on such an awfully great scale.

We have been a very happy New Years Day party just assembled in time for that day which has three claims to family notice. It is Fanny's (Mrs. Wilson's) wedding day, my little niece Mary Anne Fox's birthday, and my birthday. We had both my sisters Butler and Fox and their two husbands and Mrs. Fox's three children; both my younger brothers Francis and Pakenham added to our usual family circle.

One of our delights was hearing the Antiquary read again by Harriet who reads Scotch dialect and indeed everything well. The Antiquary like every work of genius and of real merit gains upon a reperusal. There are many beauties in the preparation for the appearance of characters and for coming events, many beauties of well-managed contrasts between what precedes and follows in composition which can never be so well appreciated at first as at a second reading, not only because curiosity carries us away and absorbs our attention from these objects but because till we know the whole it is impossible to see the connection or to judge of the proportion of the parts, and this perception of proportion, good ordering, and exquisite art of preparation and putting together form new and high sources of admiration and delight.

Sir Walter Scott's new edition of his novels with notes and prefaces is very popular and has brought him ten thousand pounds. I am almost ashamed to say all I could wish to say of the introduction to this work, Sir Walter Scott has spoken so very kindly of me! In such a gratifying manner. I feel more than I can say. I know you will feel this for me and that you will be pleased and gratified both by the matter and the manner.

When I was with my Aunt Ruxton near Dublin, I was within a few miles of the College Botanic garden and I saw and had a long conversation with Mr. Mackay who is at the head of that garden, the gentleman to whom you were so good to send the Jul[*ibrissins*], *etc.* He tells me they are all alive and doing well and he much obliged, very much obliged to you. I inclose a list of requests which he commissioned me to make to you, but at the same time he begged that if you find it troublesome you would not think of his requests further. Direct the box to the care of Messrs. Brown, Liverpool, to be forwarded to Mr. Williams, Packet Office, Dublin, for Mr. Mackay, College Botanic Garden.

I am now going to make a very trivial request to you and yet it is near my heart to have it complied with. Your beautifully worked veil has become yellow. I have worn it but seldom I was so choice of it, but no folding or shutting up in cabinet drawers and silver paper could protect it from the yellowing effects of time. Tell me exactly how you worked or bleached it, for I think you hinted to me that after it was worked it was washed. Give me exact directions and I will see them exactly executed. I suppose the purl was sewed on after it was washed. Was it ironed or pinned out? It is impossible to put it on as a turban because that hides all the work in folds; I wear it as a handkerchief and it never fails to attract a degree of admiration very uncommon in anything I wear. I still have the unreasonable wish that you would work for me on a bit of muslin the breadth of this fold down from the double lines [*two inches*] and exactly three times the length of those lines [*twenty-two inches*] in any pattern or stitches in cotton work you please which I may wear with a thin but not *book* or *buck* muslin. I can get the muslin for the turban easily in this country—it takes about two yards—but the border is all I want from you; that I pin round my head after I have put on my turban. I hope you will not think me insatiable. I wish my dear little friend who sent me his rice bird's wings could get a rice bird stuffed for me and send it to my sister Lucy. Lucy is now so perfectly recovered that she was able to dance for two hours at a ball lately without fatigue. She is going with Mrs. Edgeworth immediately to London to spend a few weeks with dear Fanny. Fanny will come to us in Autumn and then I shall return with her to London for the winter. You see I treat you as if you were one of the family and tell you all our little arrangements.

Ever affectionately yours
Maria Edgeworth

[Copy]

Wilmington, January 24th, 1830

I have been reproaching myself my dearest Madam for the many weeks that have elapsed since the receipt of your most kind and welcome letter. I had written a very few days previous to its arrival, after seeing in a newspaper an obituary notice of your estimable brother, and I now thank you sincerely for anticipating the request that my letter contained by giving me such details of that sad event as you rightly judged would be most interesting to me. I was relieved to find that to his affectionate family was granted the sad satisfaction of smoothing the pillow of death and administering to his last hours these offices of tenderness which soothe most sweetly from the hands of those we love. The expressions of your brother strongly reminded me of what you have written of your father at the same awful hour—both calm, collected; grateful for the assiduities of friends and resigned to the will of their Creator. I have always prayed to retain my senses to the last, and to feel, as I trust I should, a perfect resignation to the Will of my Heavenly Father. To ensure this enviable state of mind, how watchful must we be over our thoughts, our hearts and dispositions, seeking to gain an approving conscience, as earnestly as if each succeeding hour might be our last. But how difficult is this task, how imperfectly performed. The world withdraws us from ourselves sometimes, it is true, by those duties which society claims and in performing which benevolence and self denial are continually exercised; these are doubtless beneficial, but the frivolities of life will also intrude, and our reflections on *them* must always terminate in the conclusions of the wise man that "all is vanity."

It is not fair that I should at your expense thus give utterance to my crude thoughts. Let me turn to a more cheerful subject and tell you that I have within the two last months enjoyed the society of my dear father and one of my brothers, George,[195] an amiable and promising young man, valued and respected wherever he is known. The four years that have elapsed since my father last visited us have made little change in his appearance, for many years his head has borne its silvery [*blotted out*], but time has otherwise touched him with but a gentle hand, and when engaged in animated conversation he appears ten years younger than he really is. He greatly enjoyed the prattle and the caresses of his little grandchildren. My son will in a few days enter his ninth year; he is more companionable than the generality of boys at his age, exceedingly fond of argument (a propensity which I do not freely encourage), and unwilling to relinquish a subject on which doubts have arisen in his mind until his reason is perfectly satisfied. We are often amused by his recurring to some point which we have considered as finally adjusted, with, "But father I have just been thinking, *etc.*" I sometimes think as many mothers have thought before me, when looking at their children and casting a mental glance towards their most valued friends, I sometimes think with what emotions of pride (may I say?), a mother's pride and pleasure I should present to you my son and my two sweet daughters, and you, should you not even find them all that a parent's fond imagination portrays, would bestow on them a smile so full of benevolence that it might be mistaken through the same flattering medium for one of acquiescence and approval.

You have never expressed to me your opinion of Capt. Hall's travels in the United States. On this side of the water you probably know they have not been well received,[196] not so well even as

195. George Mordecai (see Appendix B).
196. Basil Hall (1788–1844), *Travels in North America in the Years 1827 and 1828* (1829). While this work did not raise the furor in America that Mrs. Frances Trol-

they deserve; extracts from the most exceptional parts of the work may truly be said to have run the gauntlet through our reviews and newspapers, and the constant reply to any inquiry respecting the book is, "I have not read it, but I have seen enough to satisfy me as to its demerits." In this unfair procedure I could not acquiesce and I read with an earnest desire to approve. What could be better calculated than his book on South America to present both the author and the man under the most agreeable aspect? In this I hoped to find a counterpart; but in some respects I must own myself disappointed. In description and detail no one can be more easy, accurate, and interesting, but when he reasons, the premises are not always correct; consequently the conclusions must be unfair. I hope I have not been influenced by that national vanity which Capt. Hall, not very unjustly, ascribes to us. I endeavoured to divest myself of all party feeling and to view the state of our society, and of our political institutions, as a disinterested observer; still it appeared to me that he beheld them through an imperfect medium which so distorted the object as to mar all its fair proportions. He has struggled with his prepossessions and prejudices but has not succeeded in restraining the one or overcoming the other. I have not hesitated to express my sentiments to you with openness because you were so well aware of my previous impressions. I hope you will use equal freedom. You need no assurance that with me your letters and remarks are sacred.

In the letter last received you mention the plants I sent as having arrived in good order and tho' you do not exactly say so I am led to suppose that the Julibrissin were also alive. I hope they will flourish and that you will some time tell me you have seen

---

lope's (1780–1863) *Domestic Manners of the Americans* (1832) was to provoke, both writers were accused in the American press of being in the pay of the Tory government in Britain to discredit democratic institutions. One of the earliest American reviews of Mrs. Trollope's book attributed it to Basil Hall as no lady could have written such coarse things; he was termed "the captain in petticoats." Other reviewers would reverse the image and have him "Mrs. Trollope in breeches."

them. There is something very agreeable in looking on an object and thinking it has once been beheld by one who loves us or whom we love. I wish you would mention if the drawing I sent ever reached you; the friend who executed it for me sometimes asks if I have heard of its having reached its destination, and I should like to reply in the affirmative. I am daily in hopes of having one of your welcome letters presented to me. Allow me if not too late to salute you with wishes for the happiness of the New Year, while I assure you, *etc*. [*Mrs. Lazarus's copy ends here.*]

[*Copy*]

Wilmington, July 25th, 1830

Our letters my dear friend do so often cross each other on the way, that as I seat myself to write, I cannot but hope that I am but anticipating your reply to my last which probably reached you some time in March.

Soon after the receipt of yours inclosing Mr. McKay's list of plants, I had the opportunity of sending him a box containing several, of which I inclose the names. I should have sent them to him with the box, but intending at the time to write to you immediately I omitted doing so. The intention has never been lost sight of, but various impediments (the chief of which has been the protracted illness of one of our daughters, who has suffered dreadfully from an attack of the Tic Douloureux,) have delayed its execution. Our poor invalid after three month's suffering is at length convalescent and we are enabled to resume with renewed cheerfulness our usual avocations. One of these has been to work the little border you wished for, and this should have been done long ago, as soon as I understood that the Handkerchief did not answer your purpose, but that, to use a technical phrase, *my hand was out*. Since my marriage I had not done a stitch of muslin work, and tho' formerly fond of it, was fearful of not succeeding, besides which, my sight has been much impaired by severe illness during my last confinement two years ago. Your request however was too flattering to be withstood, and I forthwith commenced practising, while I waited to receive a piece of India muslin for which I had sent to Charleston. It arrived, not so fine as I wished, but the best to be obtained there, and I worked the little border. But judge of my regret on finding that it had probably been injured, and would not bear a single careful doing up. My eyesight would not admit further trial and you I knew would not have wished it; our daughter Anna has done another strip for me, in the same pattern, and I send both, the one to lie in your drawer, the other, as I hope, to be worn.

I wish I could have said to you all this; it occupies so many lines and might in such an instant be verbally communicated. Yet I must not quarrel with a medium through which some of my greatest enjoyments are derived. I will only condole with my correspondent who is subjected to such an imposition. Before I turn to something else let me reply to your inquiry respecting the bobbinet Handkerchief. Have a fine lather made of soap and warm water, fold the lace and lay it in, let it stand in the sun, and when the water appears discoloured squeeze it gently out and lay it in a fresh suds, continuing to change it as often as requisite till the yellowness is removed; then dip it in one or two clear waters till sufficiently rinsed and pin it out quite tight on a smooth cushion, a minikin pin in each scallop, observing to pin each corner, and then the middle of each side first, that it may be drawn quite straight and square. In half an hour or less it will be dry and even the appearance of the pearling will hardly be in-jured (it was sewed on after washing). Should the work not be perfectly dry when unpinned, it may be laid between two nap-kins and ironed quickly with a hot smoothing iron, the pearling if disordered being previously drawn gently into place. While on the cushion the eyelet holes in the work should be repierced with an ivory piercer, and now the whole operation is I believe happily accomplished. A professed blancheuse would laugh outright at these minute directions, but you begged me to tell you exactly, and you will admit that I have done so. I wish it were as easy to send the stuffed rice bird. I tried to do and to have it done, at the time my son sent the wings, but could not succeed, tho' as far as practicable I followed directions. The Humming bird I obtained from a museum in Philadelphia after finding it required more skill than any one here possessed to clean and prepare it in a proper manner. Lovely little creatures! I wish you could see them as we now do, humming and dipping their long slender bills into the tubes of woodbine, as we sit at breakfast. Our woodbine, sometimes called "Coral Jessamine" from its bright scarlet colour, is not I believe the same as yours, for it has no fragrance, and your "casements *sweet* woodbine creeps wantonly round." It is however very beautiful, and I put a root or two of that, as well as of one or two other flowering vines and plants into the box sent to Mr. McKay. Will you let me know if any have lived?

I have a sister-in-law staying with me at present, the intimate friend of a Miss Yates of Liverpool, who she tells me sent you some time since an ornamented portfolio, executed by herself, as a proof of esteem and gratitude to the author of "Harrington." Was it handsome and were you pleased with it? With the intention I know you were. We have been reading the debates in the British Parliament on the subject of Jewish Emancipation, as I believe it is termed, which could not be otherwise than exceedingly interesting. Is it supposed that the bill will pass in the House of Lords?

What is there new and admirable in your literary world, *valuable* I should add, for in the multitude of new publications there may be found much to admire (as in the Pelham novels for instance) while there is little to prize, little to excuse the portion of time occupied in their perusal. What think you of Moore's Byron?[197] I was in hope that no life of that talented but unhappy man would be published; we already knew enough. Never could the concluding lines of Gray's beautiful epitaph have been better

197. Thomas Moore (1799–1852), *Letters and Journals of Lord Byron with Notices of his Life*, 2 vols. (1830–31).

applied than to Lord Byron. Tell me if you have seen a little book entitled "Colburn's Mental Arithmetick."[198] If you have not I will send it to you for Mrs. Fox's little son, who when I last had a peep at him was exercising his prowess against an overbearing Turkey Cock but is now I dare say striving to attain nobler ends by nobler means.

I thank you my dear kind friend for your detail of family arrangements, *etc.* You know how agreeable it is to me to be in any manner brought as much into your vicinity as possible. Let me tell you in return that the birth of my sister Eliza's first child, a son, makes me feel almost as if I were a grandmother in reality. She has been a wife nearly three years. [*Mrs. Lazarus's copy ends here.*]

[*London*], December 16, 1830

My dear Mrs. Lazarus,

I have only time at this moment to write a few lines and must abruptly note the needful—which is just to warn you that no more letters or packets to me can be sent under cover to Lord Rosse, because he has resigned his office of postmaster general and instead of being able to frank them to me he would have to pay a great deal for them himself.

Direct to me (if you write so as to reach England before May)

Miss Edgeworth, 1 North Audley Street, London, and enclose your packet to

Robt. W. Hay, Esquire,[199] U. Secy. for Colonies, Downing Street, London.

Enclose to him according to his direction at all events. But if your letter be not likely to reach England before May, direct the en-

198. Warren Colburn (1793–1833), *Colburn's First Lessons. Intellectual Arithmetic, upon the Inductive Method of Instruction* (1826).
199. Robert Hay (1799–1863), Egyptologist and archaeologist. ME met him in 1821 when he was private secretary to Lord Melville, first lord of the admiralty.

closure to Edgeworthstown where I shall again be in May.

I am now on a visit to my dear sister Fanny and my brother-in-law Mr. Wilson, with whom I shall remain till May. She is perfectly happy. I wish I could say perfectly well, but though her health is certainly much improved it is still very delicate.

I left Mrs. Edgeworth well at home and all our family at Edgeworthstown well. But I have lost since last I wrote you an aunt and friend who has been from my childhood most kind and most dear to me, my father's only sister, more like him than anybody I ever knew in mind, manner, and person. She preserved that likeness to the last, in generosity of heart and brilliancy of intellect and quickness of sympathy for all her friends to fine old age. She was eighty-three. She died without pain, in the arms of her children, respected, beloved, regretted in no common degree by all who knew her of all ranks.

To me the loss is irreparable. But I am thankful for having had the blessing so long, and for having still so many friends left to me. My sister Sophy Fox's children are growing into charming little objects of interest. My Brother Pakenham has left the India College at Haylebury[200] with all the prizes for successful application and testimonies to good conduct which his mother could desire. He will go out as a writer to India, to Calcutta, in May.

Of course my interest in all books relating to India has been keenly increased on his account, but independently of this I think I must have been deeply interested in Munro's delightful Life and Letters,[201] I mean with all of his *own* in the book; the editor is *tiresome*. There is in the *Foreign Quarterly* for September last an admirable review of books on India. In it is mentioned a novel called "Life in India"[202] which I have read in consequence of the

200. Haileybury College, located in Hertford, Hertfordshire, England, was founded in 1805 by the East India Company for civil service students; its emphasis was on the study of Asian languages.

201. George Robert Gleig (1796–1888), *The Life of Major-General Sir T. Munro, Bart. . . . Late Governor of Madras. With Extracts from his Correspondence and Private Papers*, 3 vols. (1830).

202. In the review of this work in "The English in India," *Foreign Quarterly Review* 6 (1830): 149, the title is given as *Calcutta, or Life in India*. Since the review surmises female authorship it must have been published anonymously.

honorable mention there made of it. Upon the whole, though the account of the passage out in the first volume is wearisome commonplace, I found the book fully answered, surpassed my expectations in all that relates to the picture of the country and manners of India, both of Europeans and natives, quite new and warranted true, and all that part admirably written. Much false taste in heaping together wonderful adventures and distresses (especially a lady scratching with her own fingers in the sand her husband's grave), but these are faults easily laughed at. The book has beauties and merits it would be difficult to imitate and information and food for thought never before laid before an English reader.

Who wrote it I know not but shall soon know from Mr. Lockhart (Sir Walter Scott's son-in-law). A great share of the pleasure I have had and expect to have in London society depends on our intimacy with Mr. and Mrs. Lockhart both of whom I like much. Her eldest son, the little boy to whom those charming Grandfather's Tales are addressed, has in consequence of a spine complaint become deformed and a most melancholy sight. His mother had not been sensible of the progress of the deformity till she was separated from him for some little time and on seeing him again she was quite shocked. She has two other children, beautiful, healthy, and promising in every way, a boy, the most handsome likeness imaginable of Sir Walter Scott with all his intelligence and benevolence of countenance, and a most engaging little girl, the image of her mother.

England has been much disturbed of late by riots and burnings; the object of the mobs has been to lower tithes and raise wages.[203] Imprudent and cowardly concessions made to these mobs have increased the evil, but the late changes of ministers and measures give hope that *steadiness* and *reasonable* reform will

203. Most of the riots at this time were taking place in the industrial north of England. The Birmingham Political Union was the most important group outside Parliament in the struggles for political and economic reforms. The Whig Reform Bill was introduced by Grey in 1831; it passed the following year.

produce and maintain tranquility. Ireland is at present the quietest and best behaved country of the two. The *party* raised against the Union I hope will not succeed; it is merely a *party*. All persons of candor, sense, and experience are convinced of the advantage of the Union and know that the desolving [of] it would throw Ireland back into barbarism. Of French affairs I know no more than the newspapers tell you. Talleyrand[204] who is French Ambassador here says that he is now come "to complete the restoration of the Bourbons." He means to support the only Bourbon (the present King)[205] who has sense enough to keep his seat on the throne. It is thought he will get through his difficulties though they are great.

I think that before I left Ireland I wrote to you my dear friend to thank you for the nice work you sent me, but perhaps as it too often happens with me, I imagine that I have written when the thoughts and feelings have only passed in my mind and have never been committed to paper. Believe me whether I have said so or not I am *very* grateful to you and to your sister for these proofs of your kindness. It was most provoking that the muslin you worked on so treacherously shrunk away from your beautiful work. And after all your pains and eyesight wasted! No, not wasted for I am *obliged*. And thank your sister, pray, most particularly. The work has been admired by all who see it and I am now in the midst of good judges.

Read Sir Stamford Raffles life. I hope soon to be acquainted with his admirable widow.[206]

Believe me to be ever affectionately your friend,
Maria Edgeworth

204. Charles Maurice de Talleyrand-Périgord (1754–1838), French statesman, had a truly remarkable record in adapting to political changes, justifying his multiple allegiances with the claim that he had always served France.
205. Louis-Philippe, duc d'Orléans (1773–1850), king of the French. ME met Louis Philippe and his duchess in June 1820; when she was invited to spend a quiet evening with the duke and duchess in Neuilly, he showed ME pictures of himself in America, as an exile who taught school there. ME also dined with his mother, the dowager duchess, widow of Philippe Egalité, at Ivry.
206. Sir Thomas Stamford Raffles (1781–1826), English colonial adminis-

London
1 North Audley Street
January 1, 1831

I wrote to you my dear friend lately (on the 16th Dec.) to beg you not to enclose any more to the Earl of Rose but to direct to
Robt. Hay, Esquire
U. Secy. of Colonies
Downing Street, London.

I now write only to enclose the little rings which I have found at last and to add to them an *English heart* (Derbyshire spar), cold and hard, but warm when worn by a friend. Try and wear it for the sake of one who wishes all manner of happiness this new year and every year of your life.

I am well and happy with my dear Fanny and her husband with whom I shall stay in London till May.

Yours affectionately in haste,

Maria Edgeworth

[Copy]

Wilmington, May 1st, 1831

My dear friend

Will I hope receive this soon after her return home and amidst the happy countenances by which she will be there surrounded, imagine one more, eager to greet her with an affectionate welcome and to listen (if that indeed might be) to the amusing and interesting details which have been reserved for the hour of meeting. I too spent a part of this winter abroad, with my husband's family in Charleston, very pleasantly, but my happiness in returning appeared to acquire an additional zest from my

---

trator, founder of Singapore. *The Memoir of Sir Thomas Stamford Raffles* (1830) was by his widow, Sophia Hull Raffles.

temporary absence as I looked around me, and I was ever emphatically repeating "sweet, sweet home! There's no place like home!" Nor can there be when so many duties, combining cares and pleasures, centre as they do with me in that one favoured spot. Another interesting little claimant has been added to our family since I last addressed you, a third daughter, Julia,[207] and now if I may only retain these without adding to their number I shall be truly thankful. I should grieve to find my duties multiplied beyond my power of fulfillment. Time never seems to fly more rapidly than when viewed in reference to the growth and advancement of children. I can hardly realize the years that have flown when I behold my son in his 10th, my eldest daughter in her 6th year and my anxiety is constantly increased to see them improve every passing moment. Young persons of the present day have delightful facilities afforded them for acquiring useful knowledge, and in the number of their benefactors they may proudly and gratefully reckon Sir Walter Scott whose tales in approaching our own times become doubly useful and interesting. I have remarked especially the detail and reasonings relative to the union between England and Scotland, which tho' in themselves sufficiently complicated are without being divested of dignity rendered so perfectly clear that a child of nine years reads, understands, and is deep rested in them. How unfortunate that the little boy to whom they are addressed should be so sorely afflicted. It is to be hoped that his mind and understanding will be disciplined accordingly, that he may escape the misery which an undue sensitiveness entailed on Lord Byron. I am acquainted with a gentleman, a Presbyterian minister, who became deformed in this manner at six years of age and I always view him with less of pity than of admiration; he has a fine head and face, and great benevolence and urbanity of manners. He told me that on first entering into life his feelings of mortification would have amounted to despondency had it not been for

207. Judith Julia, born 9 October, 1830 (see Appendix B).

the counsel and encouragement of his mother which upheld and taught him to seek beyond himself for tranquillity and resignation. He sought and he has found them.

But I am forgetting that with which I intended to commence my letter—thanks, which tho' delayed are not less sincere for the *heart* and rings which I received quite safely and shall ever value as evidences of that remembrance and esteem which I so highly prize. They are accompanied with too many agreeable associations not to be worn with gratitude and pleasure. The heart is my favourite but the rings are very pretty and ingenious. You say, "I inclose the little rings which I have found at last." The mode of expression leads me to suppose that you must have mentioned them in some previous letter; if so, I never received it. Were they made by any one of your family? That will bestow on them an additional value. As to the name in the motto it would be much easier to imagine my own in its place, than to transform myself as you advise into the Rebecca of Sir W.S. I am impatient for the appearance of Robert of France.[208] We were alarmed as all the civilized world must have been by the late report of Sir Walter having been attacked by paralysis, and proportionably relieved in its contradiction. We cannot bear to be reminded that so bright an intelligence must be subjected to all the evils of poor humanity, that his light too must be extinguished. May the period be averted so long as life may be deemed by him a desirable possession.

I have always felt much interested in the accounts you have given me of your late venerable relative Mrs. Ruxton. Her death appears to have been as enviable as her latter years were tranquil and happy; it is only under such circumstances that long life is desirable, and an old age like hers in which the faculties and the sympathetick affections are retained to the last is lovely and touching in the highest degree. You mention the indisposition of your sister Mrs. Wilson. I hope you left her in better health. Is she yet a mother? It is in this month that you expect to part with your

208. Sir Walter Scott, *Count Robert of Paris* (1831).

brother for India. It will be an anxious and distressing period, tho'
so long anticipated, but you will have numerous pleasing anticipations to buoy up your spirits, and I am well aware that you possess that true and useful philosophy which turns to the bright
side, except where wisdom teaches that the foresight of evils may
serve to avert them. My sister Ellen has within a few weeks set
out on a journey to Mobile which a few years since would have
appeared almost equal to an East India voyage, but now by the
facilities afforded by rail roads and steam boats it is accomplished
with little either of fatigue or danger. She mentions an intelligent
fellow traveller who had been farther west and was describing
the fertility of the State of Missouri. He had stopped he said at the
house of a farmer who lived in abundance and who told him that
he had little else to do but to sow his seeds and reap his harvest,
that he had kept a memorandum of the number of days in which
he had laboured during one year (and he had no assistance).
They amounted to no more than fifteen. There can be no doubt
however that more time might be employed to advantage in a
neater system of farming than is there generally practised, but
this is all that was positively requisite. What a country for emigrants! What an exchange would that be for the oppressed Poles,
should they at length be forced to seek refuge from tyranny. I behold their struggle with deep interest and shall rejoice if they succeed in shaking off the yoke and obtaining once more their station
among the nations of Europe. [Copy ends here.]

[Undated, but letterbook
records 1 August 1831]

My dear Mrs. Lazarus,
    I am almost certain that I wrote you last autumn to convey to
you very particularly Mr. Mackay's thanks for the cargo of American plants which you were so kind as to send him and to tell you
that I had seen them and that they were all flourishing, except the
Dionae Musipula which unfortunatley he had again lost. I re-

ceived a note from Mr. Mackay in August begging me to apply to you for a fresh supply of the Dionae, and I think it must have been in September that I wrote to you. I cannot call to mind any thing that I said in that letter, but I have a recollection of its being of several pages length and of my having felt my conscience relieved when I had finished it by the sense that I had told you all that I thought you could wish to hear from me, and I know that I was vexed by not finding the rings and heart which I had intended to enclose. The hearts are of Derbyshire spar; the rings I mentioned in the lost letter were made by boys at Lovell's school. I enclose one other.

I am quite pleased and touched by your being so constantly awake to whatever interests me. You seem to be always up to whatever I am doing and to know where I am and all my domestic concerns as well as if you were near me and one of ourselves.

I have spent three quarters of a year with my dear sister Fanny and can hardly believe it, the time went so pleasantly and so fast. Her new house is delightful, with a library at the back of the drawing rooms which was as free from noise and interruption as if in the country. Fanny has every blessing that it is possible to enjoy except perfect health and children. Her health is however much better than it was. I left her with this best of consolations; till her health be quite strong I ask nothing else in my prayers for her.

I was such gratified in London by the constancy of old friends and enjoyed much the variety of literary and scientific and what is called fashionable society which all together mix better in London than in any other capital I ever visited. But I much prefer Country to Town Life for permanent residence. There are more materials for thinking in town but less time for thought, more presented to the mind but less exertion of the mind itself—at least so my mind has always felt it. I am so much amused and in such admiration of others' minds that I cannot feel any necessity for exertion of my own.

A gentleman who is called *Conversation* Sharpe[209] was in some company in London when he heard me reproached for not writing more for the public and Fanny told me that he answered, "Oh she is too busy being happy." This shewed a penetration into my character which surprised me, and I always like his the better for it.

I am exceedingly happy now; I have returned home and cannot feel sufficiently grateful for the uncommon felicity of my lot in this life to be able to go from friends to friends as I do, still loved and loving and enjoying such pleasure in esteeming as well as loving so many for various and permanent qualities. I leave the pleasure of hating to whoever *can* enjoy it.

Steam carriages on railroads are really wonderfully convenient inventions. Did I mention to you that I went on the railroad between Liverpool and Manchester at the rate of twenty miles an hour? It is now the constant mode of communication and the rate is thirty miles an hour; goods to a great amount carried every day, 200 people at a time I saw in nine carriages chained together and moved by one engine.

I have the pleasure to tell you that I have this day heard good accounts of Sir Walter Scott's health. It has so much improved that the physicians say that he may yet with care last long. When the physicians said to him, "You must not exert your mind so much. You must not think so much," he answered, "You might as well tell the tea kettle that is on the fire not to boil." He is gone with his son-in-law Mr. Lockhart on a tour into the Highlands. How he will enjoy it with all his traditionary knowledge, love of that country, and power of turning every thing to account in so many different ways.

Your admiration of the Tales of my Grandfather and all relating to the history of Scotland delights me. Those books are some of the best among the best, and the manner of addressing the grandson is as you say most charmingly judicious. Your own

209. Richard Sharpe (1759–1835), British member of Parliament. He published *Letters and Essays in Prose and Verse* (1834).

anecdote of the clergyman who was so happy, amiable, and useful in spite of his bodily disadvantages is admirable. I wish I could make use of it.

I fear that the grandson of Sir Walter Scott will never live to be a man. I saw a good deal of him when I was in London. He is very amiable and intelligent but he is of very weak health and too great sensibility for his circumstances. I was with him and a little party of friends of his on Twelfth Night and *hunted the slipper* with them and observed that poor boy suffering much, mind and body. His mother, Sir Walter's favorite daughter, Sophia, is most amiable and engaging.

Politics is so wide a field I dare not enter it lest I should never come to an end. I will only say that there is almost equal danger in granting too much or too little to the reformists and that parties run so very high that few can tell what they really think best. The defeat of their adversaries is the first wish, the good of the country the second. There is however in the middle ranks in England a fund of good sense and of property which will resist revolution and yet require rational reform; upon this we depend.

The distress in Ireland is nearly over. It has never existed in the County of Longford. It is difficult to understand. There has been corn *exported* and exporting while people in some parts of Ireland were famishing, and not many miles assunder lay famine and plenty. Money wanting, not provisions, England has been very generous and has sent money. But woe to the nation that lives upon charity.

An excellent book has lately been published by Mr. Jones[210] (whom I know) "On the Distribution of Wealth." The first volume only has yet come out; this is chiefly on the influence of the various modes of paying rent in different countries, *Ryot* rents in India, *Metayerie* rents in Switzerland and Italy, *Farmers'* rents in England, *Cotters'* rents in Ireland, *etc*.

210. Richard Jones (1790–1855), English economist. He succeeded Malthus in the chair of political economy at Haileybury. His *Essay on the Distribution of Wealth and the Sources of Taxation* (1831) was a pragmatic rather than a theoretical approach to the subject.

Captain Hall has published a most entertaining little book in three small volumes called Fragments of Travels and Voyages, or more properly by the Edinburgh Reviewers "Sketches of Naval Life."[211] Pray read it. I do not approve of his patronage notions but those excepted I very much like the book. His forte is not reasoning but lively narration and description and humor.

Destiny is a delightful novel, by the author of Marriage.[212] There is a character of Molly Macaulay that is quite charming and really does one good; [she] recurs to the mind as an example of most amiable, cheerful contentedness which must make one ashamed of ever being discontented. Sir Walter Scott has published a new edition of his poems with introductions to them all compressed in a ninth volume. These are as delightful as his prefaces to his novels.

Mr. Herschel's Essay on the Progress of Natural Philosophy published as a volume of Lardner's Cabinet Cyclopedia is by far the first book of this age—price 7/6![213]

I am well and am about to go on with my novel.

Ever affectionately your friend,
Maria Edgeworth

[P.S.] Do not fear the multiplication of your duties; with you this will be the multiplication of pleasures. Your children must be delights to you. I wish I could see them.

[A letter from Mrs. Lazarus is missing here. Maria Edgeworth refers to its date as September, Mrs. Lazarus as October 1831. She wrote of the Negro uprising known as the Nat Turner Rebellion. As will be

---

211. Basil Hall, Fragments of Voyages and Travels, 3 vols. (1832).

212. Susan Edmonstone Ferrier (1782–1854), Scottish novelist: Marriage (1818) and Destiny (1831). The latter was dedicated to Sir Walter Scott, a personal friend. Like Scott's, Miss Ferrier's novels were published anonymously.

213. Sir John Frederick William Herschel's "Preliminary Discourse on the Study of Natural Philosophy" was published in 1830 as the first volume of Dionysius Lardner's (1793–1859) Cabinet Cyclopaedia.

seen, when Maria Edgeworth read that the insurrection affected Wilmington, she immediately wrote her friend, alarmed for the safety of the Lazarus family. Mrs. Lazarus, anticipating Maria Edgeworth's concern, wrote to reassure her. Others were likewise concerned for the Lazarus family when they read the lurid accounts in the newspapers; it is conceivable that Mrs. Lazarus wrote Maria Edgeworth somewhat in the same vein that she wrote her brother George Mordecai in Raleigh on 6 October 1831:

I can readily conceive the alarm and anxiety which must have been excited in your mind by the shocking reports of us which have been circulated far and wide. During the period of the first and greatest commotion among our townsfolk, I thought the accounts (as they eventually proved) so vague that I felt merely a state of discomfort from the scene of indefinable terror and confusion around me without realizing sufficiently to partake of them, and as Washington no doubt informed you, we remained quietly at home during the day and night (a very inclement one), when many were exposing themselves in the streets or crowding into the bank and other houses on the front street. The horrible disclosures which have subsequently been made have made a total change in my feelings, and I view the condition of the southern states as one of the most unenviable that can be conceived. To be necessarily surrounded by those in whom we cannot permit ourselves to feel confidence, to know that unremitted vigilance is our only safeguard, and that soon or late we or our descendants will become the certain victims of a band of lawless wretches who will deem murder and outrage just retribution is deplorable in the extreme. The United States government might possibly find a remedy by rendering some equivalent to slave owners and exporting the slaves in as large numbers as practicable to Africa. But I do not know whether if such a plan were proposed it would be acceded to by any considerable majority; people are too short sighted, too unwilling to relinquish present convenience from the fear of future ill or for the prospect of future good. Mr. Lazarus regrets holding so much property here, and if not actually tied down to the place, would gladly remove to the north, and I cannot help hoping that we may at some period be enabled to do so.][214]

214. The editor is indebted to C. F. W. Coker of the Department of Archives and History in Raleigh for locating this letter from RML to George Mordecai. It is part of the large collection of Mordecai papers held by the State Archives of North Carolina.

Edgeworthstown, November 4th, 1831

My Dear Mrs. Lazarus,

I am expressly anxious to hear from you since I have seen in the newspapers the terrible accounts of the revolt of the Blacks in Virginia and [*they*] specially mentioned Wilmington. I pray you to take pen in hand the day you receive this and write to relieve my true anxiety if you can by the assurance at least of your own safety and of that of all *who* and *which* are dear to you. I hope neither life nor property in which you are interested has suffered.

No part of the *civilised* world, old or new, appears now to be quite safe for civilised people to inhabit—what with the march of intellect and the march of troops. The instructors of the people do not seem to consider sufficiently that it is not sufficient or rather it is too much to set the intellect marching unless they clearly know and can direct to what good purpose it is marching; to give *power* without the certain and good direction of that power is most dangerous either in mechanics or education—or legislation.

We in England and in Ireland are now in most perilous circumstances. The refusal of the Reform Bill in the House of Lords has enraged the people so that (as this day's paper tells us) furious mobs are doing mischief in various parts of England: In Bristol the jail opened, then destroyed, prisoners who had been committed for riot set free; Jail Mansion, house of the Lord Mayor and two sides of Queen Square, a large square in Bristol, pillaged and burned. The troops brought out against the mob fired—above 500 lives lost. It is *said*, but not yet confirmed, that one regiment of dragoons sided with the people. If this, which Heaven forbid, be true there must be a revolution in England. Nov. 5th. To-day's papers say the troops behaved well and that the whole blame rests upon the Lord Mayor and civil magistrates who did not allow the troops to act early enough. The mob is now quelled and was I believe more *local* and [*acted*] less on revolutionary principle than I yesterday thought. The Lord Mayor's *wine cellars* contributed much to the mischief.

The most judicious persons of both parties agree that some

reform was and is necessary; even the special Tory friends of the Duke of Wellington now declare that his Grace's declaration that he would grant No Reform (that declaration which was the cause of his going out of ministry) ought never to have been understood literally!

As far as I can hear or judge the most sensible of the Whigs think that Lord Grey's Bill for reform was not well framed, that it would throw too much power into the hands of the democracy, not only more than the *Constitution* (that indefinable word) allows, but what is of far greater importance, more than is good for the *Constitution*—more than is good for the people themselves. They after all are very like the children in Berquin's story,[215] "Les enfants qui veulent se gouvener," with this difference, unfortunately for us, that we are all in the boat with them and if they get drunk and have hold of helm and oar we shall go down along with them.

The rage for revolutions seems to be catching, from all our neighbors on the Continent—France especially. We have more reason to dread it than the Cholera morbus; bad as that is, there are specifics for that. But where is the Oil of Cajeput,[216] or oil of any name, which will "medicine" to a State diseased?

It seems to me that at certain periods of wealth and population Nations must have revolutions, that if not from the rivalship of machinery, from over-population, from the accumulation of property and power in the higher classes, from the corruption of morals and the hardening of hearts; from all these causes co-operating, the poor become too poor to endure their poverty well and too numerous to endure it at all without combining for the destruction of those who are richer and happier than themselves

215. Arnaud Berquin (1749–91), French writer and moralist. His *L'Ami des Enfants (Children's Friend)* had many editions and translations. "Les enfants qui veulent se gouverner" may be translated as "The children who wish to do as they please."

216. The East India tree *cajeput* yields a pungent, greenish oil known as oil of cajeput, used, among other purposes, as an anodyne.

and whom they consider (whether they are or not) as the sole causes of their sufferings.

When a State comes to this critical state, the frequent changes of ministers and the violence of parties are but signs of the times, signs of the impossibility of governing those who will not longer submit to be governed, signs of the general sense of danger, the fear, the cowardice on all sides which turns as fear is ever prone to do into hatred and cruelty towards opponents. Party spirit is one of the worst signs of bad times, alternately cause and effect.

I am surprised to find I have written so much of what I scarcely ever write—*Politics*. But though I feel it is not a woman's department and that as she can do nothing, she had better say nothing; yet all is so out of its place now that I have got out of mine.

I will only add for your satisfaction about ourselves that this neighborhood is as yet perfectly quiet, that my brother's rents have all been paid in full to May 1831, that we have not yet had any disturbances about tithes or cess—or Reform Bill. But other parts of Ireland are much disturbed and the causes lie so deep and untouchable that I cannot form an idea how it will end, except by general convulsion. In which case, the apparent present quiet of this country only lulls us treacherously. I fear there are secret associations all over Ireland as in the time of Lord E. Fitzgerald.[217] I suppose Moore's Life of him has reached you; he was made for an amiable and domestic creature, not for the commander of a revolution for which he had none of the requisite talents and qualities, good or bad.

If you have time or spirits to amuse yourself pray read Captain Hall's last book, three small volumes, "Naval Sketches" the reviewers call it, a better title than his own, which is "Stray frag-

217. Lord Edward Fitzgerald (1763–98), Irish revolutionist. As a young man he served in the American Revolution; he became a member of the Irish parliament and later sought the establishment of an independent Irish republic. Thomas Moore, *The Life and Death of Lord Edward Fitzgerald* (1832).

ments of voyages and travels." You will find them delightfully entertaining and well written. I do not agree with him of course in his love of Patronage; indeed I wish he would not deal so much in general reflexions, national, political, or moral, in which he does not excel though he thinks he does, and he is not sufficiently aware of his powers of humor and of lively narration and description.

These observations I make not only on his books but on his conversation of which I had last season in London opportunity of hearing a good deal. He is an exceedingly good and good natured man, with an irritable temper and an unmanageable or ill-managed egotism, and yet in spite of this I should say that he is rather an humble than vain man; he talks more than he *thinks* of himself. He does not over value himself *altogether* nor does he value himself sufficiently altogether, tho' he puts the value on wrong parts. He is both very candid and very positive, very desirous in general to do right and justice and quite unable to do so in particular cases; his temper and his prejudices will not let him see to do what is right. He has been the means of doing a great good lately to my dear Sir Walter Scott, and that I may say is a national, a universal good. It was he who applied to the Admiralty to obtain a Government frigate to carry Sir W. to Naples. When Sir James Graham[218] who is at the head of the Admiralty mentioned the matter to the King, his Majesty said he would have it done as a personal favor to himself, and the King desired Sir J. Graham to write to Captain Pigott,[219] the Captain of the best frigate in the service, requesting him to take Sir Walter Scott.

Sir W. is accompanied by his son Major Scott and his unmarried daughter Anne; his youngest son Charles he will find at Naples in some diplomatic situation; so he will be surrounded by his family, and wherever he goes his glory and, better, his amiable character will follow-precede him, and his charming temper will make him enjoy everywhere all that can be enjoyed and

218. Sir James Robert George Graham (1792–1861), British statesman.
219. Sir Hugh Pigot (1775–1857), British Admiral, not to be confused with two other naval Hugh Pigots who died in 1792 and 1797.

endure all that must be endured with pious and charitable patience.

I fear I shall never see him more and how heavily this weighs upon my heart I cannot express. Joanna Baillie who has lately seen him describes him to me as very feeble in body, unable to cross the room without pain and difficulty, tho' still the same in mind.

Her own words are so touching I must give them to you, "I went the other morning to Lockharts (his son-in-law) to pay a second, a last visit to the Bard, for the Bard the great Bard he still is to me though this high distinction seems at present to be sunk and forgotten in that of the novelist. He looked cheerful and told me some pleasant Scotch stories as usual; but we took no leave of each other; though it was pressing on the minds of both that we may probably never meet again. How differently such scenes pass in real life to those which are imagined even in the simplest story. May God bless him wherever he goes."

I must now my dear kind Mrs. Lazarus bid you adieu, having many other letters to write and business of various kinds to work upon. I have been absent from home for a month on visits to various friends, and a most pleasant tour I had ending with a few days at each of my sisters Harriet Butler's and Sophy Fox's. Mrs. E., Lucy and I were at the christening of my sister Fox's last boy, William Waller Fox, Waller from his mother's aunt *Waller*, a descendant of the English poet of that name. My sister Fox is quite in round-faced health after having been very delicate. This encourages me to hope I may one day see Fanny round-faced. She is much improved in health, and her dear good husband brought her with him most unexpectedly last month to see us. She took me with her to the north of Ireland and they returned by Scotland.

My brother Pakenham is by this time in India, at Madras or Calcutta. Read Sir Thomas Munroe's life and letters, a new 3rd volume just published.

Ever yours affectionately,
Maria Edgeworth

[P.S.] Your observations on the preface and whole spirit of Tales of my Grandfather delight me. That poor boy I fear will not live. I wish I knew your amiable deformed friend.

Edgeworthstown, Dec. 29, 1831

My dear kind Mrs. Lazarus,

I have just received your letter dated in September last, in which you complain of one of mine then before you having no date. I must have been in a desperate London hurry when that was written; I particularly pique myself on the punctuality of my dates, having been reformed on that point by the perpetual reproaches of my family.

I will not proceed to any other subject before I have answered the questions of yours to which you say you have not received reply. I certainly did answer them in some letter of mine which has missed fire. I now repeat I am very much obliged to your friend who was so good as to draw for me the view of your residence. It gave me great pleasure and I have it carefully preserved in a drawer full of treasured presents from distant friends, a drawer stored with many, many of yours with which I amuse young and old friends who come to visit us. In the pauses of conversation or in the flagging it is very agreeable to have some things to look at which suggest new ideas and pleasing feelings, more pleasing feeling than gratitude, and gratitude for proofs of affection can scarcely be raised in the mind.

I particularly remember having answered your question about Miss Yates's portfolio. It is beautiful outside and still more beautiful inside. It is made in the neatest manner and I assure you has been preserved with so much silver-paper care that the rose colored silk lining and strings have not faded a single shade and the flowers on the white velvet are as natural as when first laid down. Miss Yates may be assured that her present gave me all the pleasure which she intended.

In two letters you have mentioned hair rings which it seems I twice said I had sent and twice omitted to enclose in my letter. I perfectly recollect one of these omissions, and I find in my letter book the entry of the letter in which I repaired the omission and I am quite certain that I inserted in that letter the rings and heart mentioned thus:

"1831. Jan. 9th. To Mrs. Lazarus—with two hair rings and a purple Derbyshire spar heart. Sent by Mr. Millar of Henrietta Street No. 13 Covent Garden, London, along with ten other letters from our poor Irish neighbours to their friends in America."

I have been of the opinion that all the letters which I have forwarded for poor people to America by favor of Mr. Millar have reached their destinations; it is odd that my own should fail. In the letter which you mention having from me without a date did I mention a purple heart as well as hair rings? Pray answer this question that I may make out where the failure has been.

I now sew down to this paper three hair rings, one for yourself on which is inscribed Maria to Rebecca, one for your sister Maria to Ellen, one for any of your children whom it will fit—with Maria on it.

I am sorry to have filled so much paper with these troublesome explanations but it is quite worth while to find out what mode of sending letters proves most safe. Direct your next by way of experiment as follows, your letters thus: To Miss Edgeworth, Edgeworthstown, Ireland, and the outer cover in which you enclose it To the Clerk of the Council in Waiting, Council Office, London. Thus enclosed any weight under that of an Edinburgh or Quarterly Review, for example, may be sent.

I hope your intended *wee-wee* cap of your sister's work may come safe, for I am sure that my dear Fanny will much value the kindness. Alas, I do not hear of her having any prospect of applying it to use. Her health however has much improved and I am thankful and contented with that great blessing.

Your account of the Negro rebellion is horribly interesting.

You will receive a letter of mine dated Nov. last which must have crossed yours on the road, in which I particularly begged you to give me some account of this Negro insurrection of which we had seen accounts in our newspapers that alarmed me for you as it was in your neighbourhood. You anticipated my wishes and I thank you for being sure of my feeling for you.

What will be the end of the threatening appearances in these countries I cannot venture to predict, nor can I even venture selfishly to say "Après nous le déluge." The waterspout is over our heads.

I enclose a few lines of Sir Walter Scott's handwriting as you desire, and I assure you there are very few people to whom I would part with a line of his, but you are welcome. I have a print, a very good likeness of Sir Walter which I would willingly send to you if I could be secure of its reaching you safely. Tell me if you can how to convey it from Liverpool or London and to whom it should be directed in New York, to which place I think it would be most easy for me to send.

All my family are now assembled for my birthday and Fanny's wedding day on the 1st of January. My sister Harriet Butler and her clerical husband and my sister Sophy Fox and her military husband and all her little ones, a charming train: Maxwell, a fine black-eyed boy, and Marianne and Charlotte, Mother's darlings and worthy to be so, and a little baby boy, William Waller Fox. Her mother's family (Mrs. E's.) [is] descended from Waller the poet. I have also a naval nephew here, a most amiable youth and very handsome moreover, Henry Beddoes, son of Dr. Beddoes.[220] He has just now been describing to me a naval day of misfortunes which would make a fine contrast to Rosamond's day of misfortunes, with which I hope your little girl is acquainted.

The variety of professions in a family makes an agreeable di-

220. Son of Anna Edgeworth and Dr. Beddoes (see Appendix A).

versity of character and variety of interests and ideas, all assimilating where there is affection and union.

Even when any event happens which does not quite please us this is lightened by our all drawing together. My amiable and very clever brother Francis, whom I believe I have more than once mentioned to you as a young man of considerable talents, has within these few days married at twenty-two a young Spanish emigrant General's daughter, between sixteen and seventeen. It has been a very sudden romantic affair. I fear they have not enough to live upon, but this marriage may stimulate him to the exertion of his talents in some profitable way and the cause of having new duties may steady his character. Rosa Florentina is the name of my new sister-in-law; Francis calls her *Simplicitas*. I have not yet seen her but I hear from Fanny that she has very good sense and that she is a sort of person of whom she thinks "she could grow very fond." If she could I am clear that I could. We are all resolved to make the best of it, and my brother's happiness in his own way is all we desire. Long may it continue.

We are going to read Robert of Paris. The introduction which we read last night we do not like. Sir Walter has you will see by the papers arrived at Malta under Quarantine. He has the advantage of two excellent libraries, one of them the library of the Knights of Malta. He was sent out in the best frigate in the service of England by the King's particular desire, who said he considered the health of Sir Walter Scott as a national concern. I hear from his son and daughter that his health is much improved.

That poor little deformed boy to whom the Grandfather tales are addressed is dead.[221] His death will be felt as a misfortune by his parents at first, but in time they will acknowledge it is for the best. His health was so very weak that he could never have enjoyed life for himself. He could not, like that amiable friend of yours, have made himself amends for external disadvantages by

221. See note 173.

mental and moral excellencies, and by the feeling of being useful to others, esteemed and loved.

I must now bid you adieu my dear Mrs. Lazarus, assuring you of my constant and grateful regard and esteem.

Your affectionate friend
Maria Edgeworth

[P.S.] In looking over your letters the other day I see you mention some establishment near you where young people work imitations of lace. If they work for sale I should be glad to have a scarf or mantilla worked as a specimen of American work. I have specimens of Scotch, French and English. I should not like to go beyond three guineas price, and if you are so good to bespeak this for me I will by means of my bankers, Messrs. Hoars, remit the amount of the charge. I should add that I would not have the work bespoken unless you can secure some way of sending it safely to London.

[Copy]   Wilmington, January 15th, 1832

Ere this my dear friend you have I hope received a letter written I think in October in which I gave such information relative to the insurrectionary state of our slave population as I thought might be interesting to you, and I rejoice at having written at that time since the affectionate anxiety evinced in your letter of November 4 has been the sooner dispelled. The assertion of [La] Rochefoucault[222] that we find something agreeable in the troubles of our friends has never obtained my assent, but that our own may, as [by] eliciting evidences of the regard and sympathy of friends, become in some manner a source of pleasure is more frequently felt, and more readily admitted, as your very kind letter affords ample testimony. All disturbances are effectually

222. François de la Rochefoucauld (1613–80), French writer, noted for his maxims.

quelled and as long as the impressions now made on the minds of our black population continue, there need be no apprehension of a recurrence; with this indefinite postponement of the evil we must rest contented until in its own good time an over-ruling Providence sees fit to enlighten the minds of our rulers, and enable them to devise means for its final termination.

You hope that neither life nor property in which I or mine were interested may have suffered; this unhappily I cannot say. Three of our slaves were implicated and two of them as having been aware of the plot and given it a conditional assent, were executed. But to these disturbances may be attribed an event far more afflicting, the death of Mr. Lazarus' second son, just twenty-three years of age.[223] He as well as most of our citizens had been much exposed in patrolling and his feelings greatly harrassed in attending the trials. He had lately commenced the practice of law and on one day when engaged in defending some of the accused had remained in the Court House from breakfast till a late hour of the night; a heavier supper than usual was in a few hours succeeded by violent pain, to which succeeded inflamation. Many times we were buoyed up by hope, for the progress of the disease was less rapid than usual, but the unfavourable symptoms were vainly combated and on the 19th day of his illness, we received his last sigh. His eldest sister[224] had been spending a delightful summer at the North, and during his illness was on her return, full of eager and happy anticipations. W[ashington] was aware of his precarious state and anxiously desired to see his sister once more. We wrote to prepare her for what we feared must be the event, but no letters reached her. Yet the Almight granted them the comfort of a last sad embrace. He knew and realized the happiness of seeing her, and then his passing spirit reposed I trust in the presence of his Creator. I will not dwell on the harrowing scene which succeeded. Nature demands her

223. Washington Lazarus, born 20 September 1808, died 21 November 1831.
224. Phila Cohen Lazarus, born 8 September 1806, married William Calder. She attended the Mordecai school in Warrenton.

tribute, but in well governed and pious minds a meek tho' sorrowing submission will succeed, till the heart is schooled to say, "He is the Lord; let him do that which seemeth to him good."

From this severe domestick affliction I turn to one of a general nature for which the tenor of a part of your letter prepared me. In your last you had mentioned the flattering hopes entertained by Sir W. Scott's physicians, and tho' aware of his intention to spend the winter in Italy, I was by no means prepared for the feeble and debilitated state in which Miss Baillie affectingly describes him. I felt a pang shoot through my heart as it warned of the impending fate of a personal friend. Too soon, always too soon for our wishes, will this bright, kindly luminary be extinguished, but if it depart it will be in its brightness prepared, so far as human knowledge can decide, to enter the regions of everlasting day. I have not thanked you tho' I now do for the extract from Miss Baillie's letter. I was reminded, as I frequently am, of your very great kindness in granting to me a portion of your time, when so many valuable and interesting correspondents have claims on your writing hours; you know my gratitude and therefore continue your indulgence.

We had seen the accounts of the Bristol riots some weeks since and have been pleased to observe that the private losses were less heavy than was at first supposed. The view you take of the causes of this general revolutionary spirit appears to me just and philosophical. The general peace has also its influence from the leisure it affords both bodily and mental, for it is in states as in families that the idle become the mischievous. In the United States the disturbance which was threatened at the South appears to be lulled for the present. The violence of partizans in South Carolina has been borne down for a time by the good sense and moderation of the community at large, and a reasonable modification of the Tariff will it is believed set all to rights again. The events of the present session of Congress are looked forward to with deep interest. On them the continuance of our happy Union may in a great measure depend, and as a true lover of my country, I for one, should not wish to live to witness the dissolution of that Union.

We have just read Herschel's preliminary discourse, which you lately mentioned to me, and have read it with admiration and delight. Embracing a variety of subjects, with some of which we were not familiar yet in a style so lucid as to render all intelligible and interesting; the master hand, the unclouded intellect are evident throughout. How great a happiness for such a father, to have been the father of such a son! and more that the son should excel in those pursuits in which the father was distinguished, which is less frequently the case even where both possess talents than it would seem reasonable to expect. I have not read "Hall's Sketches" but shall do so before I write again. I could not but smile at the contrarieties in your delineation of Capt. Hall's character, yet I do not doubt its accuracy; no two men could appear more dissimilar than the benevolent, amiable writer of the travels in South America and the prejudiced, petulant author of those in the United States. I felt not only regret but a singular species of mortification in finding those books different in many respects from what I expected and could have wished them to be. You probably know that as an individual he did not please in this country; he was thought self-sufficient, overbearing, sometimes rude, and I am really glad to hear from you that he is both "a good and a good natured man," for I confess I had been led to fear that the latter at least was not the case. I read lately a very interesting and well written book "Stewart's journal of a Voyage to the Sandwich Islands."[225] The rapid advancement in civilization and knowledge made by those poor Islanders is truly astonishing, and were these accounts not too well attested to admit a doubt, one might be excusable in questioning their veracity. As it is, nothing can be more pleasing and satisfactory than to become acquainted with the valuable results of the missionary labours in those remote countries, and every virtuous mind must sym-

225. Charles Samuel Stewart (1795–1870), *Private Journal of a Voyage to the Pacific Ocean, and Residence at the Sandwich Islands* . . . (1828).

pathize in the benevolent gratification of those, who having left behind them country, friends, the world, or rather society and its enjoyments, are thus enabled to witness the blessed effect of their toils and privations.

I have to apologize to Mr. McCay for not having sooner attended to his wish respecting the Dionae. Circumstances must plead my excuse until lately when I have waited for a direct conveyance from this place to Liverpool which on several accounts I prefer. [*End of copy.*]

[*Copy*]

Wilmington, March 10th, 1832

My dear friend

I have just been examining the dates of your letters and find I have received all that you mention except that of the 1st August 1831, unless it be that without date in which you say "I inclose another ring" which as I told you was forgotten. Those previously sent *with* the *heart* I received in February 1831, and you must have received the acknowledgment of them from me, as I have a letter of yours in reply; that of December 29th, 1831, inclosing three more rings is now before me, and for my sister Ellen as well as myself I thank you for them. Ellen has not yet returned from Mobile, but promises me a visit on her way home when I shall have the pleasure of presenting your gift; I know she will prize it highly. "Maria" I shall keep till my daughter Ellen's finger *will fit it*; "Ireland to America" I will send to my young sister Laura, because I know you would like if you knew her, and it will please her so very much, and the two *Rebecca's* and the Heart I retain in remembrance of my ever kind friend. But before I leave this subject let me tell you that you only *promised* to inclose a few lines of Sir Walter Scott's writing; it was forgotten I dare say and will be sent in your next. That with the print may be inclosed to me under cover to Isaac Arnold, Esqr., New York. I prefer your directing to him whenever there is an inclosure; it will render the receipt more safe as well as less expensive. I have written today to a friend of mine in Providence to enquire about the mantle you mention to me. I have not heard any thing of the establishment lately and am uncertain whether it is still in operation. I think it would be very safe to forward the parcel to Messrs. Brown & Co., Liverpool, with directions to await your orders for forwarding it to yourself. I could write at the same time and inform you of its being sent so that there would I think be no difficulty. My little parcels have always through this medium reached you in safety. This is all I believe in the way of details, and necessary and satisfactory as they are, nobody is ever sorry when they are concluded.

I will with pleasure reply to the little note from your sister Lucy as soon as I am enabled to do it in a satisfactory manner. I have never seen the book to which she alludes but have sent for that and for another book on the Religion of the Indians of North America, to New York, and will write again when I have received and read them. No arguments that I have seen on the subject have, I own, appeared to me otherwise than visionary; perhaps those advanced by Mrs. Simon[226] may be more feasible. We have read Moore's life of Sir E. Fitzgerald and were interested in his letters and character though compiled with little judgment and connected with as little skill. So much repetition too as if the principal object might be to collect a given number of pages and make of them a book. How is it that Moore, who as a poet is rich and mellifluous sometimes almost to a fault, should in his prose writings be so dry and uninteresting? Biography which seems to be his favourite exercise certainly requires ease and admits of the graces of composition, but in Moore we seek in vain for either; he has certainly mistaken his talent. I wish he would charm us anew

226. Barbara Anne Simon, *The Hope of Israel; . . . Evidence That the Aborigines of the Western Hemisphere Are Descended from the Ten Missing Tribes of Israel* (1829) and *The Ten Tribes of Israel Identified as the Aborigines of the Western Hemisphere* (1836).

by his melody and leave the task of Biographer to some inferior but more competent genius. Robert of Paris is just received. I have not yet read it. Some of my friends think it a failure; if so I am sorry. If it should be one of Sir Walter's last I wish it might be one of his best; so bright a luminary ought to set in Glory.

I had seen in a newspaper the death of Mr. Lockhart's son before I received your letter. I think with you that after a time his parents will acknowledge that he has in Mercy been removed from a world in which more than an ordinary share of pain was destined as his portion.

And so your poor young brother Francis is married; how time flies. It seems but the other day that you mentioned him as a school boy, happy on his return home during vacation to be allowed to mount his wall-eyed favourite Grace Nugent. I hope he will enjoy all the happiness he has promised himself and that you will all find reason to be pleased with his choice. We have just received Eugene Aram; I am half inclined to let it remain with Paul Clifford[227] unread by me. Bulwer is eloquent and interesting but I dislike books which have a demoralizing tendency; this very dislike might act as an antidote and prevent injury to myself, but in truth I like to choose my books as I do my companions, for some innate good quality. If I disapprove their sentiments and feel a consciousness of being more injured than benefitted by my intercourse with them, I rather avoid than seek their society. Besides to look a little beyond self, to the young and unreflecting the elegance of style and variety of incident are but additional snares; immorality appears in a splendid and becoming garb and they gaze at and become familiarized with her appearance without seeking to raise the veil and behold her in her native deformity. Did you see in the newspapers a copy of The will of Stephen Girard,[228] a rich banker who lately died in Philadelphia? If you

227. Edward George Earle Lytton Bulwer-Lytton, *Eugene Aram, a Tale*, 3 vols. (1832), and *Paul Clifford*, 3 vols. (1830).
228. Stephen Girard (1750–1831), American merchant, banker, and philanthropist, founder of Girard College in Philadelphia.

have, tell me what you think of his plan of educating youth at a seminary at which though morality will be inculcated, every tendency to religion or religious exercises is to be studiously avoided, even to the extent of forbidding any clergyman from entering the grounds on which his college is to be erected. By some it is thought that virtuous sentiments and liberal opinions will be the certain result of such a course; for my part I should fear that liberal might be converted into libertine, or else that those who had never before heard of religion might, on becoming acquainted with it on entering the world, find its doctrines in themselves so lovely, that from a shale of total ignorance and unbelief they would pass to the other extreme and become Zealots. Mrs. Barbauld's essay on prejudice offers the best possible commentary on this scheme. I asked your opinion and did not intend giving mine; here however you have it. Tell me how far our opinions coincide. I cannot write more just now than the oft repeated assurance of affectionate regard

with which I am my dear Madem
your friend—R.L.

[*Mrs. Lazarus received a book or books accompanied by the following note. The original doubtless was pasted in Mrs. Lazarus's gift. The copy gives no place or date.*]

My dear Mrs. Lazarus,

This will be short and I hope sweet. It is only to let you know that I have directed the publishers of a new edition of my tales and novels to transmit them monthly as the volumes come out in numbers to you to New York in care of the gentleman you mentioned in your last letter. The name I cannot at the moment remember and your letter is in my mother's possession and this letter must go before I can see her. But it is sent to the man you desired. My booksellers send a volume or two this month and will send the books every month in their monthly parcel to their agent Mr. William Jackson of New York.

I have seen only two numbers of this edition. The binding is very elegant and the engravings good but not as the Editors are pleased to say *superb*. I have nothing to do with the edition except having furnished corrections. The booksellers have undertaken it at their own risks and I hope it may answer to them.

But what I am much more anxious about I hope you will like this little offering as a mark of my sincere esteem and regard. I wish I was in London that I might write in the first page of them for you that they are the gift of the author. Perhaps this can be pasted in.

[in margins]

Mantle you say. The thing I meant to have worked was a scarf that should be long enough to put on as the Spanish mantilla is put on over the head and hanging over the shoulders. By your word *mantle* I am afraid you understood a cloak which would be a much larger and grander affair than I meant. But I entreat you not to trouble yourself about it if you find that the ladies of the establishment you mentioned no longer work or if there be any difficulty. It is not a matter near my heart.

[Copy]   Wilmington, August 10th, 1832

You are too, too kind my ever dear friend thus to remember and to seek my gratification; favoured, honoured as I feel by the valuable and elegant testimonial of that regard which has for so many years been to me a source of the highest enjoyment, those terms are cold and inadequate to express the emotions of grateful affection which fill my heart. That you have deemed me worthy of such a proof of remembrance and esteem is my sole claim to such distinction, but this consciousness renders it not the less dear and delightful. If I knew how I would express my thanks for the oft repeated instances in which I have experienced your kindness and affectionate regard, but words would say too much and yet too little. Better that I trust to your own grateful heart to understand and to interpret the language of mine. The only circumstance which could serve to enhance the value of such a gift you have not forgotten [is] the indication to others that it is from yourself I receive a copy of those works which have served alike to delight and to improve mankind. It will I hope be a better feeling than vanity which will induce me to place in the initial volume the concluding lines of your note. I shall request Mr. Arnold to forward the first numbers as soon as they are received and I hope to welcome them in a few days.

"The mantle," Mantle is the term by which we designate every article of the Scarf kind, whether long and straight, or of more dressy kind with fancy cape and collar. The one selected for you will I hope prove of the kind you wish. I received a letter from my friend in Providence dated May 10th in which she says, "I regret that through indisposition I have unavoidably kept you in a state of suspense relative to your commission. I have selected a mantle at $15 (about 2 guineas), the pattern of which is very beautiful, and the quality of the lace superior; it is to be finished in about four weeks." I wrote immediately, annexing an order for the money, and requested that it should be forwarded to me as soon as completed, but as we find the order has not been presented, I have again written to enquire the cause of the delay and waited to hear before I again addressed you, but am still without reply. This must also apologise to my dear Miss Lucy for my seeming negligence, but to her I must take the pleasure of saying a little word for myself.

Our country is in a state of extreme distress and apprehension from the prevalence of Cholera in New York and several other cities. Its ravages have been dreadful and tho' on the decline in those parts of the country where it first made its appearance, it is advancing with fearful strides towards the south, and some cases are already reported in our state. It is impossible to be aware of the existence and comparative vicinity of so harrowing a scourge without feelings of dread and awe, but further I cannot say that mine are influenced. Happily my mind is free from anxiety while willing to employ every precautionary measure that prudence may suggest. I feel as if thrown more immediately on the care of Providence and I can almost say that I experience a sort of calm satisfaction in confiding myself and those I love in a more peculiar manner to the protection of the Most High, praying in any event to be enabled to submit without repining to his unerring dispensations.

In this country as in Europe the ravages of this disease have been principally confined to the lower class, to the imprudent and the dissipated, but there have been many exceptions; several physicians in New York, a clergyman and his whole family are among its victims. You have perhaps seen in our papers the disastrous fate of a detachment lately sent to quell some disturbances which had broken out among some tribes of North Western Indians. My brother Alfred lately promoted to a Captaincy has been ordered, not with the regiment in service, but on military business in Detroit, Michigan Territory. He writes thus, "The troops happened to arrive here, just when that peculiar constitution of the atmosphere which predisposes to that disease prevailed, and being many of them fit subjects, the mortality was dreadful. In the foremost boat the only one of whose arrival at Chicago we have yet heard, in which General Scott with about 200 men was embarked, the disease appeared in all its violence; for some time men were thrown overboard at the rate of one every hour, and although the disease began to abate soon after their landing they have lost as many as 65 or 70 of their small detachment. Nothing could exceed its horrors as you may suppose from the great mortality and the dreadful character of the complaints. Another detachment was landed with the disease upon them at the foot of Lake Huron (Ft. Grahot) and in the panic most of them fled without ceremony from the port; of these many perished miserably in the woods or by the roadside, the terror of the people preventing any relief being offered to them. Many of them fled into Canada, and yesterday I went over there authorised by the Secretary of War to offer them pardon for the desertion if they will return to duty." I will not apologise for this long extract, believing it cannot prove uninteresting.

I am uncertain whether Irving's new work "Tales of the Alhambra"[229] is published simultaneously here and in London and shall direct it to be sent from New York with this; the two volumes put up separately will hardly exceed a Review in bulk and I will order the address as heretofore. It is pervaded by the author's usual vein of good humour and suavity, and forms a pleasing addition to his sketch book. I hope you receive gratifying accounts from your brother in India and that Mrs. Wilson's health is improving. I remark with regret the lingering but certainly declining state of your great and estimable friend Sir W. Scott, and with wonder the announcement of two new works from his pen. Unless his parting notes be like those ascribed to the swan I could hope they may be withheld. The charm which has so long detained us entranced ought not now to be broken.

Adieu my dear friend

[Copy]   Wilmington, September 23rd, 1832

I have so much to thank you for in this letter my dear friend that I scarcely know with which to begin; to render myself intelligible however, let me tell you that I have received the valuable little case containing the engraved likenesses of Sir Walter Scott and Dr. Darwin, and the penciled view of your residence; and tho' last not least, the billet written by that hand whose traces have charmed and improved the whole civilized world, that hand

229. Washington Irving (1783–1859), American author and diplomat, *The Alhambra: A Series of Tales and Sketches of the Moors and Spaniards*, 2 vols. (1832).

which even now, Alas! may be in the chill grasp of death. I cannot tire of gazing on that mild thoughtful countenance and would fain unclose the volume in his hand and trace if possible the subject of his meditation. The note, though of so few words, is certainly characteristick. Sir Walter's fondness for dogs is almost proverbial and who I wonder is not acquainted with Fangs, or with [blank]?

I never look at a view of Edgeworth's Town house without imagining Harry and Lucy seated at their breakfast under one of those fine trees near the hall door. The trellised portico if I mistake not opens into the library, but tell me if the windows of your apartment are visible and where I must look for them, and do not think me too childish in venturing the inquiry. By the date of your note within the packet I find that it was sent in January last! Where it has been lying all this time it is impossible to say. I rejoice that it is mine at last.

When you receive my letter of [March 10] and find me reminding you of the billet, you will I dare say pronounce me an excellent dun, but you pardon the liberty and all is well. I have received the 1st Vol. of Moral Tales, the 2nd of the Monthly Series. Another is on its way—the 1st I hope—and that it may contain "Griselda" and "Castle Rackrent," the former one of my prime favourites. Many years ago, before I dreamed of being allowed the happiness of thus conversing with you, after reading "Griselda" again and again, I copied into a commonplace book the delineation of her character, as if by transcribing I could have claimed some property in that which attracted so strongly my love and admiration. Permit me once more to thank you for this delightful and highly valued testimonial of your friendship and regard; to my husband and myself, and in after times to our children, it will be a source of pride and pleasure that Miss Edgeworth (tho' consulting her own kind heart far more than my deserving) should have bestowed on me such distinction. When you receive this, probably in chill November, borrow if you can prince Ali's glass, and you may behold us seated round a cheerful fire, with some "the shining needle plies its busy task," all set in pleased attention, while the delightfully instructive page, "by one made vocal, for the amusement of the rest, beguiles the night!" Has not this magick glass the power of revealing even the title of the book? Yes, it is Edgeworth who is charming anew! The regular series is irresistible, and like an old and intimate acquaintance returned in a new dress from abroad, we welcome and crowd round to listen to its details. Our usual reader is the eldest daughter of Mr. L. who to the agreeable talent of reading well, unites the happy faculty of never becoming fatigued with the effort.

I hope you have received the letter I wrote you last month, and the Alhambra which accompanied it, the two volumes in separate inclosures. I have now the pleasure of transmitting a small box containing the mantle, and a little cap for Mrs. Wilson if agreeable to you and to herself. The cap is the work of our daughter Almira, the border that of my sister Julia. I preferred it to imported lace, because I thought you would like it as a pretty specimen of needle work.

I fear the Mantle will not entirely please you; it is not so fine, nor is the work as well done as I could have wished; but not being on the spot, I had no alternative but to receive it when sent. The cost is at your limit, three guineas. I shall send the box to Messrs Brown of Liverpool to await your order for being forwarded. This letter I send separately inclosed as usual. Be so kind as to write soon after receiving the box as I shall be anxious to hear of its safety.

I have not told you how much pleasure we have found in the perusal of "Hall's fragments" which you some time since mentioned to me. Capt. Hall describes admirably and possesses a most agreeable vein of humour, besides which there is so much good sense in his remarks and so much of novelty to us in the sort of information conveyed that we read his book with avidity and own that it possesses equal attraction for the boy and the man. We remarked with pleasure his gentlemanlike notice of the reception of his previous work in the United States and the friendly heartiness of his expressions of good will. *I*, for one, believe them sincere and I am pleased with his assurance of not having read the remarks of our American Editors, and with the motive that dictated his forbearance. I do not think that it was by his remarks on our government and institutions that Capt. H. gave offence, so much as by a sort of testiness which he often evinces in his remarks on the rapid growth of our country, and above all, by repeatedly declaring himself wearied with *"sight seeing,"* and with the attentions (perhaps officious, but certainly well meant) of persons who wished to point out to him all that might be deemed most interesting to a stranger. On some occasions when one route was proposed to him as more pleasant, exhibiting a finer country than another, he misinterprets the probable intention of the adviser, construing it into a wish to conceal the defects of the country, and to exhibit it only as it were in gala dress. These remarks are only intended to shew the general grounds on which the travels in the U.S. were rendered unpopular, not by any means as an attack upon the work itself. Its merits with me very far overbalance its imperfections and I have sometimes been good-humouredly bantered by my friends for standing out as Capt. Hall's champion. I hope he is preparing something more for our entertainment; the reception given to his naval sketches has been sufficiently flattering to offer an inducement. You will be tired with this long letter and though there are several other little matters pressing to the tip of my pen, I must bid them away and close my desk, after begging you to present my best regards to my kind Miss Lucy and to accept for yourself my dear Miss E

the affection of your ever obliged friend
R.L.

Edgeworthstown, November 7, 1832

My dear Friend,

That I may not again mistake I have a specimen of Sir Walter's writing now in my hand for you. I have cut the piece of one of his letters and though it may seem but an insignificant scrap there are not six people breathing out of my own family to whom I would give it. It was written to me just when he was first coming to Ireland and to pay his long promised visit to Edgeworthstown. He wrote to plan his future journey to Killarney which we took together. It was the bridal excursion of his son and daughter-in-law, they and Miss Scott and Mr. Lockhart, my sister Harriet now Mrs. Butler, and myself. A happier party never travelled and my dear most amiable Sir Walter was not only the head but the heart and soul of it. Most delightful in manners and temper he certainly was: those charming manners that are of *no* fashion and of the best fashion of all times and circumstances, good sense and good feelings being the foundation of all real good breeding such as his.

It is impossible to represent to you fully the sensation which his death has produced in public and in private, more in private than in public; the newspapers will work their way to you and will give you some measure of the public feeling. You will see that the towns through which his remains were carried the deepest sorrow was shown, in Edinburgh for a whole day, the shops shut, all the inhabitants in mourning. You will see that subscriptions have been set on foot for two purposes: to raise a monument to him and to free his estate of Abbotsford from all encumbrances.

Mr. Lockhart wrote me word a few days ago in answer to enquiries I made in alarm from the accounts I had seen in the newspapers of the disastrous state of Sir Walter's affairs, that they are not so bad as the papers represent and that I must not believe what the newspapers say about him as the real state of the case is known only to a few of his friends and none of them have sent or will send any information to the newspapers. Mr. Lockhart for my own satisfaction assures me that though—to use his own expression—Sir Walter's affairs are "bad enough" his family are not left in anything like want. The eldest son will live as he always has done on his pay and the interest of his wife's fortune which was large. The second is in a good diplomatic situation in Italy and will be well befriended in his profession for his father's sake and for his own. Anne will have a home with her sister Sophia and Mr. Lockhart who is a man of great feeling and has shown it during Sir Walter's illness and since his death. Mr. Lockhart is I hope in good circumstances himself. He is Editor of the Quarterly which brings in an income of Lbs. 1500 per annum or should bring that income but all literary speculations now are declining in England. It is said that one only of the great *firms* is *firm, i.e.* Longman, Hunt, and Rees. Lockhart's bookseller is Murray;[230] he has been hurt by a newspaper speculation and is in a precarious way, but Lockhart has besides the Editorship of the Quarterly some place under government which affords him some hundreds a year so that I hope he will do well and he has such abilities that as long as England lasts he must be able to earn money by intellectual exertions some how or other.

I am told that Lord Brougham at the meeting of Parliament intends to propose a public grant of money to redeem Abbotsford Estate for the family of Sir Walter Scott, upon the same principle that the Nation gave Blenheim to Marlborough and Stratfieldsay to Wellington as superior in arms. As superior in arts and literature this is due to Sir Walter and will be honorable to Britain.

But even if Parliament should not make this grant, I am sure private subscriptions will effect the purpose. And I think a subscription for redeeming Abbotsford from the load of debt will be much better than a subscription for a monument for him whose works are his best monument—deathless fame. The

230. John Murray (1778–1843), London publisher, one of the founders of the *Quarterly Review* (February 1809), publisher of Byron and other leading writers of the day.

monument would only in fact preserve perhaps the names of the subscribers! It is dreadful to think that the almost super-human exertions this great genius made to pay the immense debt which Constable[231] the bookseller's failure brought upon him was the cause of the premature loss of those devinely gifted faculties and of that most precious life. For several months previous to his death he did not know those he had loved best except at intervals for a few minutes. Conceive what their sufferings must have been! Lockhart in his letter to me in very touching words says, "We are beginning to recover the bright image of him we had such as he was before his illness—loved by all who knew him from the first hour to the last." I have omitted what I was most intent on saying, that I have written to my friend Mr. Ralston of Philadelphia to ask him to apply to some of your influential people in America to suggest that it would be honorable to the New World to send some testimonial of national regard to the memory of him who they have so much valued. Could there be an American subscription for the Abbotsford purpose, mention it to any whom you think would foster it. I cannot pour out my own feelings for this dear friend; they are too deep. Look at what he says of me in his introduction to his works and then think of what I must feel. So there is an end of this matter forever; there is no such being left on this earth.

I will now turn to your letter and I thank you for your account of your Brother and his perils in the cholera boat; how anxious you must have been about him. I hope [*Here she breaks off*].

Nov. 8

Yesterday I was obliged to stop, to lay down my pen and go to bed, I had such a sick headache and bilious stomach. Today I

231. Archibald Constable (1774–1827), Scottish publisher of the *Edinburgh Review* and several editions of the *Encyclopaedia Britannica*. Through overspeculation his business failed in 1826, a failure that involved Sir Walter Scott. James Ballantyne and Co., with whom Scott also was involved, failed at the same time.

am medicined into perfect health and find that what I thought an evil yesterday proves a good. It was fortunate that I was unable to finish this letter and send it off because this morning Mrs. Edgeworth who always brings me good, brought to the side of my bed a cordial in the shape of a letter from you my dear friend (dated Sept. 23) as I may well call you when you feel so much kindness for me and only too much, a great deal too much gratitude for the very little proofs I can give you of my regard. I am glad to find that the 2nd volume of the series of my books reached you and shall write immediately to my bookseller to warn him that the 1st has not yet reached you. Pray always give me warning if there is any failure because it is more easy to remedy this at the time than it would be afterwards.

As I find that you *have* received the specimen of Sir Walter's handwriting I will not send the scrap I mentioned in the beginning of this letter.

Lucy begs me to ask if you know any of the old Hebrew psalm tunes such as they sang in the old times of King David?

I write today about the box, *etc*. [*Here the copy appears to skip a passage relative to the arrival in Liverpool of the box containing the mantle.*] I am sorry that I cannot say I like the Alhambra as much as you seem to do; I like the introduction, the journey to the Alhambra very much; that is in Washington Irving's best manner. But the rest appears to me too much manufactured, too like bookmaking. I think it bad taste to hang so many flimsy fictions upon that venerable ruin. Real plain unadorned anecdotes, historical or of individuals who had been connected with the Alhambra *naturally*, would have satisfied me better. This book seems to me much ado about nothing and however prettily that sort of work is done it is never useful and therefore seldom agreeable. But when you have sent me the Alhambra it is ungracious to say all this. No, because I shall prize your kindness in the gift just as much and probably the more than if I had not told the plain truth.

We are all well and happy. We hope that this country will

not come to an explosion and that O'Connell[232] who has no real regard for anything but the hurrahs of the mob will not succeed in effecting a dissolution of the union between England and Ireland which would dissolve all remains of law in Ireland and would leave all property at the mercy of those who want it, not those merely in misery but of the turbulent numbers who want to obtain property. Whatever watchwords may be used by any party this is the fact.

My sister Lucy has returned to us not strong; she has done too much for others while absent with them and taken too little care of herself.

My sister Honora or some other sister or brother will do a sketch of the house where I live and also of the other end of the house which leads to the library. There is a portico at that end as you shall see, but the verandah of which you have the view leads to the dining room where three windows down to the ground give on the verandah. I have left myself scarcely room to say it but nevertheless you will believe that I am

Your sincere friend
Maria Edgeworth

[*Copy*] Wilmington, March 24th, 1833

My dear friend

I ought to be ashamed and so I really am at having suffered so many weeks to elapse since the receipt of your last welcome letter. Were it not that I am a declared enemy to epistolary apologies I might dare say offer some that you would deem valid and which your kindness would allow to plead in behalf even were the loss

232. Daniel O'Connell (1775–1847), Irish statesman. He was the leader of the Irish Catholic movement against the repressive English rule and was instrumental in bringing about reforms against tithes and in advancing Catholics to positions of trust and power in the state. ME's fears relative to property appear unfounded as he was to prove his regard for the claims of property.

on your side. As it is I account myself the only sufferer by delay, and the offence if voluntary would bear its penalty along with it. In the letter now before me you mention the arrival of your little box in Liverpool and I am wishing to hear if the Mantle in any degree equalled your expectations. I hope you will be as candid with me in this as you were in giving your opinion of the Alhambra which on more than one account particularly obliged me. Its justness I at once admitted tho' I confess I had viewed the little work with an eye of favour as the production of our very amiable and gifted countryman. I had read it too on board a steam boat where so light a production appeared to the best advantage, and writing to you immediately after, I directed it to be sent before its novelty wore off. It would have been more judicious in the author to have presented this little work to the publick in the form of an Annual; it has just sufficient fibre for one of those evanescent productions. You ask, "Is it not ungenerous in me to [*say*] to you what I have?" On the contrary I felt it a kindness and a compliment and hope you will always treat me with similar openness.

I need not say to you that every word contained in your letter relative to the world's lamented Sir Walter Scott was read with deep interest. I was gratified that your wishes respecting a tribute of respect from some of his admirers on this side of the Atlantick had been anticipated. Meetings were held in several of our principal cities for the purpose of raising a fund to be appropriated in some manner indicative of the estimation in which this great and good man had been held among us. Some proposed the erection of a statue, others that of a monument, while a third party more judiciously in my opinion suggested that the funds thus raised should be employed as a contribution towards the purchase of Abbotsford. What has been decided on I have been unable to learn tho' I have made frequent inquiries; when I hear the result if not from the Newspapers, you shall know it. We not long since recommenced Scott's works in regular series for our evening entertainment; it appears to me that new beauties, new sources of delight are continually presenting themselves, and on finishing a work I feel as if I could recommence it immediately without a feeling of satiety. But why expatiate on a subject far beyond my powers in words tho' my feelings, could they find utterance, would discourse most eloquently.

I thank you my dear friend for having written to the publisher of your works in London for the still delinquent first volume. Messrs. [blank] have also applied for it, so that I have good hope it will yet come to hand. I forgot to mention in its proper place that your draft answered my purpose perfectly well, especially as I was just making a remittance to Liverpool.

I have not told you that we are preparing for an excursion; about the 1st of May we expect to leave home on a visit to my parents in Richmond, Virginia, and leaving our children with them Mr. L. and myself propose taking a tour through the Northern and Eastern States. After being for several years completely domesticated I anticipate much gratification from change of scene and of society exclusive of the happiness which will precede in a meeting with my beloved parents and family. Your letters meantime may be addressed to the Care of James De Peyster, Esqr., New York, and will be forwarded to me more readily than from this place.

You speak of your sweet sister Lucy not being well. I hope this is no longer the case. It gives me pleasure to be enabled to comply with her wish relative to some of the ancient Hebrew Musick. That which I send has been sung in the synagogues from time immemorial and was most probably composed by one of David's own musicians. My father obtained it for me and wrote the Hebrew words in English characters with the translation.

I find in your new edition a letter annexed to the story of Rosanna which is not contained in any that I have before seen and which appears to be really written by the character supposed. Will you tell me if it is so and if the story is founded on fact? Have you seen a little book from the German, The life of Kaspar

Hauser,[233] a boy who was confined in a solitary cell from infancy till the age of seventeen? The account tho' not well written is very interesting; it is much to be regretted that so unique a subject for experiment on the philosophy of the human mind should in a great measure have been lost by falling into injudicious hands. I really sympathized with the poor boy when with a Universe of Wonders around him, he was required to commit the rules of a latin grammar to memory. Nothing short of the actual want of common sense could have suggested such a course. Do you know whether he has been brought over to England and in what way the Earl of Stanhope has disposed of him? How are you pleased with the letters of Prince Puckler Muskau?[234] Are they supposed to be written by him, or by some Englishman who chose to appropriate his name and title. I am rather inclined to the latter opinion. [*Mrs. Lazarus's copy ends here.*]

Edgeworthstown, June 27, 1833

I promised to write you my dear friend when I could inform you of the safe arrival of the Mantilla. I have now the pleasure to tell you that it has at last arrived safely. It is very handsome and a prodigious size. But it certainly has not the lightness and elegance of your own and your sisters' work. The cap is most beautiful. Will you give *my* most cordial thanks to the kind person who worked it? Will she for some time be content with my poor

233. Kaspar Hauser (1812?–1833), a German youth whose mysterious origins and subsequent history excited wide speculation that he was of noble birth. He was placed in the care of a schoolmaster, a Professor George Friedrich Daumer, and later was sent by Earl Stanhope to study under a Dr. Meyer. His death was likewise the cause of rumor and speculation. RML probably refers to a translation of Professor Daumer's *Mitteilungen uber Kaspar Hauser* (Nuremberg, 1832).

234. Prince Herman von Pückler-Muskau (1785–1817), *Tour in Germany, Holland, and England in the Years 1826, 1827, and 1828 in a Series of Letters by a German Prince*, 4 vols. (1832). This work was widely appreciated in America as the author's strictures against England were strikingly similar to Mrs. Trollope's attacks on America.

thanks. I wish to keep the cap for some while in my own possession till a favorable moment, or I should in hopes that a favorable time may in future occur for presenting it to Fanny. Her health is now improving so much and her general strength increasing so much that we are not without hope she may hereafter have the blessing which she has till now been too weak even to desire for her. I am certain that though she and her husband, my dear Lestock, have foreborne to repine and indeed have always said it was for the best, yet they are both so fond of children that no doubt a family of their own would add much to their happiness. And I would if you and your kind sister permit, refrain from sending the cap to Fanny at present. It may give infinitely more pleasure hereafter. If our hopes from her increasing strength should never be realized it will be time enough still to give the pretty kindness to her and she may then preserve it as a memorial of friendship in America, from whence so much has come to her family.

Before I go on to any thing else I am anxious to mention lest I should forget it that my booksellers answered a letter I wrote to them to say that the 1st Volume had not reached you. They assured me that it had been sent and they doubted not would in due course reach you. Pray let me know whether you have it or not and whether the volumes reach you regularly. Nine volumes have come out monthly; the Absentee is the last.

I omitted in my last to beg the favor of you to send for Mr. Mackay this spring some plants of *the beautiful* (as he terms it) *Sarracenia flava*—all his plants have failed—and "any other species of that interesting genus." He also wishes for another Dionae Muscipula.

And I very much wish for a *Spotless Anemone*. No botanic name did I ever hear for this delicate little flower. It was sent to me by a friend of yours from New York and we have nursed it in a greenhouse and beautiful it was for two years and I gave a little rooted *scion* from it to my sister Sophy who admired it much. But this year all have died. It is a white, very delicate flower about the size of *Everlasting* on a very tender flexible stalk. If you can make out what I mean and can favor me with it, pray give me your directions how to take care of it or what soil and degree of heat it requires. I suspect we have succored it too tenderly. Should it live out of doors or in a greenhouse?

I wrote you so lately that I have nothing new to tell you, except that Madame d'Arblay,[235] the author of Evelina, Cecilia, and Camilla all of which I assume you know and like, has lately published memoirs of her father, in which there are many interesting anecdotes both of her father and of her own publications and the great family affection among all her family, and also several curious anecdotes and characters of some of the most illustrious in literature and in every department of the arts of her father's day— Johnson, Garrick, Reynolds, Wyndham, Erskine, Madam Piozzi, Miss Carter, Mrs. Montague, *etc.*[236]

In this respect it is curious: when she lets people speak naturally and when she writes naturally herself, she is very entertaining, but unfortunately she who wrote so well formerly in painting characters humorous and serious has whenever she speaks of herself some false shame, some affectation of humility or timidity, or I know not what, which spoils her style. She has a strange notion that it is more humble or prettier or better taste to call herself the *Recluse of West Hamble* or *your unworthy humble servant* or *the present memorialist* than simply to use the short pronoun *I*. This false theory leads to much circumlocution, awkwardness, and an appearance of pedantry and affectation. It

235. Madame d'Arblay, better known as Fanny Burney (1752–1840), English novelist. *Evelina; or, a Young Lady's Entrance into the World* (1778) was a wide success. It was followed by *Cecilia; or, Memoirs of an Heiress*, 5 vols. (1782). *Camilla: or A Picture of Youth*, 5 vols. (1796) was less admired. *The Memoirs of Dr. Burney, Arranged from his Own Manuscripts, from Family Papers and from Personal Recollections*, 3 vols. (1832) is noted for its extraordinary affectations.

236. The celebrated Samuel Johnson (1709–84), critic and lexicographer; David Garrick (1717–79), English actor; Sir Joshua Reynolds (1723–92), English painter; William Windham (1750–1810), English statesman; Thomas Erskine (1750–1823), first Baron Erskine, lord chancellor of England in Grenville's administration; Hester Lynch Piozzi (1741–1821), better known as Mrs. Thrale, English writer; Elizabeth Carter (1717–1806), English poet and writer; Elizabeth Robinson Montagu (1720–1800), English hostess to intellectual society.

becomes tiresome and ridiculous; the whole style of the book is *stilted*. But she is really so good and so good natured and her work is so free from all slander, all that can in any way injure others, that she should be treated with the same lenity she shews to others.

Mrs. Trollope's novel has great merits but not this merit of *lenity*. I wish very much to know what is thought of it in America, I mean of "The Refugees in America."[237] The picture of Rochester, as to slander and gossiping, might be that of any remote English country town forty years back, all except the language spoken. Is it American? It certainly is quite new to native English. Pray write to me fully about Mrs. Trollope's novel. I am so anxious to know the opinion of a well educated, impartial American, and to learn the plain fact whether the representations of language and manners be just. She has given all the *villains* of her story to *England* and only the *ridiculous* personages and vulgarity to the Americans. Mrs. Trollope appears to me to be very inelegant herself. I have heard from those who have seen and know her that she is an unpolished person. I am sure her [*model*] of an English young lady who cannot pour out coffee is absurd, pert, and ill-bred.

Enclose your letter under cover to The Clerk of the Council in Waiting, Council office, London.

[*Having written around the margin on three sides, Maria Edgeworth probably overlooked the fact that she had not signed the letter.*]

[Original]   Niagara Falls, July 18th, 1833

How very many times within the last three days have I thought of you my dear friend and wished you at my side. The date will tell you why. I will not aim at description where both the

237. Frances Trollope, *The Refugee in America: A Novel*, 3 vols. (1832).

pen and the pencil in far more skillful hands have proved inadequate. The stupendous majesty of the scene can find no representative in language. I have gazed and pondered

Till every sense seemed lost in infinite
And one vast object filled my aching sight.

As I stand and behold and dwell on its immensity, its endurance,
from the beginning of time till it shall be lost in Eternity—how do
myself and all other worldly objects sink into insignificance.
From the window of the chamber in which I write, the Rapids
above the fall are but a few yards distant, and the view even of
these with the wild scenery around them, accompanied by their
incessant dash and foam and roar, is in itself almost a compensation for our long journey.

Why my dear Miss Edgeworth can you not come to this great
western world of ours and view its charms and wonders?

The last two months have been to me a period of enjoyment
unallayed except by the pain of a temporary separation from my
children. You have no doubt received a letter written a few days
before I left home, in which I mentioned our intended journey
and acknowledged the receipt of one from you, just as mine was
completed. After paying a visit to Richmond and confiding our
children to the care of their grandparents, we proceeded north-
wardly and have spent some time in most of the principal towns,
as well as in the cities of Washington, Philadelphia, New York
and Boston, proceeding through a beautifully varied and fertile
country, exhibiting at this season all the luxuriant richness that
judicious cultivation can bestow, while the people healthy and
robust, labouring cheerfully and reaping for themselves an
ample harvest, formed a combination on which the mind of a
philanthropist might delight to dwell. I cannot conceive how
travellers can feel disposed to cavil, or how ill humour can find
food to nourish it, in an extensive and thriving country, in which
peace and prosperity seem to have chosen their abode. I write of
my own country it is true, and might be deemed a partial ob-

server but of this I am unconscious. I see things as they are, and under different circumstances I should equally sympathize in the apparent happiness of so large a portion of my fellow creatures.

I wish you could see the neat and beautifully situated manufacturing town of Lowell in Massachusetts. It is one of those which has sprung like Minerva at a single bound at once into being and maturity. Ten years since a gentleman travelling through the country was struck with this situation, at the confluence of two fine rivers, as affording great facilities for a manufacturing place. The land was purchased by a company of mercantile men who erected all the necessary buildings and either retained or disposed of them as applied for. The water is conducted by means of canals to every factory, and water power alone being employed they are susceptible of being kept in a state of greater comfort and neatness than is compatible with the use of steam. Order appears to be the governing principle. There is great uniformity in the style of the buildings, each factory having a set of houses adjacent, in which the persons employed are accommodated with board and lodging at regulated prices. Thus unnecessary exposure to inclement weather is avoided, and extortion prevented. Few males are employed except in cloth and carpet weaving, and in the machine shops, where all the implements used in the factories are made. Girls from the age of fifteen and upwards form the great majority.

It was in this town as you may have remarked if you have looked over late American papers that between 4 and 5000 young women neatly dressed and arranged in companies by the different proprietors formed a novel procession to meet and welcome the President on his arrival at their town. Their appearance is at all times decent and respectable; all look healthy and cheerful, indeed they have no cause to be otherwise. Their wages are in proportion to their skill and industry and there is sufficient incentive to both. I fear I have fatigued you with this minute account. I was myself so much pleased and interested that I could not forbear in reviewing our route, to pause and introduce you to the thriving young town of Lowell.

Immediately after receiving your letter, I read "the Refugee." You tell me you are anxious to hear from an unprejudiced person if Mrs. Trollope's representations are true. So many competent judges of facts have since given their voice against her that the addition of mine is scarcely requisite. I noted her assertions at the time, and wrote you fully on the subject, but her absurdities were so broad that in contradicting or exposing them I became disgusted and destroyed the letter.

Mr. Stewart[238] tells truth, but he is too much a matter-of-fact journalist to interest, except in cases in which such details are desirable. Mr. Veine's book[239] is well spoken of; I have neither read that, nor Major Hamilton's[240] which has this week appeared.

[*Same letter*]

New York, August 10th

This letter has travelled in my portfolio through Lake Ontario and the St. Lawrence to Montreal and Quebec. I was interrupted and have since been too much busied in looking and seeing and roving to resume my pen except for family letters. I have not time for farther details even if I could hope to render them interesting; our tour has been delightful and seems to have given a new spring to my existence.

I have called on Mr. Prince at his Botanic Garden and requested him to send the plant you wished for. He thinks he can ascertain what it is, and insists on sending you another in his own behalf. I begged him to select something rare and beautiful as its companion and sent [*it*] for me, which he promised, saying, "I must reflect before I decide what it shall be; nothing but what is pure and elegant will suit Miss Edgeworth."

I close in haste but with renewed assurances

of regard from your friend
R. Lazarus

238. James Stuart, *Three Years in North America*, 2 vols. (1833).
239. Godfrey Thomas Vigne (1801–63), *Six Months in America*, 2 vols. (1832).
240. See note 172.

[*Butler copy*]

Edgeworthstown, Dec. 2, 1833

My dear friend,

I have seen—we have seen your dear Brother Alfred, and in one word he is dear to us now. We really feel that he has created an interest in our minds which quite surprises us considering the short time we have actually known him. We were, it is true, prepared and predisposed to like him for your sake and by knowing that he had excited so much affection in his own family, always a sure proof of something amiable in the character. But we really did not expect that we should have become so intimate with him, especially as he is not very talkative, nor at all desirous to talk of himself, or to show at once all that is in him. Nevertheless we have found it all out and the very last words I said to him when he left this library were, "We hope to see you again. Before we had seen you, we were desirous to see you on your sister's account, but now—entirely on your own."

I hope this will not affront you. He promises that if he possibly can he will pay us another visit when he returns from the Continent; he is now as I daresay you know in Paris. I believe my pleasure in seeing him was enhanced by the danger I ran of missing that pleasure. When he arrived at Edgeworthstown, I was far, far away in the ultimate wilds of Connemara.

When I heard from my sister Honora that Mrs. Lazarus' brother was at Edgeworthstown, you may imagine my impatience. She said he had waited some days in hopes of seeing me and she was afraid he could not wait any longer. But he let himself be prevailed upon and here I found him, and I do not think we were long before we completely understood and—I will boldly say it—liked one another. For I firmly believe his truthtelling expression of countenance and mild persuasive voice. Most gratifying and delightful was it to me to see reflected as it were in him the regard and partial opinion you have of me. He assured me that he had grown up from childhood with these kind sentiments towards me and all this family. That it had been the pleasant dream of his childhood that he should be some day amongst us, and that now his dream was become reality and that he was really at Edgeworthstown, he could hardly believe it or describe the sensation. His smile however showed that it was not a disagreeable sensation, and though all might be different from what he expected, his good nature would not let us see that he was disappointed. His own easy quiet manners and conversation full of sense and information, his amiable disposition and gentleman-like manly character surpassed our expectations. It is very delightful to me to feel that with perfect sincerity I can say this of the brother you love so much. I wish he may with equal sincerity be able to tell you that he was happy here; the best proof will be his coming again.

Thank you for your account of your tour which unlike mine was in truth a tour of pleasure. Your cultivated mind and cheerful temper peculiarly fit you for the enjoyment of travelling. It was very kind of you to think of me and to take the trouble to give me so full an account of your enjoyment. I shall be very glad to receive good Mr. Prince. [*Here the copy breaks off. Since he was the subject, Alfred Mordecai may have kept the original before returning the letters to Edgeworthstown the second time.*]

[*Original*]

Wilmington, March 9th, 1834

Who is there my dear Madam that knows so well as you how to say the kindest most acceptable things in the kindest and most acceptable manner. Had I not long ago discovered this, your very gratifying letter just received would at once have convinced me of the fact, and I feel so well assured of your sincerity that I should almost as soon think of doubting the reality of my own sentiments towards my brother, as those which you so kindly, so flatteringly express. I hoped that you would like him, tho' as you have perceived, he does not show off at once all that he is worth, but then as is natural you know, I had my misgivings and the receipt of your letter was at once a relief and a delight to my heart. You see there is no danger of my being affronted that you now regard him *entirely* on his own account.

His journal had been delayed and I received it a day or two after your letter, so that this week may be recorded as abounding in sources of pleasure for me. He dwells minutely on his visit to Edgeworth's town, knowing that he could not be too particular for me, tells me of your apartment which Miss Honora had the goodness to shew him and of your little writing table in the library which must have all the insensibility of wood if it has imbibed no portion of the wit, intelligence, and information which have been indited on its surface. Alfred was conscious of having made his appearance rather too unceremoniously, but he says he was in fact fearful of making enquiries lest their result might prevent his visit to Edgeworth's town by informing him that you were absent, and if you and your sisters forgive him I am glad that he went straight forward as he did. He is very sensible of the politeness, the kindness with which he was treated; all was entirely suited to his taste and inclination, and tho' conscious that he had trespassed full long on your hospitality, he took his departure with regret. More than once he remarks, "Here I am a stranger in a foreign land, yet I can hardly realize it, my feelings are so much those of home; I feel at ease and at liberty because I cannot perceive that my presence interrupts the usual routine of the family. I enjoy more fully the pleasures of such society because the kindness bestowed on me imposes no restraint on themselves; this is true politeness." He was charmed with Mrs. Fox and her interesting little group of children who he says are just such as you would expect to find in the Edgeworth family. This my dear madam is not saying a little. He mentions your kindness and that of Mrs. Fox in pressing him to repeat his visit, and in conclusion says I am charmed with all I have seen of this family and shall not willingly forego the temptation of repeating my visit. Both your letter and his journal were far too interesting to be withheld for a moment from my parents and sisters. I forewarded them immediately that they might partake my enjoyment.

I will send you as soon as I can ascertain that it is in a fair way to thrive a layer of my Nondescript rose which Alfred said you would like. I see no reason why it should not thrive in your climate. It is a perennial, and the beauty of its winter foliage renders it a valuable ornament to our gardens. In London as you have heard, Alfred had the pleasure of presenting your letter to Mrs. Wilson of whom he only saw enough to render him desirous of seeing much more. He is much pleased with all he has seen of England and praises English neatness, comfort, and convenience at every turn. I seem to be forgetting that his details do not possess all the interest for you that they do for me, but I am so much used to your indulgence that I am apt to claim it on every occasion. Let me now renew my thanks for your most acceptable and valuable present, the 18th volume of which arrived a few weeks since. The first which by some accident never arrived, I have been fortunate in replacing by one of the same edition so that I have them complete. Alfred was informed by Mrs. Sneyd that you had laid aside the novel which we saw announced some time ago but that you have another in the press,[241] published no doubt by this time, a new pleasure in anticipation for me.

My winter has formed a perfect contrast to the summer, having been devoted to domestick employments and the education of my children. I have four. My son will leave home in June; except for the languages he has scarcely known any instructor but his mother whose tuition is now insufficient, even if the imperceptible indulgences of home were altogether admissible. It will cost us an effort to part with him but we shall I trust be compensated by his improvement. The conversation on this subject in your sequel to Frank seems to have been written on purpose for *me*. My little girls are promising and it is very delightful to me to watch and assist the gradual development of their minds and dispositions. Ellen is reading the Parent's Assistant and wants to know why Miss. E. did not write a great many more volumes

241. *Helen: A Tale*, 3 vols. (London, 1834); 2 vols. (Philadelphia, 1834).

than "just *three* Mother." Mary Kate is very happy just now in the society of Mrs. Barbauld, and Julia, three years of age, lively and observant, stands at her side and listens for the hundredth time to the story of the foolish little lamb which would not mind the shepherd and was carried by the wolf into his "dismal dark den." And then she details the catastrophe with all due emphasis and impressiveness of tone and gesture to all who lend a willing ear. I hope when you next write to hear that your amiable suffering sister Lucy is again improving. Oblige me by presenting my respectful remembrances to Mrs. E. and to each of your sisters, and believe me

affectionately your friend
R. Lazarus

[*Copy*]

Wilmington, May 25th, 1834

My dear friend

I have just completed, reluctantly and with much hesitation, a very inconsiderable task, that of writing an introductory letter. Will you forgive the liberty I have taken in presenting to your acquaintance Mr. Hamilton Murray of New York, a gentleman entirely unknown to me, but for whom the favour is so earnestly solicited by a friend of his whom I love and esteem that tho' I feel the indiscretion I know not how to refuse and have resolved rather to throw myself on your indulgence than to hurt her feelings by my noncompliance. My friend speaks of Mr. Murray in the highest terms and assures me that if I knew him I should feel no hesitation in complying with his wish to know one whom he has always admired. He takes letters of the first respectability and intends travelling for some months in Europe. Do not fear future indiscretion of this sort. It is very natural that every one should be desirous of seeing Miss Edgeworth, but [*it*] would be very unfair that her time and convenience should be sacrificed without a probable equivalent. Say that you forgive me now, and I will turn to another subject.

A most delightful subject too—"Helen," which I finished last night, borne along but too rapidly by the engrossing interest of the story, which is still the least of its merits. Will it be presumption in me to say that I read your works with the scrutinizing jealously of friendship anxious of detecting any thing to which an objection could be raised; pardon the presumption since it has doubled my enjoyment. I found excellence in every point. (One wee wee exception—Are you aware of the frequent quotations from the Ode to Adversity? I know you will not call me impertinent.) The variety of well defined, well drawn character[s], the sterling sense, playful wit, elegant allusion and sound morality unite their claims to admiration, and we lay down the volume with the comfortable reflection—it has done me good. One only regret is left on my mind, that that dear, delightful, improving useful pen was not sooner resumed. Lady Davenant's character pleases me particularly—such dignity, such genuine greatness of mind combined with feminine tenderness of feeling and with just enough of human frailty to keep it on a level with its kind. I know not exactly why, but she brought Lady Russell[242] frequently to my mind. Do you think there is any real similarity? Miss Clarendon is an original; I like her much. The conversation in which Beauclerk bursts forth into his eloquent eulogium on Sir Walter Scott went to my heart. Ah! had he lived till now how would he have enjoyed, have sympathized in your complete success. Not very long since I had taken part in a similar discussion, whether or not the desire to see great men has any more laudable motive than the indulgence of curiosity. It was therefore particularly gratifying to find the matter here so clearly, so satisfactorily defined. Autographs too, tho' not a professed collector, I have a great respect for and now it is sanctioned.

242. See note 134.

I have been too impatient in this first perusal to do half justice to this book. Could I but read it again seated beside you! Too great an enjoyment that would be, but I did wish it and shall wish it more, when fairly *reading* and reflecting on the parts that form the animated, the improving whole.

I wrote you in March, I think, immediately after receiving your kind and gratifying letter announcing the visit of my brother Alfred. His last dates to me are Marseilles on the eve of proceeding to Italy. I hope he will have time to avail himself of your kindness and pay Edgeworth's town another visit before his return home.

Adieu my dear friend, I must close here after a word of enquiry relative to your dear sister Lucy, who I hope is better—

ever affectionately
R. Lazarus

Edgeworthstown, September 18, 1834

My dear friend,

I have really nothing to tell you new or entertaining and yet am impatient to write to you to tell you how much pleasure your letter gave me with such full and flattering (and yet *not flattering*) approbation of Helen. However much you over value the writing and the talents of the writer yet your exactly seizing the views I had in writing Helen and shewing me that the very effect I wished to be produced was produced on your mind, so convinced me of *your judgment* and your *taste* that I could not help being completely charmed with *myself*. I have one letter from Mrs. Herschel giving me her husband's opinion and her own and this letter and yours are those which have given me the greatest pleasure I have felt independently of the sympathy of my own family. I wish you could know how much gratification your letter gave to all my sisters and to Mrs. Edgeworth; they thank you for it as much as I do. Fanny particularly admires your letters for their joining all the simplicity of nature and of truth as she says and all the refinement of high cultivation and of all that is supposed to be the result of being in what we call *high society*.

Captain Hall would we think acknowledge on reading your letters that he must make exceptions to all the severe remarks he makes on the want of delicacy and refinement of manners in America. I find from an American gentleman with whom I have lately been conversing that the author of Cyril Thornton, Major Hamilton, has by his late publication hurt the American feelings more than either Captain Hall or Mrs. Trollope. Miss Martineau[243] has gone out to America now and I hope she will give us the result of her observations in a form that shall not be invidious or tend to set nations at variance instead of making them good friends, and emulous, not envious, of each other, giving each other the advantages of their respective differences in character and manners resulting from their different *ages* in society and positions in the world. America is in fact placed in circumstances in which no other nation, of whom we have any tradition, was ever placed before. She has not gone through the regular gradation in civilization from childhood to age, from savage to polished life, but began as it were in manhood, and without savage ancestors. As to laws, government, *etc.* this observation holds, and I wish instead of dwelling upon such trivialities as "eating with a two-prong instead of a three-prong fork" some author of more enlarged views would develop all that needs so much to be developed respecting America.

The American gentleman of whom I just now spoke is Mr. Cruger of New York, who called upon me in consequence of his having married a Miss Douglas, a rich lady of New York who a few years ago travelled in these countries and who had by some

243. Harriet Martineau (1802–76), English writer. Her series of tales entitled *Illustrations of Political Economy* brought her wide success in 1831. Her visit to the U.S. in 1834 resulted in *Society in America* (1837) and *Retrospect of Western Travel* (1838). Her sympathy with the abolitionists was unpopular with many Americans, but her scorn of Mrs. Trollope's *Domestic Manners* pleased them. Novels, travel accounts, histories, and numerous articles flowed from her pen.

circumstances (much too long to tell you) interested us for her. We rejoiced to find that she is at last married to a countryman of her own who seems to have sense and steadiness enough for both, and to whom she is much attached.

Among other curious facts which were told me by Mr. Cruger in a conversation of a few hours, he mentioned the project now formed of making the voyage from New York to the port of Valentia in Ireland in the course of eight or ten days in steam packets, supplied with the fuel of anthracite coal which lasts so much longer and gives out so much more heat compared with its bulk than any other fuel that ever has been tried in steam vessels. This c[oal is] not to be found in these countries, certainly not in England. Kilkenny coal in Ireland comes nearest to it but is not the same. Kilkenny gives out clouds of smoke and smothering smell. But your anthracite coal (if *not too much* puffed [*over-exaggerated*]) emits little smoke and lasts longer than I can tell or conceive. It is peculiar to one district (I think near Philadelphia). The American coal mine will be more valuable to that country and to all countries than any mine of lead, gold, or jewels that ever was wrought (the famous mine of Malachite in Russia not excepted). It is scarcely possible to calculate the future extent of the consequences of thus having a monopoly of the fuel which is *essential* to the quickest possible communication between civilized nations, [*even*] between civilized and uncivilized nations, in short for all the purposes of barter, commerce, intercourse, improvement, or conquest. Civil, commercial, military, literary, and scientific—what a range! And what a new and higher order and progress of ideas open to imagination, not merely "Visions of glory!"

Thank you for your observation about the Ode to Adversity quotations so frequently recurring. We have cut them out in consequence. Just in time your hint came for the corrections for a second edition of Helen.

We are at this moment enjoying a visit which is to last only one month (alas) from Mrs. Edgeworth. My sister Harriet Butler went over to Clifton to take care of Lucy while Mrs. Edgeworth came over to us. Harriet was to have gone on an excursion with her husband to Scotland and would have been in Edinburgh at the time of the grand meeting of all the scientific people there of which you have seen or will see an account in the newspapers. I do not know many people who would have enjoyed that more than Harriet but she still more enjoys being with her sister Lucy and doing this kindness and service to us all. Lucy is we hope considerably better and we trust will soon be able again to leave her weary couch and enjoy fresh air again and the *life* of *youth*.

I beg leave to observe, not meaning to be either impatient or reproachful, that the Spotless Anemone which Lucy brought to my mind has never reached me yet, nor that pretty flower or shrub, whatever it was to be, which your friend said he would chuse for me himself. I hope you will not think me quite a sturdy beggar. Several of the American plants you sent me are alive and beautiful, especially some that grew from seed—Edwardsia, Clethra, *etc*. But till more of the Spotless Anemone comes I am not completely happy. I hope your purple crocuses live and blow still *purple*. And I hope your brother Alfred still remembers us with kindness as we shall always remember him.

Love me and Farewell,
Maria Edgeworth

[P.S.] You gave us a plant of Phytolacca or Virginian Pokeweed. It is flourishing. We read in an odd little American letter book that Pokeweed is sovereign for killing beetles. We pray you to tell us how we are to kill beetles with it. Our kitchen and all the lower story of our house is overrun with black beetles and we much, and our cook and housekeeper still more, desire to get rid of this plague.

Edgeworthstown, November 10th, 1834

My dear friend,

This is to tell you a sad disaster, that the nondescript rose has been swept over board. I wrote to Liverpool to Messrs.

Brown to inquire for it the moment I heard that the Caledonia had arrived, and this was my answer. I cannot tell you how much I am disappointed both that I have lost my rose and that you have lost this opportunity of giving me pleasure. Will you without being quite discouraged try it once more and the next will I hope reach me. The captain of the ship must have it recommended to his special care and he shall have my special thanks if it reach me safely. I beg you will tell me what sort of treatment, soil, and degree of watering or manuring or non-manuring it requires. Tell me also why you call it *Nondescript*. Has it no Botanic or vulgar name, and what are its flowers and its leaves? To an Irish woman you know you may *describe* a *nondescript*.

The Spotless Anemone has never reached me. Pray tell my kind friend that I am pining for it. Also for some beautiful plant he promised to chuse for me and on which my imagination has been living ever since.

Your praises of Helen are so elegantly expressed as well as with such warmth of regard for the author that they have given more pleasure to myself and all my family than almost any others we have received excepting from Mr. and Mrs. Herschel.

The scene of the next story I write, if ever I do write again, shall be in Ireland.

We are quiet at present. The tithe business will I trust settle itself without more agitation, and I hope the clergy of both persuasions will be rendered independent of this odious mode of payment, and then they will be more loved and respected when they have no mixture of worldly interests in their religious zeal.

I recommend to you Mrs. Hannah More's letters[244] though there is much in them that will tire you and much that you may not be able to enter into, nor I neither. But she herself is good and sincere and amiable.

244. Hannah More (1745–1833), English writer of plays and religious tracts. ME probably refers to the letters published by W. Roberts, *Memoirs of the Life and Correspondence of . . . Hannah More* (1834).

I am interrupted and must hurry off this letter.

Ever yours affectionately,
Maria Edgeworth

[*Original*]

Wilmington, January 1st, 1835

A Happy New Year to you my dear friend, and may many joyful returns of this interesting anniversary be yours. Yesterday when my husband entered at the dinner hour he presented me a letter with your superscription, saying, "Look at the New Year's gift I have brought you!" It was indeed an unexpected pleasure, but I was sorry to find on opening it that it announced a source of disappointment to us both, in the loss of the Nondescript: *Rosa Laevigata*.[245] I had requested my friend who forwarded it from New York to place it under the especial care of the Captain of one of the Liverpool packets, but I fear the solicitation had little weight. The loss however is too easily repaired to permit it to call forth more than a momentary expression of regret. I will send another as soon as I ascertain that it has taken root and is in thriving condition. It is also termed the Cherokee or Georgia evergreen rose, being indigenous to that part of the U.S., and when first observed, as no description of it was to be found in any work on Botany, it received the popular name of Non-de-script. It flourishes in rich light soil, requires no particular care, being with us in the latitude of 35° a hardy evergreen. In your more Northern clime it might require some protection, as straw round the roots during the winter, but I think you might venture it in the open air. It is beautiful when in bud; the flower when expanded does not bear examination, consisting of four simple white petals, but the appearance of an arbour covered with it when in full bloom could not fail to elicit

245. Mrs. Lazarus at last discovered the botanical name for her Cherokee rose.

admiration. Intermixed with the daily rose, it forms a very beautiful and impervious hedge, the branches being well provided with strong and sharp thorns. How glad I shall be when you say "I have it, safe and thriving." Patience till next summer. I wrote to Mr. Prince on the very day on which I received your previous letter, urging him to send both the Anemone and the other plant or plants immediately. No reply has yet reached me; if I do not hear soon, I shall renew the application.

And now let me say that if you saw the half finished letter dated November 23rd, which now lies before me, you would think me less stupid and ungrateful than I must have appeared in having so long delayed replying to your delightful, may I use your own words and say "flattering, and yet not flattering letter" of September 28th. The epithet in its common acceptation, we mutually reject as inapplicable, where each does justice to the other's sincerity. Yet what term can I find so expressive of my feelings when assured of being thus highly appreciated by persons whose judgment I respect, whose opinion I value, and whose sincerity gives sterling worth to every expression of regard or commendation. It delights me to have given you pleasure, to be told that Mrs. Edgeworth regards me with kindness, and that the charming Mrs. Wilson, your own dear Fanny, gives me credit for being not only all that I am, but all that I may desire to be. I hope you received a note written, I believe in August, in which I acknowledged the receipt of the copy you had sent me of "Helen"; a second perusal has only served to confirm the justness of my first impressions. Why is "Taking for Granted"[246] again announced yet still invisible? Is it again only anticipated and will you not give it to the world? You say "*if* I ever write again." I hope the *if* may be changed into *when*, and I acknowledge that the scene being laid in Ireland would form with me an

246. ME worked over an outline or rough draft of a story with the title "Take for Granted" for a number of years. It was to illustrate the comic and tragic consequences of taking for granted as true something that was in verity false. Her main problem was to develop a story that would carry the moral but not be obvious. She apparently never quite gave up, but she never finished it.

additional attraction. The Absentee, Ennui, and Ormond have always been among my reigning favourites.

I have not yet told you that preparations for the marriage of Mr. L's third daughter, Anna, which took place early in December, and a subsequent visit from my brothers George and Alfred, laid an embargo on my pen and caused the delay above alluded to. Alfred found me an untiring listener, and he indulged me with many an interesting detail. I shewed him your letter, and he begged me to express his gratified sense of your kindness, and to assure you of his warm and respectful remembrance and regard. He often speaks of Mrs. Fox and of her children as some of the most attractive he has ever met with. When he read the letter in which you mentioned his visit to Edgeworth's Town, he said that had he seen it while in England he could not have resisted his inclination to repeat the visit. Thank you for the penciled sketch of Loch Katrine. He brought me Dumont's *Mirabeau*[247] and read aloud for me "The Last days of Pompeii,"[248] unequally written I think, but withal full of incident and very interesting. It has the merit, too, in which too many of his works are deficient, of not offending against morality.

Do you not like Capt. Marriott's novels?[249] "The King's Own" has this evening afforded us great amusement. I shall not

247. Pierre Étienne Louis Dumont (1759–1829), Swiss political writer. His *Souvenirs sur Mirabeau* was published posthumously in 1832. He was a close friend of ME's and helped her with the manuscript of her father's *Memoirs*. He visited frequently in England, and ME visited him in Geneva in 1821.

248. Edward George Earle Lytton Bulwer-Lytton, *The Last Days of Pompeii*, 3 vols. (1834).

249. Frederick Marryat (1792–1848), English sailor and novelist, *Frank Mildmay or The Naval Officer* (1829) and *The King's Own* (1830). He retired from service in 1830; thereafter his popularity as a novelist elicited a steady flow of works including numerous tales written for boys. He is considered a link in the development of the novel between the eighteenth-century novelists and Dickens. Marryat also contributed to the accounts of English impressions of the United States with *A Diary in America*, 3 vols. (1839). He stated as his motives: "My object was to examine and ascertain what were the effects of a democratic form of government and climate upon a people which, with all its foreign admixture, may still be considered English" (p. 10). He praised the beauty of the girls but joined the other British travelers in denouncing the American habit of self-praise with expectations of concurrence.

neglect to profit by your recommendation of Hannah More's letters. The excellent sense and fervent piety conspicuous in her writings, with the almost unequalled flow of eloquence in which they are conveyed, have always placed them high in my estimation, and where I cannot fully concur in her views, I do not the less esteem and respect her sincere and ardent desire to increase the sum of human happiness.

The information given you by Mr. Cruger relative to Major Hamilton's work on America is correct. It was deemed unfair in many of its representations. Major H. as well as Capt. Hall seems to have felt a sort of contempt or indifference toward publick opinion, which, by rendering him less attractive than he might have been in society, had the effect of preventing his seeing it in many instances to the best advantage. By this term I do not mean in the way of shewing off, but under the influence of native good feeling, and that best kind of ease and politeness which are its result. In the *reality* of both these gentlemen I own myself sadly disappointed: the one I had delineated under the most agreeable aspect, from the impression left on my mind by his South America. The other had completely identified himself with his hero Cyril Thornton and was my beau ideal of all that is amiable and interesting. What a novice! you will say, and truly, but I had almost unconsciously yielded to the illusion, and to have one's day dreams thus rudely interrupted is enough to discourage the dreamer from ever again being lulled by the voice of the charmer, charm he never so wisely.

Miss Martineau has selected rather an unfortunate period for her visit to America. The tone given to the political world and in some measure to general society by the mistaken opinions and unprecedented line of conduct pursued by our First Magistrate [*Andrew Jackson*] render it difficult amid conflicting elements to ascertain the true American Character. I do not love my country less, but I am less proud of it than formerly because I see much to disapprove. This is a painful, it would be a humiliating confession did I deem the error radical. I trust it is not, and that the people, dazzled and misled by the pretensions of the Hero of New Orleans, may ere it be too late dispel the illusion and turn once more to the guidance of that solid sense and true patriotism by which their independence was achieved, and by which alone it can be rendered permanent. I have been led to say more than I intended, and yet have not perhaps rendered myself very intelligible—*n'importe*, here let it rest.

The Anthracite or Lehigh coal is found in the neighbourhood of a small river of that name in the vicinity or rather not very distant from Philadelphia. Its properties are highly and I believe justly extolled, but there are some difficulties attending the use of it: it is difficult to ignite and requires grates of a peculiar construction, but when once lighted burns with a fervid heat and without any of the unpleasant accompaniments of a coal fire. I trust the experiments now in course may prove successful in enabling its powers to be fully tested. When we reflect on all that has been done within the last age, nothing appears too difficult to be compassed by the ingenuity of man. Are you aware that the hardness and brilliancy of the Anthracite coal are such as to admit of its being manufactured into earrings, bracelets, and a variety of ornaments which are hardly distinguishable from jet?

I wish I could relieve your domestick annoyance by replying efficaciously to your inquiry about poke weed; you are aware that its root and its leaves when full grown are poisonous, tho' the young shoots are used as an early spring vegetable. Now there can be no doubt that a decoction made from either the root or the leaves and left in the way of the beetles would destroy them, but the experiment, even supposing the liquid to possess an attraction for them, would be too hazardous. I have been consulting our domestick Cyclopaedia and here is the result. "That very troublesome insect the Black beetle may be extirpated, by placing a hedge hog in the kitchen during the summer nights. A German writer recommends to place a bundle of pea straw near the holes, as they are fond of creeping into it, and after a short time, it should be suddenly taken away and burned. Another simple method is to place a vessel with any liquid, with boards in an oblique direction to facilitate their ascent to the mouth of the vessel, over which they will fall into the liquid." And this is all I can find on the subject. Will it be of any service to you?

Why cannot I congratulate both you and myself on the flourishing state of the purple "Crocuses"? They bloomed for three years; the next I sought them in vain; one solitary flower was all that appeared. I removed its bulb into a box in the hope of at least preserving that, but it shewed its pretty purple head no more. I would not tell you, because I knew you would be sorry for my disappointment and would perhaps with the kindness I had repeatedly experienced send me a fresh supply. This I can hardly wish, lest after all my care, they should meet with a similar fate. I do not believe I can be charged in a general way with want of perseverance, but in some cases I would rather avoid than incur the risk of disappointment.

I have twenty things more to say, and you will thank fortune that twice twenty interruptions since I commenced this letter have driven half out of my head, and now a new one obliges me to close without an effort to recall them. Let me just congratulate you on the improving health of your dear invalid Lucy, and then place in my cap the plume of smartness which you award as my due for unravelling the mystic phrase of "thy servant not being a dog may come."[250] Harael is too old an acquaintance not to be recognized even when disguised by a negative. Pray tell me if the Mrs. Herschel to whose letter you allude is the wife of the Mr. H. who wrote "a preliminary discourse on the study of Natural Philosophy." I wonder if it is idle curiosity that prompts the wish that I might see that letter. If you think it neither idle nor impertinent will you not indulge me? May I ask too, for a copy of the little poem suggested by the "Transmigrations of

250. RML appears to refer to a puzzle in one of the annuals that ME sent her.

Indur" from which there is an extract in one of the volumes of Early Lessons? If you send it, address to the Care of Messrs. DePeyster & Whitmarsh, Merchants, New York.

I send with this a little work, which Mrs. Fox will perhaps do me the favour to accept for the use of her children, "The Child's book on the soul"; the author, Mr. Gaulaudet,[251] was for many years at the [*illegible*] an institution for the education of the Deaf & Dumb [*at*] Hartford, Connecticut.

Not one word more.

ever affectionately yours
R. Lazarus

Edgeworthstown, March 23, 1835

In return for your long and delightfully kind letter, my dear friend, I can at this moment write only a few lines to tell you that by a young countryman of mine who is setting out this morning on his way to the United States via London, I am going to send for you a little old fan case and an old tin pipe full of native Irish earth and damp moss and cuttings of a rose tree called the Macartney Rose and rooted plants of Irish heath and of another heath named [*American*], also a few roots of the purple crocus which I entreat you never to regret if they die. The rose I send because it is beautiful in itself, a thick petal, cream colored white, and shining evergreen leaf; from this description, even before you see it in flower or in leaf, you will perhaps guess my second reason for sending it. You will suspect what I suspect, that our Macartney Rose and your Nondescript may be the very same roses.[252]

---

251. Thomas Hopkins Gallaudet (1787–1851), educator of the deaf, *The Child's Book on The Soul* (1830).

252. ME's and RML's roses were not the same but closely related. ME's Macartney is the *Rosa bracteata*, whereas RML's Nondescript is the *Rosa laevigata*, both natives of China.

I fear however that thy rose and my crocuses will never have one fibre alive by the time they reach you, spite of all the pains our gardener has taken in packing them. Probably you take too much care of the purple crocuses. Put them into the ground in the garden and let them take their chance. In this country they like being let alone and they strike very deep into the earth. Mice are very fond of eating them. Again I say never grieve or reproach yourself if they die, only enjoy them if they live. They are of no value and it is not the least trouble to send them. I hope you will receive with this parcel a little "New years gift" (for 1830) which contains the little poem you asked me for, "The Transmigrations of Indur" by my brother Sneyd Edgeworth.

I wish your amiable brother Alfred would repeat his visit to Europe and to England and Ireland. My whole family are gratified by what you say of his half repentance when he saw how much we had liked his first visit. We are no flatterers, and not in general sudden in our likings.

[*Same page*]

March 24, 1835

I am ashamed of the hurry in which I wrote yesterday and of all the blots and scratchings in and out which I have made. But as the record such as it is of what I have sent in the old fan case and tin pipe is correct, I will not waste my time writing it over again for the mere fairness of the looks.

I have now determined to send this letter by the post instead of by the young man who carried the parcel. I only hope that the direction I have given is right, to have the parcel left at Messrs. De Peysback [*De Peyster*] and Whitmarsh, New York, directing upon the parcel to have it forwarded to Mrs. Lazarus, Wilmington, North Carolina, and stating that it contains plants. The vessel *The Mexico* sails the 10th of April with a cargo for Philadelphia.

Mrs. Fox and I are very much obliged to you for the child's book on the soul by Mr. Gaulaudet. She likes it much and thinks it will be useful to her children. But there is one little caution I must give you, never to send a half bound [*pound?*] book again under cover to the Clerk of the Council. He, Mr. Bathurst, wrote me a remonstrance when he forwarded the packet and warned me that he might really lose his place by receiving too-heavy packets in these reforming times when molehills of abuses are made mountains (and mountains molehills). I am afraid it was all my own fault and not yours, and that I told you you might send any weight, which was quite a mistake. I now beg for complete security that nothing but *letters* may be sent to Council Office and those may be of any number of sheets that you can be kind enough to write to me. Be so kind as *not* to write the direction to Miss Edgeworth, *etc.*, upon the outside of your letter but fasten it on a slip of paper to the letter as you will see that I fasten a slip to this letter merely to serve as a pattern.

I am sorry to plague you with this prosing explanation. To make some amends I will copy some pretty lines which we have just received from my dear brother Pakenham from India (from Amballah where he is now assistant to Mr. Clarke, Political agent). We don't know whose the lines are. Pakenham says that he met with them just after he had finished reading Helen and that he thought them so expressive of what might have been General Clarendon's feelings at the moment when he exclaimed "Beautiful creature!" that he could not help sending them to his sister Harriet.

> Fare thee well, thou lovely one,
> Lovely still tho dear no more.
> Once the soul of truth is gone
> Love's sweet life is o'er.
>
> What e'er thy words the flatt'ring tale
> Could ne'er have thus deceived,
> But eyes that tell the truth so well
> Were sure to be believed.

I have desired my sister Fanny to send with the parcel to New York a copy of a French translation of my own little Snow Woman joined to a story called Perseverance written by Madame Belloc, the lady who has so well translated Helen and Early Lessons and the Conclusion of Harry and Lucy. She is a very amiable and *persevering* lady, not rich, wife to a painter who is at the head of one of the Parisian Government schools.

The story of *Perseverance* has for its hero an imaginary son of a real person, Bernard Palissy,[253] who was a most shocking instance of Perseverance, an enameller or porcelain manufacturer who flourished as well as I remember in the time of Henry the 3rd or Henry the 4th of France. In Chaptal's Chemistry there is a note containing his history which I remember marking with pencil about thirty years ago for my little brother Henry to read. I cannot think that any fiction can on this subject be so entertaining or so exciting to children or grown up people as the simple truth. But if I remember rightly the real Pallisy threw his last remains of clothes into the furnace and died just as Henry III/IV had granted him a pension. This would not be such good encouragement for children as there ought to be for Perseverance. I have not yet seen Madame Belloc's story, but Fanny has two copies for me and I desire her to send you one. If you should wish to have any translations of my Early Lessons in French or Italian (or German) I could send you both for your young people. Tell me if you think it worthwhile, but do not burden yourself with them unless wanted.

My sister Fanny is recovering we hope and Lucy [is] much better, and Mrs. Edgeworth will consequently leave them both and return to us in a few days, we hope for some time.

253. Bernard Palissy (1510–89), French potter, who worked much of his life in a vain attempt to reproduce Chinese porcelain. His work, however, came to the attention of Catherine de Médicis and her sons, and he set up his kilns on what later was to become known as the Tuileries. When almost eighty he was imprisoned because he was a Protestant. Offered his freedom by Henry III if he would recant, he refused and died in prison.

Believe me my dear friend very sincerely and affectionately Yours

Maria Edgeworth

[*Note accompanying the box of plants directed to DePeyster and Whitmarsh, New York*]:

FOR MRS. LAZARUS, WILMINGTON, NORTH CAROLINA

This case contains

A Macartney rose, so called because Lord Macartney brought it from China.

A bit of Irish heath, indigenous.

Another kind of heath called *American heath*, common in these countries in gardens. But Botanists say that no heaths grow in America.

The case also contains a bit of Irish Shamrock which is neither more nor less than common white clover.

Witness my hand St. Patrick's Day (17 March 1835).

[*Copy*]

Wilmington, January 10th, 1836

If it is not too late, and it can hardly ever be too late for the expression of kind and affectionate feelings, if it is not too late then, let me congratulate you my dear friend on the arrival of another birthday, and convey my sincere wishes that the newly entered year, like many of its predecessors, may be to you a period of health and of happiness, as little allayed as is compatible with our present state of existence. Soon after I last wrote you, acknowledging a letter which I received in Raleigh, I saw an account in one of the papers of your having been hurt by a fall. I have been constantly hoping that a reply to that letter might inform me of your recovery and also of the restored health of Mrs. Wilson, and have now resolved to disclose my anxiety and remind you, worthless as my letters are, that you have permitted me to assert my claims upon you, and that you are in my debt. When I last addressed you I was recovering from a protracted fit of illness; my health I am happy to say is now perfectly restored, and I have been since the middle of October at home and enabled once more to enter on the performance of my duties. During my absence the flower roots had been received and planted though without a hope of their reviving, nor have they ever sent forth a shoot. The pretty little souvenir being of less perishable nature has survived all delays and dangers, has been read with pleasure by Mr. L and myself and with delight by my little daughter Ellen, who became a perfect Scheherezade during its perusal. I have always wished for the little poem of Indur, and am quite as much pleased with it as I had expected to be; the change in the plan of the original is well imagined and the story of the Elephant and the Indian mother happily introduced. I am sure if Mrs. Barbauld ever saw this little production she must have been pleased with it. You as well as myself have, I know, been interested in Madame Belloc's admirable little story "Perseverance." I believe it is the first time since my childhood that I have ever been tempted to anticipate the course of fictitious events and peep at the catastrophe, but actually while our little friend Bernard was watching the furnace I could not control my breathless impatience to know the result, and I fairly turned over and caught him in his unfortunate slumber. Of Garry Owen[254] I would fain say that like every other production of the same hand, the charm of the story is only equalled by the value of the lesson it conveys. The translation too is so spirited and yet so judicious, not too *french* for an English tale, and yet availing itself of those pleasing turns of expression for which our language has no parallel. My children have been delighted with both tales, as I read the translation to them, tho' my English did not possess the charm of Madame Belloc's french or of your original. I have been wasting some little time lately

254. ME wrote *Garry Owen, or the Snow-Woman* and *Poor Bob, The Chimney-sweeper* (1832).

over two or three new American Novels chiefly on account of the growing celebrity of the authors. "The Lenvilles"[255] by Miss Sedgwick among the number is not among her most fortunate efforts. She has written pleasingly in several of the Annuals but her novels since "Hope Leslie" have I think been failures.

If you see our papers you must have remarked the efforts that are making for the Abolition of Slavery, an end to be desired by all, tho' the means too inconsiderately adopted are in every point of view unjustifiable. The excellent, the Philanthropick Wilberforce[256] who spent his best years in the advancement of this labour of love viewed the subject with wisdom and humanity. But what can be said of men who blindly, madly urge the slave to seek his freedom through a sea of blood, who promise to aid him in the commission of crime, without even glancing at the too-certain consequences, and who, while pledging themselves in the cause of suffering humanity, would spread horror and devastation among their brethren and over one half of their mother land? Their mischievous purposes will I trust in Heaven be averted, and the removal of this mighty evil, of which we of the South are not insensible, be left to our own legislators whose wisdom will find means gradually but surely to effect the end.

We will not dignify this scrap by the name of letter; it will have fulfilled its destiny if it serve to recall to remembrance and assure you of the

> affectionate respect and regard of
> Your friend
> R.L.

255. Here RML appears to have mistakenly written "the Lenvilles" for Catherine Maria Sedgwick's *The Linwoods; or, "Sixty Years Since" in America* (1835).

256. William Wilberforce (1759–1833), English member of Parliament and philanthropist. He was a proponent along with Pitt of the abolition of the slave trade, but the Emancipation Bill did not pass until a month after his death.

Edgeworthstown, April 15th, 1836

My dear friend,

My legs are quite safe and I am sorry that you wasted your sympathy upon me. The lady whose leg was in question was a Miss Edgeworth, a distant relation of mine, and as perhaps you may kindly extend your interest to her name I will mention that she has recovered the use of her leg which was not broken as the newspaper announced, only sprained, I believe only the ankle sprained. But Miss E. lives at a distance from us and we are scarcely acquainted with her; therefore I am even now giving you only second-hand information. Thank you for your birthday greetings, quite in season.

Though I had not the excuse of a broken leg or a sprained ankle for not writing to you yet I hope you will pardon me, for I really have numerous letters to write both on business and to a great number of family friends who live at a distance and also many claims from literary correspondents, so that it is often as much as I can do to get the business of the day done before the dinner bell rings, and I am then forced to dress in *no time*, while the rest of the family or guests are going downstairs from their several rooms. This is literally the fact I am sure three days out of seven in every week, and I might with truth state a much larger proportion. I have very little time for writing for the public, and in truth I have written so much that I ought to fear falling into the common fault from which even my admired and admirable friend Sir Walter Scott could not, did not escape. Perhaps he was forced on by his desire to fulfil his engagements with his creditors, but as I have no reason of that kind to urge me to write I should be inexcusable if I were to *overdo* and to leave my friends to regret that I wrote so much, instead of what they now kindly say and I am sure feel. Friends deceive themselves upon this point often and mislead authors without meaning to flatter. The Booksellers, the publisher are the only advisers to be depended upon because both their interest and their knowledge of the facts by which they should judge of the *public* taste and feelings enable them to judge and advise well. My publisher has written to ask me to give him another book, and I believe I shall. But I shall not hurry myself. I will finish as well as I can, and then I should with a good conscience leave it as a posthumous work if I should not live. I have always thought it disgracefully mean in literary manufacturers to trade upon their name and to put off ill-finished works upon credit. That is what I never will do. And I am sure you, my dear Madam, who I consider as one of my real friends and whose moral feelings and moral taste I respect and love, will agree with me in these sentiments and will wish for me to abide by these principles. I have said too much about myself and my writings, but I was led into it partly by belief in the interest you take in me and partly by the fear that you might think me idle and that I am not.

I am now finishing "Take for Granted" which I had to new model and which after all will be a very slight story, not above the length of "To-morrow," and after turning and tossing it in every way I cannot make it half so entertaining. I *must* finish it however among two volumes perhaps of several Tales which may better suit various tastes better than having only one novel.

In our domestic life we have been very anxious for my Aunt Mary Sneyd; she is eighty-six and has had for above a year a bad leg which threatened mortification. At the same time she had an attack of cough and inflamation on her chest and the swelling in the leg suddenly ceased. An eminent physician and surgeon we had from Dublin gave her up, but at the same time continued his skilful and most carefully chosen remedies. Contrary to all human expectations she has been spared to us and she is now so much better that we have every reason to hope she may enjoy life some time longer. Her understanding is so perfect and her feelings and sympathy with all her friends so young that you would never know her age from them. My sister Fanny for whom you so kindly inquire is better and was certainly benefited by her journey to the Baths at Ems, but she is not yet in good health and I fear never will be strong, but she has so many of the blessings of life that she is, dear patient creature, content and cheerful. I do not know whether she will have strength to undertake a journey to Ireland this year. Lucy, another sister of mine about whom you are interested, is wonderfully recovered and is now up and walking about, *soberly*. She is at Bath paying a visit to a friend and will soon go to spend some time with her brother Francis and his Spanish wife Rosa. That romantic match has turned out much better than many worldly interested matches do, much better than many of those which Parisians call *mariages de convenance*, which often end in divorce legally or illegally *pour incompatibilité d'humeur*. Rosa's disposition and her husband's admirably suit, and she has a strength and uprightness of character and a warmth of affection and an originality of thought and expression in conversation and writing which make her altogether a very interesting and estimable relation and loved by all her husband's family as well as by him and worth more to us in our way of valuing money, *i.e.* by the happiness it does or does not produce, than if she had a large share in the mines of Peru without her good qualities. They have a charming little boy now several months old, replacing the eldest who died. Aunt Mary, the first work she could do when able to sit up after her illness, knit for this infant a nice, warm, pretty lamb's wool shawl which has delighted him and his parents.

And now having filled an egotistical sheet it is time to tell you that I am sincerely glad you have recovered your health and are again able, to your own satisfaction, to fulfil all your domestic duties. I know how dreadful the weight upon the mind is in illness from the sense of not being able to do what we wish and think we ought to do. There is no "medicining" that feeling of disquiet "to repose."

I hope you are often out in your garden and among your shrubs and flowers. I am sorry that the crocuses did not live and will not live with you. Very foolish and very bad taste in those crocuses! I enclose some seeds of *German*-aster and some seeds from the East Indies which my brother Pakenham E. sent to his mother and which with her kind regards she shares with you. As you know they come from a hot climate; you must treat them accordingly. The German Aster on the contrary is from cold regions and very hardy. I send you also a few larkspur seeds— from the South of Europe you know these are. I hope they will prosper with you.

I have had a visit last week from an American literary gentleman of eminence who resides at Albany, Doctor Sprague.[257] He is a presbyterian minister, has published some eloquent sermons and what I think more of is a liberal, and mild, benevolent man who is sufficiently candid to see and to say where he thinks his own enthusiasm has gone and carried others too far. Perhaps you will think he has bribed my judgment when I confess to you that he has promised me a fine plant of the Spotless Anemone. Mine is very puny. I forgot to ask him to tell me what treatment and what soil it likes. We keep it in a pot in a greenhouse, and it has grown less and less pretty, delicate creature, and threatens to vanish quite away.

I have never seen the last novel of Miss Sedgwick which you name. But I have a great admiration for her talents as I saw them in Hope Leslie. I have lately seen in a North American Review honorable mention of her and a comparison of her and myself, of which I have only to say that I am gratified by what is allowed to me and convinced of the justice of what is given against me. Not that I think, as some I believe do, that what is given to another is taken from oneself. I remember that my

257. William Buell Sprague (1795–1876), clergyman, biographer, collector. After graduation from Yale in 1815 he spent the following year at Woodlawn, near Mount Vernon, as tutor in the family of Major Lawrence Lewis, a nephew of George Washington. While there he was given permission by Bushrod Washington to select whatever Washington letters he wanted provided he left copies. He thus came into possession of some fifteen hundred letters. He was the most widely known American clergyman of his day and a prolific writer on a number of subjects. His publications number more than 150 titles.

The Rev. Mr. Sprague visted ME in Edgeworthstown in 1856 and recorded his visit in a work entitled *Visits to European Celebrities* (1855).

friend, now no more, the late excellent Mr. Ricardo[258] once upheld in argument with me a doctrine of Mr. Milne's[259] set forth in some Encyclopedia that there can be no reward given publickly without its being a punishment to some other body— whose relative position is changed by the comparison I suppose. I could no ways understand the principle, and after arguing the matter with Ricardo he, who was the most candid of men, acknowledged that he was convinced Milne's doctrine was erroneous. In fact, the establishing of it would be a mere sacrifice to Envy and Demerit.

I agree with all you say about the abolition of slavery. The slaves must be prepared by education to be free and to provide for themselves before they can be set free without danger to others and destruction and misery to themselves and society. Dr. Sprague was living on Washington's estate with his niece Mrs. Lewis[260] [*illegible*] the slaves there whom Washington had liberated; he told me that a more *worthless* and *more wretched* set [*of beings*] than they had become never did he behold.

Remember us to your brother. Send us more such visitors if you can and believe me affectionately your friend

Maria Edgeworth

[P.S.] I am glad you like Garry Owen, French and English, and still more glad that you liked Indur, and the Annual I sent you. Did I mention MacIntosh's Memoirs and Letters by his son?[261]

258. David Ricardo (1772–1823), English economist. His chief work was *Principles of Political Economy and Taxation* (1817). ME visited the Ricardos at Gatcomb Park and in London attended his breakfasts where political economy was the main topic discussed.

259. Joshua Milne (1776–1851), English statistician. His main work is *A Treatise on the Valuation of Annuities and Assurances on Lives and Survivorships; or the Construction of Tables of Mortality; and on the Probabilities and Expectations of Life* (1815). He contributed to the *Encyclopaedia Britannica*, 4th ed. (1800–1810), articles on "Annuities," "Bills of Mortality," and "Law of Mortality."

260. Mrs. Lewis was the wife of Major Lawrence Lewis, Washington's nephew. She was Eleanor Parke Custis, granddaughter of Martha Washington. The pronoun "his" refers to Washington, not to Dr. Sprague.

261. Sir James Mackintosh (1765–1832), Scottish parliamentarian, professor of law, and writer. His interests and culture were wide. His *Life* was published in 1836 by his son R. J. Mackintosh.

The most interesting of modern publications, and I would also recommend or rather ask your opinion of Mrs. Carmichael's Sketches of Manners in the West Indies,[262] meaning Trinidad and St. Vincent's specially. Joanna Baillie has published three new volumes of Dramas.[263] The tragedies are worthy of her, and have been (two of them) acted with applause. Of the comedies we need not speak. Joanna is the most amiable of authoresses and the kindest of friends and I rejoice in the success of this last work.

[*Original*]

Wilmington, January 1st, 1837

Acknowledge, my dear friend, that I have been considerate, and give me credit for my self-denial in having thus long delayed replying to your last welcome letter. Knowing as I do how little mine have to recommend them, save the sincere and warm attachment of the writer, I would not indulge myself by an immediate tax on your kindness, especially as you had shown me in your last how fully and constantly your time is occupied. To indemnify myself in some degree for this privation, I have been almost daily enjoying a delightful and never tiring intercourse with your mind, opinions, and sentiments, through the medium of these admirable works which in various editions enrich my shelves. My children are so happy with Frank or Harry and Lucy as companions, they realize so much, and make so many inquiries about Miss Edgeworth that I seem to be passing half my time in your society. Thus you are brought much nearer to me than I possibly can be to you. You cannot be

262. Mrs. A. C. Carmichael, *Domestic Manners and Social Condition of the White, Colored, and Negro Population of the West Indies*, 2 vols. (1833). Mrs. Carmichael favored colonialism believing the slaves were happy and the Methodists fostered dangerous delusions.
263. Joanna Baillie, *Dramas, by Joanna Baillie* (1836).

forgotten. Must I fear that I may? Or shall I confide in that warmth of heart and benevolence of disposition, which like the widow's cruise [?], fail not, to have your remembrance and regard continued not because I claim but because I prize them so dearly. New Year's day, always bringing with it interesting and salutary reflections, you have invested in my mind with a peculiar charm; in imagination I join your family-party to offer my congratulations on the happy return of the period which has I trust found you in the enjoyment of health and surrounded by the delights of the assembled family circle. You witness the improvement of your young nephews and nieces, and in sympathising with them and their parents, the feelings of by-gone years are renewed; you almost fancy that time has stepped back and placed you amidst these days when the parents were themselves happy, intelligent, well-instructed children. One dear venerated countenance is sought in vain, but he is gone to receive the recompense of a well spent life, and who would diminish his felicity if by a wish he could be recalled! Dear Aunt Mary Sneyd! She had just regained her health when you last wrote. Has she retained it? And is she this evening seated at the fire side, cheering all hearts by her benign and tempered cheerfulness? I trust it is so, and that years of peace and comfort may yet be hers. And you my dear friend, with so many to love, as much to enjoy, can I wish for you aught better than a continuance of these blessings? With what sweet satisfaction must you review the past, with what well grounded hope anticipate the future! How few have passed a life of so extensive usefulness and well-earned fame, so little chequered by the evils incident to humanity. I would say that to your state and feelings those beautiful lines of Addison's are peculiarly applicable:

Ten thousand, thousand precious gifts
My daily thanks employ,
Nor is the least a cheerful heart,
That tastes those gifts with joy.

I am happy to hear that your volumes of tales are in a state of forwardness. We seem to have been tantalized with Taking for Granted! It has been so often promised in the papers for you, and now I am doubly pleased to think that the agreeable morsel will not again be withdrawn.

Your best and most solicitous friends need not fear your sending forth any work prematurely, tho' they may and do regret the cautious diffidence in your own powers of pleasing which creates and fosters the fear of writing too long and too much. Yet will they be too chary of your fame to press you further than your own excellent judgment decides that you should go.

Helen was a precious addition to the treasures of preceding years; of this a third reading has afforded ample proof; it will live and do good when many of its brilliant contemporaries are neglected or forgotten.

I was unfortunate in not being able to obtain either the Memoirs of Sir J. McIntosh, of which I have seen only a review, or Mrs. Carmichael's sketches, both of which you recommend in your last. They have not or had not last summer been republished here, and English editions are seldom to be obtained. Miss Baillie's tragedies interested me exceedingly; they possess much of that dignity and pathos, that refined delicacy and beauty of expression which in her writings have so often charmed the ear, riveted the attention, and touched the heart. It is a pity that the comedies were not suppressed; how difficult in many instances it appears for even the wise to decide with accuracy on the value of their own performances.

I have lately read and been disappointed in the Memorials of Mrs. Hemans.[264] Her poems replete with tenderness, and feeling, had cast a charm round her ideal portrait which this publication has in a great measure broken. Her papers could not have fallen into judicious hands, for surely the greater part of

264. Felicia Dorothea Hemans (1793–1835), English poet. Popular in her day and a friend of Scott, her *Memorials* appeared in 1836.

her letters are little worthy of preservation. Few biographers have the tact to set aside personal feelings and look with a single eye to the public taste when they form their selections from the letters of a deceased friend. They seem to forget that they themselves are in possession of certain links, which will be wanting to others, and that divested of these associations the letters are either flat, or impertinent in revealing things which ought not to pass the sacred limits of domestic privacy.

This fourth page has taken me by surprise, and I have not yet told you of my brother Alfred's marriage. His wife is gentle, amiable, and devotedly attached to him; he deserves to be happy and I trust will be so. I must tell you too that I have my son at home after an absence of two years. He is now nearly fifteen, a sensible unassuming boy, not free from faults, but giving promise of becoming such as our wishes would have him. He will not remain at home tho' we have not exactly determined where he shall complete his studies. I will not say complete his education. Our daughter Ellen is absent at school; the two younger, Mary and Julia, occupy much of my time and more of my solicitude. They are good and promising, the one eight and the other six years of age.

Let me hope my dear friend to hear from you without very long delay; it is such a gratification to me, and I endeavour not to be unreasonable. Will you have the kindness to make my regards acceptable to Mrs. E. and to your aunts and sisters, and believe me ever affectionately your friend

R. Lazarus

[*In margin*]

Astoria[265]—how could I forget it. I know that as a whole, you like and have been interested in it.

[*Bottom of page*]

How could I leave for a marginal line my expression of

---

265. Washington Irving, *Astoria*, 2 vols. (1836). Through his acquaintance with Jacob Astor, he created an interesting history of fur trading in Oregon from the records of the Astor enterprises.

thanks to Mrs. E and yourself for the flower seeds. The Iponica [*Japonica?*], the Clitoria and the Convolvulus[266] bloomed in my garden; the paper marked Larkspur I think proved to be a beautiful, sensitive [*plant*]. I hope you have received your spotless Anemone. I have reminded Mr. Prince of it repeatedly; he always apologises and promises, but does not invariably perform. Dr. Sprague is on the spot and will be more successful. Again Adieu.

Edgeworthstown, March 1st, 1837

Be assured my kind friend that you are never forgotten by me. Time adds as in justice and gratitude it ought to do to the esteem I have for the steadiness and truth of your character and the constancy of your regard and your kindness to me. Such is the feeling of all who live with me, of all my nearest and dearest friends towards you. The arrival of a letter from you is a real pleasure to us, and we are never disappointed of that expectation of pleasure with which we break the seal.

I congratulate you and your brother Alfred on his marriage which you give us reason to believe to be one of those marriages for which increasing congratulations may be given every year. Your brother Alfred we all thought remarkably well suited to domestic life, and now that he is so far off and has disposed of himself we may venture to say we looked upon [*him*] as one particularly likely to make any amiable woman he might marry happy for life. You may tell this with my congratulations to his wife. You may add that I am near seventy, so that she will not suspect that I have actually ever intended to rival her. Pray tell us the name your sister-in-law bore before she married, and tell

266. The clitoria was probably a vine known as the blue pea and the convolvulus a variety of morning glory. Mrs. Lazarus's japonica may have been another vine known as Japanese honeysuckle.

us where she lived, and as much more information as you please.

I am very glad any of the seeds we sent you prospered. Most of them were from my brother Pakenham in India. He poor fellow has had sad losses a few months ago which he has borne with admirable temper. He was employed by his superior (Mr. Clarke, Political Agent at Ambala) to go to Bullawallee in the Jhend territory to settle what rate the Quimdan (farmers in short) should pay of taxes to the European Government and he thought he had at last tolerably well satisfied them of the justice of his assessment. But after dismissing them and when he was quietly going to bed in his tent, they rose in a body, seized possession of the fort, and while he went for military [aid] and before he could summon troops sufficient to his aid ransacked his tent, carried off his horses, his very valuable books, his instruments, telescopes, microscope, drawing-box, writing desk, drawings of flowers and hortus siccus which he had been collecting and painting for years! Monied value of his losses [was] about £400, but the loss was incalculable to his tastes and feelings. Three of the horses, great favorites, after some weeks he recovered. They were turned loose and strayed back in sad condition, cruelly used, but they were so glad to see him again, rubbed their heads against him most affectionately, so that it was almost worth while to have undergone the parting to have this meeting again with his grateful, faithful brute friends.

He has no society where he lives at Ambala (near the Himalaya Mountains, a charming climate) except Mr. and Mrs. Clarke and the surgeon. With the tastes for Botany and Entomology which he has and his love for reading, this want of society is endurable; he who makes the best of everything says *delightful* compared with what might have been his lot, the being forced to bear the interruptions of vulgar idle company.

[*Same letter*]   March 1.

This day brought us a letter from Pakenham, to his mother, via Alexandria, dated Ambala, Nov. 13,—by a steamer—very quick, four months only!

My sisterly pride cannot forbear copying for you my dear *family friend* the concluding lines of this letter which came so apropos just as I was writing to you about him. He speaks so much better for himself than I can for him, and I wish you to know him. He concludes, after telling us of some brilliant prospects which might open for him in case the British keep possession of the Jhend territory:

"To a more ambitious person than myself it would be the most desirable situation in India; but I am not ambitious of any very difficult and prominent situation as I feel that I should fail and by my failure make you all unhappy. I should prefer such an appointment as I at present hold where I can perform all my duties and I trust will, to the satisfaction of those in authority over me and those under my control. When I think of it I cannot help almost shuddering at the thought of the immense responsibility I even now have (under Clarke to be sure) but still I have immense power to do harm for a person of four and twenty, in a district larger than any of the Irish provinces under me. However I try to do my best, and as long as I know that my dear mother is daily offering up her prayers for me I hope I may be enabled to do my duty. Ever my dear Mother, Your affectionate son, Michael Pakenham Edgeworth." I know my dear Mrs. Lazarus you will not see only vanity in my copying this for you, and feeling sure of your sympathy, I leave it there.

His dear mother is now at Clifton nursing two of his sisters, Fanny and Sophy (Mrs. Lestock Wilson and Mrs. Fox). For Sophy we very much fear, for Fanny we have great hopes. Sophy's case we dread is consumptive and that she is growing daily weaker; Fanny's complaint is something internal which we are assured is curing. And from the perfect recovery of Lucy under the same medical friend who is now attending her sisters we have hope for Fanny's perfect restoration [and] reason to believe that everything that can be done by human skill and kindness for Sophy has been done, is doing, and will be done. I can say no more on this painful subject and in the suspense in which we are, and must put our friends by any accounts we now give.

You kindly mention the spotless anemone which I wished for. I have never heard of it but from you. You mention Doctor Sprague. We have never had any letter from him and we are rather disappointed because we had fancied he left us with a feeling of regard that would last, as ours has for him. His friends in Scotland where he left a similar kind and good impression I know have heard *from* him and we have had pleasure in hearing *of* him from them. I rather suspect he has forgotten the receipt I gave him for directing letters to me and sending them free. After he was gone from Edgeworthstown House we found on the library table a card of directions I had written for him. If you have any means of communicating with him give him the receipt for enclosing to the Clerk of the Council Office in Waiting, Council Office, London, bidding him direct the letter he encloses in a small hand on the sealed side of the letter just by the seal. This is the last way which my official friends have prescribed to me. Warn him to put nothing but manuscript in his cover. Any parcel, either books or Spotless Anemone, may be sent to Liverpool, care Messrs. J. & W. Brown for me (I am sorry to be so tiresome).

I do not know that I have much interesting to say about books. Mrs. Trollope's J. Jefferson Whitelaw[267] I cannot bear. The character is beyond belief bad and degrading to human nature, and if it be possible to exist in certain circumstances still it must be an exception and not a general case fit for fiction or for any moral purpose, and it is invidious to give such as national character. It will tend to give Americans a notion I fear that such representations please the British and this would propagate national aversion. I do not think the book has been at all popular in England or Ireland. It is thought too horrid and disgusting. The German family are the only amiable and interesting people except the Aunt—I forget her name (Aunt Cli). She is the only *good* American Mrs. Trollope has drawn. Tell me if you know what is thought of the book in your part of the world. Perhaps you never thought of it at all.

267. Frances Trollope, *The Life and Adventures of Jonathan Jefferson Whitlaw: or Scenes on the Mississippi*, 3 vols. (1836), reissued in 1857 under the title of *Lynch Law*.

We are reading Captain Back's Arctic Expedition in which the American liberality and hospitality have honorable and just and grateful mention. This is as it should be and puts one again in good humour with one's kind and with Authors. I like Washington Irving's Astoria but think it is too finely written in some parts.

I do not know whether I ever mentioned to you "Mary's Grammar", a little book written by Mrs. Marcet[268] which I am very sure you would find useful and agreeable to your young people. I have no friend in London now Fanny is gone who could get it for me and send it to you, alas. But whenever I can I will.

Mrs. Mary Sneyd was gratified and quite touched by your kind mention of her in your last letter. She is now perfectly well (in her 87th year) and knitting beautiful pelerines, *etc.* for our little Foxes. She is listening to Captn. Back's Expedition every morning for an hour while she knits, with as much interest as the youngest in company, and in the evening with as much pleasure to the old Vicar of Wakefield which we are reading over again and comparing with some of the fashionable novels of high excitement, (dangerous I think). A very entertaining review in the Edinburgh for Jan. 1837 of Prior's life of Goldsmith[269] put it in our head to look back at his works.

We have now in our hall the original picture of Sir Joshua Reynolds from which the prints are taken. It was lent to us by our physician Dr. Nelligan whose wife was a relation of Goldsmith's (Hudson). Dr. Nelligan furnished Prior with most of the particulars in that Life.

I am going on with Taking for Granted—I am ashamed to say how slowly. But I would rather write to my family and friends than for the public.

> Ever affectionately your friend,
> My dear Mrs. Lazarus,
> Maria Edgeworth.

268. Jane Haldimand Marcet, *Mary's Grammar, Interspersed with Stories, etc.* (1835).
269. Sir James Prior, *The Life of Oliver Goldsmith*, 2 vols. (1837).

Wilmington, April 23rd, 1837

I cannot delay my thanks to you my dear friend for your delightful letter, which after so long an interval of silence I read with grateful avidity. Your expressions of kindness and regard are very precious and are dwelt on with a degree of interest and self-complacency which might be construed into vanity, did they proceed from a less pure and genuine source.

I have just finished a letter to my sister Sarah, the wife of my brother Alfred, and felt happy in communicating your message which will I know be enjoyed and prized by them both. Alfred is still commandant at the Frankford Arsenal near Philadelphia, where he married and where Mr. and Mrs. Hays,[270] the parents of his wife, reside. Mrs. Hays, the mother of Sara, is a most amiable lady, sister to the celebrated Miss Gratz of whom you may have heard through your friend Mr. Ralston. The Hays family consist of three daughters and two sons, all except the youngest son well and happily married, none, I will venture to say, more so than the wife of my brother Alfred, who, if she were looking over my shoulder as I write, would bestow on this last sentence her cordial approbation.

I have not told you that my pleasure in receiving your letter was enhanced by my having a sweet young sister to enjoy it with me, the youngest of the family, nineteen this day, called after your own *Rosamond*'s Laura,[271] and may I say it? (for I want to introduce you to her as she is) not an unfit counterpart of her namesake. How I wish that I had Prince Houssain's tapestry, how we should seat ourselves upon it and be at your side this afternoon, or perhaps you, who are intimate with the Votaries of Imagination, might more readily be accommodated with his brother's spy-glass, which if you will be so kind as to turn, with the appropriate wish, in this direction, will shew you a lovely and fair

270. Samuel and Richea Gratz Hays.
271. Laura Mordecai (see Appendix B).

haired girl, whose every smile and gesture would engage your love and sympathy; yet in these are portrayed her least attractions. Good sense, good temper, and intelligence with unaffected manners and a remarkably sweet voice both in speaking and singing render her one among the most engaging young persons I have ever known. Now tell me if I do not count largely on your benevolence and good nature, to venture such a picture with scarce one fear of incurring the censure of vanity and egotism. Perhaps if I had always known her, I should hesitate to say so much, but until within the last three months she has been personally almost a stranger to me. I had seen her at long intervals and as a child so that she was burst upon me almost as she might upon you, invested with the charm of novelty. Still I should not fear for you to see and judge for yourself.

I cannot tell you how deeply we were interested in your dear family details, how sincerely we sympathize in your anxiety for the declining health of the amiable Mrs. Fox, and how truly we rejoice in the anticipation of your favourite sister Fanny's restored health. You did not tell me before that good news of your sister Lucy. Pray offer her my friendly congratulations, and extend them to her tender, anxious mother, who will I hope through Almighty goodness have increased cause of thankfulness and the most precious recompense of her watchful care, in the recovery of her daughters.

All that you tell of your brother Pakenham met with eager attention and you should have heard our exclamations of regret at your enumerations, never, we thought, to have an end of losses so difficult, if not impossible to be repaired, and which he bore so well. Some of the articles unless wantonly destroyed would, I suppose, be so valueless to the plunderers that they might possibly be recovered from them. Do tell me if this good fortune is ever his. Those poor horses, how they loved their master and how kindly he must have treated them to inspire such uncommon brute affection. You did not misjudge me by your indulgence in making an extract from that amiable, interesting letter; let me repeat that I thank you, I thank you for allowing me to become thus acquainted with your brother's very self. As a mother it entered into my heart, and I breathed the prayer that such might at some future day be the sentiments, the language of my son.

I am glad to have it in my power to send to Dr. Sprague through the medium of a friend the direction you wish conveyed to him; she will write tomorrow and copy it in her letter. The same friend has promised me to apply to Mr. Prince on her return to N.Y., that is in the course of a month or so, for that favourite flower, which I did not think he would have neglected to send. My friend will receive it and direct it to Messrs. Brown, and I shall rejoice to hear that it once more blooms under your fostering care. If Dr. Sprague sends one it will be all the better, but mine must go too. You mention a work of Mrs. Trollope's of which we had not heard; her mis-representations of American character are so glaring, so vulgar and disgusting, that I hardly think another book of hers would bear publication on this side of the Atlantic. Laura sits by me at this moment reading for the first time her "Refugee in America," unable now and then to resist the temptation of reading aloud some superlatively absurd and ridiculous passage— such for instance as the comparison between Byron and Paulding at the Literary Soiree in Washington or the characteristick and elegant remarks of the lady from Boston in her conversation with Miss Gordon—to say nothing of the scarcity of magistrates and the absence of law in Virginia, or the posse of hungry slaves crowding in to obtain the remains of the traveller's supper. It must surely be seen that she overshoots her mark. I cannot imagine what has excited her virulence, and it is equally difficult to conceive how such gross falsehoods can be relished sufficiently to give encouragement to their propagation. True, all are not like Miss Edgeworth, just, liberal, benevolent; but common sense with the knowledge now generally diffused of American character and manners ought to render futile the attempts of a ridiculous woman to foster or implant national dislike, by presenting the distorted images of her own coarse fancy, which invention enables her to weave into a story of some interest, but which ought to be viewed as it is and taken for just what it is worth, and that is—nothing at all. I did not intend to bestow half so many words on this lady or her writing, but I find from a reference that Laura has just made to one of your letters written just after the Refugees appeared, that I am perhaps for the first time replying fully to your enquiry respecting the authenticity of her descriptions and details. You ask in the letter referred to if the language is American, adding that it is not English. I reply that it is as new to us as to you, and Mrs. Trollope deserves the entire credit of its invention. I do not wonder at your preference of the good single [sic] hearted Vicar of Wakefield to some of the fashionable novels. Henrietta Temple[272] for instance, to like which appears to me a libel on good taste and common decency; putting morality out of the question, we were quite satisfied with what we saw of it in the 1st Volume and felt no inclination to pursue the detail further. D'Israeli has, we know, genius, ingenuity and wit, but when these are employed to decorate base sophistry and to undermine truth and virtuous principle they merit only neglect and contempt. But I am growing cross and disagreeable and who would be so or continue to be so when conversing, even on paper, with Miss E. Let me turn to Col. Napier[273] as a more congenial mind and express my admiration unqualified and genuine of his Peninsular War. Laura has been reading aloud to me those parts which not relating to military tactics we both could comprehend and relish. What can be more deeply interesting than his account from first to last of Sir John Moore? I knew not until now

272. Benjamin Disraeli, *Henrietta Temple, a Love Story* (1836) is notable for not touching on politics.
273. Sir William Francis Patrick Napier (1785–1860), British soldier and military historian. His *History of the War in the Peninsula and the South of France from the Year 1807 to the Year 1814*, undertaken primarily to defend the memory of Sir John Moore against the popularity of Wellington, appeared between 1828 and 1840. It excited extended commentaries by the many officers who had taken part in the Peninsular War.

that the spot where his honoured remains were laid is marked by a monument reared by a soldier, a noble foe! His descriptions of the seiges and sufferings at Saragossa and at Badajoz are fearfully vivid and tho' these are details to which we have often listened in breathless expectation of the event, they acquire new and increased interest from his nervous pen. Do you know Col. Napier? And is he the noble independent man his work would seem to indicate?

I should very much like to see the little work you mention by Mrs. Marcet. All her elementary writings that I have seen are admirable and I dare say her Mary's Grammar is no less so. Tell me if Peter Parley's (alias Samuel Goodrich)[274] works have found their way to England; some of them are extensively used in the elementary schools that have been established in Greece. His style is original and very attractive to children after they become accustomed to it, tho' his language seems at first above their comprehension. His aim seems to be to raise them by degrees to his standard, not to place himself on a level with theirs. His works are various and, filled with all kinds of information, form a juvenile library of themselves.

You speak of Mrs. Fox's children. Are they with you during their mother's absence? I am gratified that my expressions of remembrance, if I may so term it, were acceptable to Mrs. Mary Sneyd. How could I help feeling interested in the welfare of a venerable and amiable lady, ladies rather, whom I have known and loved ever since I read the life of Mr. Edgeworth? Alfred too gave me so picturesque yet so true a description of each member of your family that if placed in the midst of them I think I could not mistake a single individual.

I am glad you are going on with Taking for Granted. Surely, I dare say, if slowly, you have done so much for me and for the

274. Samuel Griswold Goodrich (1793–1860), American author. Under the nom de plume of Peter Parley he supervised the writing of more than one hundred didactic juvenile books. The series grew out of the popularity of *The Tales of Peter Parley about America* (1827).

world that it would be ungenerous to encourage a feeling of impatience tho' we may be allowed to look forward with eager anticipation to the pleasure and profit, which we know to be in store for us. I am going to make a very silly request of you and must be satisfied if you set me down as a mere simpleton when I tell you that I want the solution of a certain riddle contained in Friendship's Offering for 1825. It commences

My first the proud but hapless, *etc*.

You sent me the little Volume and recurring to the riddles contained in it for amusement one evening last winter, this one proved too deep for any Oedipus of us all, and I recollected to have been put to the same nonplus some time before. Pray compassionate my stupidity and add one more to the favours already bestowed on

Your very grateful and affectionate friend
R.L.

Edgeworthstown, July 11th, 1837

My dear Mrs. Lazarus,

Your April letter brought me pleasure, as yours always do, from all the expressions of affection and esteem, and a gratitude quite disproportionate indeed to the very small attentions I have it in my power to shew you; but disproportionate as it may be, it is so sincere and does you so much credit and me so much pleasure that I nothing loth swallow it down with great eagerness. I rejoice to hear that your brother Alfred has married so happily, and that his wife is so justly sensible of her own good fortune in having drawn such a prize in Cupid's lottery in which the blind urchin has so many blanks and never sees to whom he gives his prizes. I am the more interested in your brother's choice because I well recollect the opinion we formed of his domestic character. I recollect too, and it struck both my sister Honora and myself, that he had a just perception of the excellence as wife and mother, of the feminine character, merits, and peculiar grace and softness of our beloved Sophy. She *was*—"*There was*"—and Oh, how many sorrows crowd "Into these two brief words!"

And yet there is a sad sweet pleasure in recalling what she was.

Thank you my dear friend for all your sympathy and all your kind wishes for my Mother being spared the affliction which has fallen upon her, but which has not, thank Heaven, ultimately hurt her health. She underwent great fatigue of body as you may imagine as well as great anxiety of heart. She has the incomparable satisfaction of feeling that no one comfort or soothing to the last moment that her power could afford to her daughter was wanting, that her own bodily or mental power could bestow. And when she was no more [*Sophy Fox*], every thing that the living had wished was performed by that tender mother and by Lucy who was with her in the very last days and able to sustain the great trial.

Lucy is now quite well and is with Fanny at Clifton. Fanny is recovering we trust and we hope that she will come here this autumn as she can come from Clifton to Dublin by water, and from Dublin to Mullingar, or to a town within seven miles of Edgeworthstown, she could travel by the canal, which would not fatigue or hurt her.

Her complaint is not consumptive like poor Sophy's but some internal derangement, I know not what since her poor only child was born dead. I am not very sure that I did not tell you all about Sophy and Fanny before. Excuse me if I did.

Sophy's four children are now in this house under Mrs. E.'s care and their father is also with us. The eldest boy, Maxwell, now eleven years old, is here for his holiday . The two girls Mary Anne and Charlotte and Waller the youngest boy, six years old, are usually under the charge of Harriet Butler and Mr. Butler who, having no children of their own, offered to take care of them. They had been under Harriet's care during their mother's illness, and this and the certainty of their being educated in the very manner she would herself have wished was of the greatest comfort to Sophy. Barry Fox her husband who was most fondly attached to her has left the children with Harriet as he thought their mother would wish it. You know she lives but a morning's drive from us and is often here with them so that Mrs. Edgeworth will have her just grandmamma's share both of the pleasure and the care of these well befriended orphans, orphans by the mother's side as we use the term in Ireland.

Charles Fox the present member for our County is Barry's youngest brother. We are now in daily expectation of a dissolution of Parliament and all the turmoil of a new election. The last, and the *petition* which seated Charles Fox and unseated the Catholic Member who had been elected by illegal votes, proved rather an expensive triumph to Charles. In money it cost *him* two thousand, six hundred pounds, independently of all the public subscriptions of his Conservative party. Charles is not married and has a good fortune and is prudent so that he will at all events hurt no one but himself and I hope will not much injure himself. He is at the Irish Bar and has a profession, excellent character, and attached friends to fall back upon and console him if he be disappointed in the career of ambition. I hope his health will not be injured nor his taste for independence, and if that prayer be granted I shall not regret his being a little impoverished; smart money paid for ambition often saves from severe pain.

The Dowager Queen of England[275] has interested all parties of her subjects by shewing the national feelings of a good woman and good wife and tending the King her husband in his last illness as though she had not been a queen. They had lived together sixteen years. The late Queen was pleased at my request, and with very gracious expressions towards me, to become patronness of the Edgeworthstown Institution for the education of the sons of the distressed clergy. It is going on well under a Committee of gentlemen who manage it. This family has nothing to do

275. Adelaide of Saxe-Meiningen (1792–1849), queen of William IV.

with it, except in heartily wishing it well and subscribing to it and having procured some subscriptions of note, *i.e.* Duke and Duchess of Northumberland, *etc*.

The present little Queen[276] has shewn much grace and discretion in her first appearance in public, in Council, *etc*. She went forward a few steps and gave her hand to the Duke of Wellington when first he appeared to pay his duty, tho' it is said some of her advisers "twitched her royal sleeve to keep her back."

She shewed great feeling and burst into tears on hearing the first burst of acclamation of Long live the Queen Victoria from the assembled crowds when first she shewed herself upon the balcony.

But what gives me more evidence of good feeling was her conduct towards the Duchess of Northumberland who you know had been her governess. When the Duchess appeared, the Queen *ran* to her and threw her arms about her neck. I am not of the opinion of those who think that the character of the Sovereign or Sovereigness has little influence on the public welfare or character. I think it has very considerable influence both by sympathy on the good and wise and by awe and fashion over even the bad or weak or foolish.

We are all anxious to hear what you think of Miss Martineau's work on America. If you have not read it I pray you to read it and to tell me your own opinion most particularly and that of your countrymen. I have read as yet only two volumes. I think it written with more ability than any work I have read on America except De Tocqueville.[277] But it appears to me that all the facts she

276. Victoria (1819–1901) became queen on 20 June 1837, three weeks before the writing of this letter.

277. Alexis de Tocqueville (1805–59). Sent by the French government in 1831 to observe the American penal system, Tocqueville also began to gather data for his masterful analysis *Democracy in America*, which was published in two volumes (1835 and 1840) in both French and an English translation. Considered by some the greatest work ever written about one country by a citizen of another, the book continues to hold interest as a political treatise of great insight and prophetic judgment.

produces—that these are in greater number and more new to me than *any* I have seen in any other publication—*all* tell heavily against a democratic form of government and against the spirit of democracy. While on the contrary Miss Martineau's opinion, theory, arguments, soul and body are in favor of absolute democracy. She would have not only universal and equal suffrage among all men but would have women to have votes and make part of her majority. As far as I can make out her meaning, which by the by is difficult through the first half of the first volume, I understand that she thinks the excellence, safety, permanence and self-correcting power of the American Constitution, or of any government, is founded upon its constant appeal to the *will* of the majority of the people. The will of course includes the sense she thinks. But the point still to be proved, still to be enquired into, is whether the majority of *numbers* necessarily includes the majority of sense, judgment, moral feeling, and all that should form the legislative and governing preponderance in any nation.

Miss Martineau has brought a list of atrocities committed under Republican form of government such as I had never seen arrayed against a Republican government of such long standing and experience before, and her saying that all these are small evils because they will all be corrected in time by the wisdom of the majority when it comes to rejudge the whole and repair injustice, *etc.*, *may* prove true or *may* not; that is still to be proved. Meanwhile here are "the damning facts" as *Othello* would say; as a man of Colour or a Black *his* language naturally recurs and forcible it is. I agree with Miss Martineau in all she says on the Slave question and on the inconsistency of American liberty and slavery.

I know this is a dangerous, a tabooed subject. Even with your dear brother Alfred, I saw he could not look at it as we do. I can hardly believe that in the American States! in a Republican government *gentlemen* burst into the post office and burnt or suppressed letters and newspapers or public papers![278] And that a

278. A little after midnight of 29–30 July, 1835, a mob entered the Charleston, S. C., post office and seized copies of the abolitionist papers *Emancipator* and *Human Rights*.

member of Council of one of the States took upon himself to approve of the postmaster's suppressing all letters and papers concerning the Slave question.

As to the folly it seems to me about as great as in the child's proverb, "Talk of the devil and he will appear," or Talk of an evil and it will exist. Very like putting a hat upon the crater of a volcano to prevent an eruption. Too like what is done at all pusillanimous courts by coward courtiers to weak monarchs, not talking of the danger till it bursts. So it was the last time with Charles X.[279] He did not know the dispositions of the people till the mob was past quelling. No matter whether it be a single sovereign or a Republic that so deceives itself, the fate will danger equal.

I hope Miss Martineau is mistaken in her *facts*, or that her *theory* in favor of the omnipotence and infallibility of appeal to majorities of the people will not mislead your wiser countrymen.

I have let out my opinion—oh don't let it prevent you from giving me yours and especially telling me about the facts. I think she has a fine, brave spirit, and I admire her indignation against *flatterers* of the people. But in all democracies there must be flatterers of the people; the many-headed tyrant loves flattery and is more voracious of it in quantities than the one-mouthed and two-eared *can* be. And all government by majority of numbers *must* become democratic.

I do not think I ever wrote so much on politics before in my life.

I am very much obliged to you for having sent or for intending to send me a spotless anemone. I have written today to Messrs. J. & W. Browne of Liverpool to warn them that such a plant may arrive for me and to entreat the ladies of their house to take care of it and water and tend it for me till I can have it by private hand carefully. I am particularly fond of it as [*was*] Sophy Fox and it was really an emblem of herself.

Thank you for forwarding the address to Dr. Sprague. In

279. Charles X (1757–1836), king of France from 1824 to 1830. His reactionary policies resulted in his loss of the throne in July 1830 to his demagogic cousin, Louis-Philippe.

consequence he sent me a very kind letter and a parcel containing valuable books, his own Lectures, Buckminster's Life and Sermons,[280] which I like much, and an Eulogy by Dr. Sprague on a Mrs. [*blank*] and on LaFayette.[281] That on Lafayette I like much for its freedom from exaggeration. But between you and I [*sic*] as I have also told Dr. Sprague I can never forgive General Lafayette for going to sleep at the moment when he ought to have been wide awake, and leaving a little gate unguarded at Versailles by which the mob rushed up to the Queen's bedchamber and massacred the life-guards. I wonder Lafayette with the feeling and conscience which I really believe him to have had could ever forgive himself for this sleep. Ah! que ne mourit il a Versailles![282] But then he would not have had your splendid feast of gratitude in America, which covers your country at least with true moral glory.

I like Mr. Buckminster's Sermons (on women particularly), independently, believe me if you can, of my own name being in such good company and so honorably and liberally mentioned. I came upon that passage quite in surprise! and could hardly believe it was *my* name when I saw it. By the by, *Maria Edgeworth* always looks to me, when I meet it accidentally in print, as a foreign German name and I feel like the little woman in the nursery story, whose petticoats were cut short when she was asleep, and who, on wakening and finding herself in that condition, sang, "Oh, says the little woman, this is none of I."

But I am sure of my identity, and of my being truly the thing I say I am, when I write that I am

Yours my dear friend, Sincerely and affectionately
Maria Edgeworth.

280. Samuel Cooper Thacker, *Sermons of the Late Joseph S. Buckminster. With a Memoir of his Life and Character* (1815).
281. William Buell Sprague. *An Oration Commemorative of the Late General Lafayette Pronounced before the Military and Civic Societies of the City of Albany, in the South Dutch Church, July 24, 1834* (1834).
282. In the early hours of 6 October 1789, Lafayette at Versailles lay down in his clothes for a short rest. Later historians are kinder than ME in her remark: "Ah, if he had only died at Versailles."

[P.S.] I am very sorry that I have not here and cannot procure before I send this letter Friendships offering to answer your riddle question. I will get it if I can before my next. Continue to enclose to The Clerk of the Council in Waiting, Council Office, London. Write the direction beside the seal of your letter to me, none on the usual side, which is left for the gentlemen to write the [*forwarding address*].

[*Copy*]

Wilmington, March 18th, 1838

I have just re-read not for the second time only, a delightful letter from my dear kind friend which has been in my possession since—yes truth bids me own, ever since October! Was it not then valued or regarded? Oh yes, most highly, and yet it has remained unanswered.

An unusually large family and a constant succession of visiters have occupied the winter I fear most unprofitably unless we may account the exercise of self-command, essential to the offices of kindness and good breeding, as of some avail and so it doubtless is; yet it requires a greater share of generosity than falls to my lot to bestow freely, unreluctantly the time which I value on those who never perhaps took care of *a minute* in their lives. Well no matter, I only mention this as a way of accounting to myself for this long silence, for you who can never have experienced it could hardly comprehend the feeling that you were incapable of collecting your thoughts to write a decent letter to an indulgent and much loved friend.

It was from the letter now before me that I first heard the painful tidings which I feared it must contain, of the loss of your sweet and amiable sister Mrs. Fox. Time has now lent his assuasive power to heal the wounds of suffering affection while the memory of her gentle virtues remains to be dwelt on with chastened delight. My brother Alfred heard of the event with sincere concern; he thought of her most high[ly] in the character of both wife and mother, and we are both interested in knowing that her children are happily situated with judicious and affectionate friends who will rear them even as their mother herself would have done. I do hope that you have had Mrs. Wilson with you and that her health is better. Think of me as feeling a sincere interest in your troubles and your pleasures, hoping always that the latter may predominate or that when misfortunes occur, as to all of human race they must, that there may be as in the present case alleviating circumstances, which may contribute in well governed minds to render them supportable.

You relate to me several pleasing anecdotes of your youthful queen whose character presents itself in a very attractive point of view, yielding to the amiable impulses of gratitude and patriotick (is the term admissible?) admiration. I am entirely of your opinion as to the influence of the character of the sovereign over that of the subject, especially under a limited monarchy, where less awe being inspired, less distance preserved, there may be and is greater assimilation in manners and greater inducements for imitation. She is fortunate in commencing her reign at a period when both internal and external commotions are either quelled or lulled into temporary tranquillity, giving her time to investigate and become acquainted with the duties of her station before being called upon to encounter any of its attendant difficulties.

Now let me turn to your request respecting Miss Martineau of whose, in many respects, sensible book I ought sooner to have endeavoured to give my opinion. At the time you wrote, you had read but two volumes (our American editions are comprised in two) and as the last part of the work is in many respects the most objectionable, I think it in some measure detracted from your good opinion of it as a whole. She is far more of an Ultra in her republican or Democratick opinions than I or any of my friends consider reasonable. The majority, the multitude are not the wise as has been proved in too many instances in which they have obtained an undue ascendancy in the control of important affairs, and Miss M. is I fear mistaken in believing that there is in a Democracy a self correcting power which will appear when the urgency of the case demands it. I should rather say, that in times of difficulty and danger some Master spirit, not of the multitude, arises, to whose voice, when unable to quiet the disturbance [they] themselves have caused, they are induced (I may not say, compelled) to yield. Witness Mr. Clay[283] and the contest for States Rights in South Carolina. Mr. Clay is not only an able politician but an honest man and a true Patriot. May Providence ever provide us with such men in the hour of need. I believe that our Federal Constitution under the restrictions contemplated by its founders is admirably adapted to promote the welfare and secure the independence of our country. Those restrictions being laid aside as they were in too many instances by our late President, Executive Patronage extended, and the majority in consequence influenced by motives of self interest, publick credit suffers, and it is still to be seen whether the evil can correct itself. Now my dear friend I trust I have not been writing incomprehensible trash; I wish I could send you a speech of Mr. Clay's just published on the subject of the Treasury, and it would give you clearer views than can be obtained from either Miss Martineau or your humble servant. As to Miss M's. opinion that marriage is the sole object in life of an American woman, I can only say that we do not understand the meaning of her assertion. True we are not called on to mingle in elections or affairs of State and we are so mean spirited as to have no ambition to do so and even to be perfectly satisfied with the limits by which she seems to think our feminine liberties are bounded. We thank her for her commiserations, tho' in fact until informed by her, we were scarcely aware of our imbecility. We walk much less it is true than English women, probably because we have not the temptation of adjacent villages

283. Henry Clay (1777–1852), American statesman. At the time RML wrote, he was in the United States Senate and about to become a candidate, for the third time, for the presidency.

with the concomitant inducements of faultless roads or shaded lanes, but we find ourselves not incompetent to exertion in the performance of domestick duties, of which all agree in admitting that we have a super-abundant share, or of those still more arduous in the chamber of sickness, which cannot unfrequently occur in a country where hired nurses are almost unknown. Miss Martineau's account of the atrocities committed in some of the Western States under the title of *Lynching*, tho' greatly, very absurdly exaggerated, has its foundation in fact. Those states imperfectly and recently settled by the ignorant and lawless, many squatters, many unprincipled fortune seekers, scattered over a large extent of country with magistrates distant, churches rare and religion still rarer, have presented instances of cruelty and irregular procedure equally horrible to us as to you, but this is a state of affairs which *will* correct *itself*. An evidence of want of subjection to law will cause the law to be more rigidly enforced, and under the influence of social and judicial regulations order will speedily take the place of brutal violence.

I have heard but one opinion expressed of Miss Martineau's book as a whole, and that is wonder that a woman of good sense could be misled or deceived in so many particulars, or that a woman (not a *lady* as she says we mawkishly use the term), a woman of probity could make assertions which have scarcely a shadow of truth. Witness for instance "the frequent enactment of the Auld Robin Gray story"—or "the habit of *intemperance*" (what could she mean by so broad an insult?) not infrequent among women of station and education in the most enlightened parts of the country, the ladies of Boston being afterwards plainly designated—equally untrue and disgusting. Then the indelicacies which she seems to feel bound by the rights of woman to give utterance were very repugnant to our over-indulged effeminate ear and, tho' she might hear it with surprise, were equally condemned by the lords of creation, from respectful submission to our whims no doubt.

I don't want to be cross, but she did sometimes put me out of patience. Now to turn to the slave question. I and very many others agree with you and Miss Martineau on the inconsistency of slavery with American liberty, but before we condemn in toto we must attend to the arrangement of historical facts. Was it the American states proud of their freedom and boasting of their rights who employed slave ships to go to Africa and bring to them hewers of wood and drawers of water? No it was English Colonies planted in America under grants from the king of Great Brittain who entailed this curse upon our land. In process of time these colonies, being denied what they deemed their rights by the mother country, laboured successfully to throw off her government, and declared themselves an Independent people. They were free from the rule of any other nation and they set about forming a government of their own. Could they at that time have loved liberty for itself alone and looked with an equally humane and philosophic eye on the miseries of the Slave and the Slave holder, all had now been well, but such ideas had not then entered into the mind even of a Wilberforce, and it would have been expecting too much from poor human nature that a people, an infant people, impoverished by war, uncertain of the issue of a newly formed constitution and employing all their faculties to maintain the advantages so hardly gained, should say, the South to the North, we would be wholly free, give us half the worth of our slaves and we will relinquish the other half and labour and till the ground with our own hands (a Utopian supposition), but the North must have replied, we are ourselves bankrupt, our continental money is worse than blank paper and our common country has no treasury and is involved in debt; we cannot assist you nor can you relinquish the only medium by which your shattered fortunes can hope to be repaired. Will you not allow that this true statement does in part excuse the inconsistency? That the system is an evil, that by it are produced a host of minor evils, is a point readily conceded; whether it is criminal in us to retain our slaves is yet to be considered, and to proceed reasonably and deliberately I would ask what would be their condition were they to be freed tomorrow. Ignorant and inconsiderate as they are, they would for the most part be unable to support or take care of themselves; they would be most uncomfortable as well as a burden to the community. Miss Martineau presents a true picture in the note which she extracts from a southern publication in which the lady is described as giving medicines to her servants and dressing their wounds with her own hands. There are few of them who will perform these offices of kindness for each other, tho' without compulsion they will, I scarce know why, shew an inclination to attend on the whites under similar circumstances. But to return, those who are most earnest on the subject of Abolition cannot point out the necessary means for its accomplishment; it would not surely be by rendering slaves discontented and instigating them to rise up in arms against their masters. They must then be exterminated in self defence. Yet this has been the means, Miss Martineau's assertion notwithstanding, by which many of those mistaken enthusiasts at the North sought to irritate the minds of our slaves. Eastern pedlars were commissioned to carry pamphlets to distribute among them filled with prints of slaves suffering under the lash and degraded in various ways with which they themselves were unacquainted. These tracts were of a most mischievous nature and calculated only to do harm. It was after the insurrection at Southampton, Virginia, and at a time when both North and South Carolina were similarly threatened that the outrage was committed on the post office in Charleston. That it was an outrage all admit, that it was sanctioned by circumstances some will argue, that its being approved by a member of the State council was an unprecedented stretch of authority none will deny. You are mistaken in supposing that this was an effort to conceal the existing evil or the possible danger from ourselves; aware of its existence the effort was made to avert or at least to prevent its being accelerated.

I do hope that means will be adopted for the gradual and judicious emancipation of slaves. The Legislature of Kentucky, a wealthy slave holding state west of and adjoining Virginia, have a bill for considering means for this purpose now under consideration; the result will be important to all its sister states. I have long averred that I would willingly undergo the hardship and inconvenience of waiting on myself were that the only alternative, to be freed from the charge and responsibility of living in a slave state. Miss Martineau has I think been deceived in many of her statements, at least they were as new and strange to me and to all with whom I have conversed on the subject as they could be to you, and some of her negro anecdotes I might venture to pronounce absolutely false, so little do they concur with our knowledge and experience of facts. I marked many passages in her book intending to note them in my reply to your letter but I believe it would be useless; your own excellent discrimination has doubtless enabled you to detect errors and contradictions which are to my mind palpable and self-evident. I have written truly and candidly as you desire, and though you may think my views too lenient, you will at least be possessed of the facts on which they are grounded, and I know you will say how far you think I may be blinded by habit or early prejudice.

I am mighty glad as we Carolinians say to find that we agree exactly in opinion as to La Fayette's conduct at Versailles; as an American I have felt grateful for his warm-hearted and disinterested services, but as a brave man, an able commander, and a loyal subject, I have always thought that on that occasion he might be weighed in the balance and found wanting.

Buckminster's Sermons I have never seen. I must try to get them. Your parallel of yourself and the little woman and the pedlar made me laugh.

My friend Miss Leppitt who forwarded for me your address to Dr. Sprague enquired in a letter the other day whether the spotless anemone had reached you safely. I do hope it has, though there has seemed to be a spell of misfortune on that same flower. If you have it not, be sure to tell me; I will take measures which cannot fail. I have not received Mary's Grammar nor the volume of Friendship's offering which you mention. Tell me if they were addressed to the care of DePeyster and Whitmarch, New York.

Edgeworthstown, June 16th, 1838

My dear kind Mrs. Lazarus,

It gave me heartfelt pleasure to see your handwriting again after so long a silence, and to find that hand, head, and heart were the same as ever good, clear, and affectionate.

Before I go any further and forget my own great interests let me observe to you that the spotless anemone you intended for me has never arrived or been heard of. The moment I received your letter first announcing it last year I wrote to Messrs. Brown at Liverpool requesting them whenever it should arrive to have it well taken care of and looked to after its voyage and forwarded well packed to Ireland, and I took precautions for its good reception in Dublin and safe conduct here. But Messrs. Brown in a letter received from them only last week assure me that no such thing has been heard of, but that if any such at any time arrive, they will attend to my request.

Now if you are not quite disheartened and sick of me and the spotless anemone you may try again. I am not superstitious, but I almost fancy that evil fate follows this poor little spotless flower or that it is too good to live and flourish in this world. My dear sister Sophy with whom I divided the plant which did reach me could not keep it; it died as she did.

Her children for whom you so kindly inquire are quite well and going on as well as heart could wish under their Aunt Harriet and her husband's care. Mary Anne, the eldest girl, is really beautiful and all of them as far as I can judge, of prepossessing appearance and with attaching qualities and good sense and early good principles. I have been spending two months most happily with them. I rejoice to hear from you of your own objects of family affection (especially of your brother who is near to us always from having been once with us and really one of us, even in the short time he stayed at Edgeworthstown) are all well.

You will find the 7th volume of Sir Walter Scott's Life[284] heartrending. It is really the most pathetic history I ever read. It is told chiefly by himself, and when that great and good mind failed at last, his son-in-law and true and tender friend continues the tale when Scott could no longer write his own history. Lockhart has fulfilled his most difficult, most delicate task with judgment and taste; the world does justice to him as a biographer, and as a man. He has risen in public opinion and what was more extraordinary he has raised Sir Walter Scott in public opinion by these courageous truth-telling memoirs. Some there are who blame the Biographer for letting any of his hero's faults be seen. But they surely neither know the duty of a biographer nor the use of biography to our own or succeeding ages, nor yet do they know what gives life and interest to Memoirs even for the mere purpose of pleasure and for their own amusement. What gives the strong, the irresistible interest the reader feels in these volumes of Lockhart is the perfect truth. We feel that we are reading of a human creature, with weaknesses and faults that keep him in human nature however superior in powers, wonderful in genius, and noble in nature. Sir Walter Scott did perhaps love the pride, pomp, and circumstance of glorious life too much, had a passion for old castles and old furniture and all that belongs to the romance of feudal or chivalrous times or Scottish Clan times. He loved Scotland with all her faults and Abbotsford with all its magnificence. It was the realisation of the early dreams of his poetic imagination. All this led him into extravagance, alas, and what is worse into associating himself with John Ballantyne and others unworthy of him and led him into all those printing and commercial speculations at once imprudent and degrading, degrading the more because he carried them on still feeling them to

284. J. G. Lockhart, *Memoirs of the Life of Sir Walter Scott*, 7 vols. (1837–38).

be degrading, ashamed of them as commercial speculation, another weakness and leading to greater and greater. How he could keep all his concerns in partnership with Ballantyne and Constable so long concealed from his family I cannot conceive. It seems incompatible with his natural openness of temper and the affectionate terms with which he lived with his wife and children. I am afraid there must have been, as Lockhart says, an inherent love of mystery confirmed by long habit, and a false shame as to his aristocracy which would have suffered by its being known to be concerned in trade, even printing. Till I read Lockhart's book I did not know that the law in Britain will not allow any man at the Bar to be of any trade or engaged in any sort of commercial business. This is some reason or cause comprehensible for Scott's concealment of the fact. But much his friends must wish and bitterly I wish that he never had done this. It is plain that he was most abominably used by his associates, that they played upon his generous nature and at last destroyed him body and mind. His exertions to redeem his fault were superhuman, and from the most generous, most noble motives!

My mind has been so filled with this subject that you must forgive me for pouring it out to you thus. It may shew you how much I depend upon your sympathy and feel that our minds will go together upon all these points. Pray tell when you have read the 6th and 7th volumes what you feel and do not be afraid of being too long. See how long I am!

I am rather sorry that Lockhart put in so much about *mystery* and so much that looked like panegyric in the last chapter. I think it was unnecessary. The readers were in possession of all the facts and had drawn their own conclusions, and the repetition being unnecessary I felt not only wearisome but weakening the previous effect.

I thank you for all you told me of your opinion of Miss Martineau's Work on America. Indignation comes with peculiar force from one of your mild temper and well regulated and well proportioned mind. I agree with all you say, and yet I think I give her more credit for the courage with which she has put forth what she *believed* to be truth, however mistaken. She means to be true tho' she positively asserts what is false. Her mind is as deaf as her ear,[285] and when positiveness and deafness go together they mutually exacerbate and exaggerate each other's infirmity and fault.

Nevertheless she has lately published a very amiable little book of advice to the deaf, which I pray you get and read because it will shew you some of the more [*the word "feminine" crossed out*] pleasing parts of her mind. I erased the word *feminine* because she would feel it as an affront applied to herself; you know she says she hates the nauseous "distinction sometimes made between lady and woman." She certainly never made practically any more than theoretically any such distinction in her own case.

I have not yet read her new Appendix work on America, but I hope you have and if you tell me it is worth reading, I will read it, not else. I can wait. An old gentleman friend of mine lately said with great naivete apparently but much arch sense and sarcasm, "I don't like to read books I cannot like. Some people like it particularly." That is some people's greatest pleasure in reading is to find fault. Not your case my dear Mrs. Lazarus, nor mine.

I have just been reading Whewell's History of the Inductive Sciences,[286] a book with which an article in the Edinburgh Review finds every fault that could possibly be found, and yet I admire the work highly and am sure you would if you had time to read or look over it, for it is the general history of the progress and causes of the progress of science or its retardment which I admire, not the particular histories of each science which no one man could possibly do accurately and which Whewell declares he does not attempt. The review is by Sir David Brewster and though I like him as my private friend I do not like the review

285. Miss Martineau turned to writing rather than teaching because of her deafness.

286. William Whewell (1794–1866), English general scientist and professor at Cambridge; *History of the Inductive Sciences: from the Earliest to the Present Time* (1837).

nor that jealous spirit which it betrays, *national* and personal. Sir David is perpetually suspecting others of a malicious intent to rob him or his country (Scotland) of the fame of inventions. I once told him apropos to some instance of this that I wondered a man who possessed a diamond mine could be vexed at seeing a pair of diamond buckles on another man's shoes even supposing he had taken them from his mine; I thought it would be unworthy of him to disturb the whole world with the cry of Stop Thief, except for the pure love of public justice. If Sir David could put his hand upon his heart and swear that were his sole motive for the trouble he takes in prosecuting offenders, it would be all well and all noble and becoming. But I fear the truth is exactly what he announced to me: "I could not bear to see another man figuring in my shoe-buckles even if I had the diamond mine as you say." Besides Sir David has a real abstract love for getting into hot water, and he boils it for himself and to the scalding point keeps it up continually, continually.

Frazer's account of the Persian Princes' visit to England is very entertaining, tho' Frazer himself is not much, nor they either.[287] But it is curious to see what things struck them in our countries.

My family has been much gratified with an account which an American gentleman, Mr. Thatcher,[288] published in the newspapers of his visit to Edgeworthstown, I presume you have seen it as Mr. Thatcher's letters were published first in an American paper—from the *Boston Transcript* I think we had them. Several of Mr. Thatcher's accounts of his visits to various places in England and Scotland are very entertaining and curious to us, from the very same cause that the Persian Princes' remarks are

287. James Baillie Fraser (1783–1856), Scottish traveler and author. When Reza Kuli Mirza and Nejeff Kuli Mirza, the exiled Persian princes, visited England, he was appointed to attend them during their stay. He wrote numerous accounts of his travels; ME here refers to his *Narrative of the Residence of the Persian Princes in London in 1835 and 1836*, 2 vols. (1838).

288. Benjamin Bussy Thatcher (1809–40), American writer. He traveled in Europe for his health in 1836–38 and contributed articles to British and American periodicals.

matters of curiosity. But none of Mr. Thatcher's please us so well of course as that from Edgeworthstown because that is all praise, infinitely more than I at least deserve. I am sure I had not any opportunity while he was here of paying him that hospitable attention I always wish to pay to foreign travellers—Americans particularly—having always received so much kindness and substantial service from Americans in their helping our poor Irish emigrants and every individual I have ever recommended to the protection of my American friends.

Mr. Thatcher seemed quite overpowered with headache while he was here, so ill that neither of the two days did he come to dinner. We thought he was actually dying. Little did we think he would write about any of us or tell about anything he saw or heard, for we conceived he could not in his sad sick state, and with one eye closed up in agony, see, hear, or understand anything.

Once a lurking smile and look of humor in his eye made me half suspect there was somewhat of the rogue in him. But I don't pretend to *say*. I only thank him for saying so well, so kindly of us. He is one of your American Professors I since find and himself an admired author—*History of the Indian Chiefs*—I see in the North American Review.

Mr. and Mrs. Ticknor[289] from Boston are delightful people, literary, highly cultivated, admirably polished, well bred, high principled, benevolent and liberal without any wild, impracticable reform notions. And most domestic and affectionate, lovers of home and of their country on comparison, reflection, and choice. We have to regret this last for our own selfish part because they were in such a hurry to get home to their own country that they could not, on their return from a two year tour on the continent, pay us a farewell visit as they had half prom-

289. George Ticknor (1791–1871), American writer and professor of modern literature at Harvard. He and Mrs. Ticknor visited Edgeworthstown in August 1835 for several days. ME compared Mr. Ticknor's conversation favorably with that of "the fashionable dinner-lions of London." He left an account of his visit which is included in *Life, Letters, and Journals of George Ticknor* (Boston, 1876).

ised they would. Wherever they are, Heaven bless them!

Forgive me I know you will, if, as it now strikes me, I have said all this to you before of these favorites of ours. I wish you could come yourself. Send us any one you love and esteem and believe me very affectionately and sincerely yours.

Maria Edgeworth

[P.S.] We are in hopes my sister Fanny, Mrs. Wilson, will be with us this summer. She is much better, Lucy quite well, Aunt Mary in her 87th year now walking about among the flowers before the library window, leaning on Honora.

Mrs. Ticknor was particularly struck with that dear, venerable aunt and with her niece's fond and never ceasing, never prominent, attentions to her. Mrs. Edgeworth gone today to Trim, thirty miles off, to see her daughter Harriet Butler and her grandchildren, Sophy's children.

Pray tell me what is meant by *Broomcorn*[290] and whether it is a common crop in America? In No. 79 of the North American Review it is mentioned that Franklin introduced Broomcorn from a single grain imported from a cornwhisk, and thence all the vast plantations of Broomcorn, the reviewer observes, so common in many parts of America. Pray enclose in your next one seed of Broomcorn for Ireland in return.

290. A variety of grass resembling Indian corn used in making brooms and brushes. The *corn* in the word may have led ME to think that it produced an edible grain to solve the problem of hunger in Ireland.

Epilogue

A note on the back of the last letter in Mr. Lazarus's hand says: "My dear children, this letter was not received before you were motherless! But it was replied to by several of your aunts and your Uncle Alfred and your father too who sent the poor anemone and the broom corn with a letter to dear kind Miss Edgeworth."

Rachel Mordecai Lazarus died on 23 June 1838 at the home of her brother and sister, Samuel and Ellen Mordecai, in Petersburg, Virginia. She had stopped there on the way from Wilmington to see her sick and dying father, Jacob Mordecai, in Richmond. This circumstance peculiarly touched Maria Edgeworth; she wrote a condoling friend in July 1838: "Thank you my dear for your sympathy about poor dear kind Mrs. Lazarus. I do indeed feel that I have lost in her an affectionate friend. I enclose her brother's touching letter giving an account of her death, a death so worthy of her life—in doing her duty—and proving her affection for her father." The death of her own father was clearly in Maria Edgeworth's mind. On 10 August 1838 she wrote a relative concerning Mrs. Lazarus: "Ever since the year 1814 she has been my constant correspondent and friend I may truly say. I am surrounded by proofs of her kindness, proofs of her continually thinking of everything that could gratify my tastes or give pleasure to my feelings and my heart. My father thought her the most sensible and amiable of all my American friends."

Maria Edgeworth wrote Mr. Lazarus on 22 November 1838: "I was much obliged by your kind letter and by the assurance it gave me that my friend Mrs. Lazarus's husband is satisfied of the sincerity of my regard for her and of the tender regret I feel for her loss. At any age the loss of such a friend must be deeply felt; at my time of life [*seventy-one*] it must be felt as irreparable even by one who is blessed with many dear friends and most excellent and kind relations.

"You do me justice in perceiving that I fully appreciated her qualities and the noble simplicty and truth of her character, and I rejoice that you and her surviving family feel this wish to continue their correspondence with me." After thanking Mr. Lazarus in detail for the plants and their conveyance, she tells him of the marriage of her sister Honora to Captain Francis Beaufort, hydrographer to the admiralty. She contined: "Be so good to tell Captain Mordecai (if you write to him) of my sister Honora's marriage. I think he appreciated her as well as my sister Sophy Fox who is no more.

Pray remember me most kindly to Mrs. Lazarus' family and your own and believe me dear Sir

Your obliged and grateful
Maria Edgeworth"

George Washington Mordecai of Raleigh, brother of Rachel and Alfred, visited Edgeworthstown the following year. By him Maria sent mementos to the children of Rachel and to Mr. Lazarus. The latter wrote thanking her on 10 August 1839. After family and plant details, he added, "I was glad, and so were all the family, to hear that your sister Honora was happily married and trust that the fondest anticipations have and will be fully realized. The marriage state is, in my opinion, though you have not shared your faith, the one in which the greatest sum of happiness may be enjoyed."

Aaron Lazarus survived his wife Rachel by only three years. He died on 2 October 1841, he too while visiting in Petersburg, Virginia, where Rachel was buried. On her deathbed, Rachel Mordecai Lazarus had become a convert to Christianity. Maria Edgeworth's "Jewish" Berenice Montenero, described in *Har-*

rington with words taken intact from Rachel Mordecai's first letter to Maria Edgeworth, was revealed at the end of the novel to be a Christian. Rachel Mordecai Lazarus was buried in old Blandford Church Cemetery. Aaron Lazarus, dying in the faith of his fathers, was buried in the Hebrew Cemetery in Richmond.

In 1837, when Maria Edgeworth took up the study of Spanish, her brother Francis laughed at her for learning a new language at the age of seventy. She continued to savor life for eleven years after the death of Rachel Lazarus. She read the new novelists, Peacock, Dickens, Balzac. When she went to London in December of 1840, she wrote the Ticknors in Boston: "I have chosen to go at this quiet time of year as I particularly wish not to encounter the bustle and dissipation and lionizing of London. For tho' I am such a minnikin lion now and so old, literally without teeth or claws, still there be, that might rattle at the gate to make me get up and come out and stand up to play tricks for them." But she was back in London again in 1843–44, attending the opening of Parliament and watching the young Queen Victoria enter the House of Lords on the arm of Prince Albert, dining at Lambeth Palace with the archbishop of Canterbury, putting the redoubtable Sydney Smith to rights about Irish affairs. The latter would write: "She does not say witty things, but there is such a perfume of wit runs through all her conversation as makes it very brilliant."

But the drama of Everyman was drawing to a close. Her brother Francis died in 1846 and her beloved Fanny in 1848. And a merciful Providence accorded Maria Edgeworth her three wishes concerning her own death: that she would die at home, that she would not burden her family with a long illness, and that Mrs. Edgeworth would be close by. On the morning of 22 May 1849 she went for a drive as usual. Feeling a pain in her side on her return, she went to her room to lie down. When Mrs. Edgeworth looked in a little later, she found Maria lying peacefully dead.

Appendix A
The Edgeworth Family

The Edgeworths were originally from Edgeworth, now Edgeware, in Middlesex, England. Two brothers, Edward and Francis Edgeworth, went to Ireland during the reign of Elizabeth, probably under the patronage of Essex and Cecil, about 1583. The elder became bishop of Down and Connor in 1593 and died without issue. Francis married Jane, daughter of Sir Francis Tuite of Sonna, Westmeath. A great-great grandson of this union was Richard Lovell Edgeworth (1744–1817), son of Jane Lovell and Richard Edgeworth, of Edgeworthstown (Mostrim), County Longford, Ireland. Christina Colvin, who has studied the primary source materials related to the Edgeworths in the greatest depth, writes of him:

R. L. Edgeworth described himself as a middling country gentleman; at his death in 1817 he had an income of about £3,700–4,000 p.a., but when he moved to Ireland in 1782 it had been perhaps half that amount. While he lived in England he had been a member of the Lunar Society of Birmingham, whose primary interest was in the application of science to industry. His own special interests were chiefly in transport engineering, the design of roads, and vehicles, but he was also deeply concerned with the theory of education and became a member of the Irish Committee on Education. He was co-author with his daughter of *Practical Education* and *Professional Education*. Because of his wider opportunities as a man he was a more interesting and open-minded person than Maria, but his reputation has been much obscured by the pompous prefaces he added to her works, and by the fact that, for differing reasons, he was not a popular man either in Ireland or in London society: in Ireland he was too educated and too unconvivial for his neighbours and, while participating in local and national politics, rejected their notorious venality; in London he was thought by many to be an egotistic and boisterous bore. But his lively mind and warm-hearted affection won him the devotion of his own family and his influence on Maria cannot be over-estimated. If he taught her to moralize he also passed on to her his own interest in the Irish, their way of life, and their turns of phrase, and without his constant encouragement it is unlikely that she would have published anything. (*Maria Edgeworth: Letters from England 1813–1844* [Oxford; Oxford University Press, 1971], pp. xxxii–iii.)

The *Memoirs of Richard Lovell Edgeworth, Esq.*, begun by himself and concluded by his daughter, Maria Edgeworth (2 vols., London) appeared in 1820. He is the subject of Desmond Clarke's *The Ingenious Mr. Edgeworth* (London; Oldbourne, 1965). He was born at Bath, 31 May, 1744. He married four times and was the father of twenty-two children.

Richard Lovell Edgeworth, while a student at Oxford, first married, in 1783, Anna Maria Elers, daughter of Mary Hungerford and Paul Elers of Black Bourton, Oxfordshire, and by her had two sons and three daughters:

Richard (May 1764–96), born in Oxfordshire, emigrated to America where he settled on the upper Pee Dee River on the North Carolina–South Carolina line and married Elizabeth Knight in 1788. He had three sons, Nathaniel Lovell, Achilles Sneyd, and Richard Lovell. Descendants of these three, widely scattered in the United States, are the only bearers of the name Edgeworth descended from Richard Lovell Edgeworth.

Lovell (1766), died an infant.

Maria (1 January 1768–22 May 1849), born in Oxfordshire, died in Edgeworthstown, Ireland. The most recent literary biography is Marilyn Butler's *Maria Edgeworth* (Oxford: Oxford University Press, 1972). Two short treatises give excellent overviews: P. H. Newby, *Maria Edgeworth* (Denver: Alan Swallow, 1950) and James Newcomer, *Maria Edgeworth* (Lewisburg: Bucknell University Press, 1973).

Emmeline (1770–1847), married (1802) John King or Konig of Clifton, a surgeon of Swiss origin who was assistant to Dr. Beddoes of the Pneumatic Institution. She had two daughters, Zoe and Emmeline.

Anna Maria (March 1773–1824), was born in London and married (1794) the celebrated physician Thomas Beddoes (1760–1808), who took his degree in medicine at Oxford and later lectured there. In 1798 he established the Pneumatic Institution at Clifton, near Bristol, to study the treatment of disease with gases. He published widely and strove to popularize medical knowledge. Anna Edgeworth was regarded by her family as flighty, but she made a favorable impression on others. Sir Humphrey Davy (1778–1829), at one time an assistant to Dr. Beddoes and a frequent visitor in Edgeworthstown, described Dr. and Mrs. Beddoes: ''He is one of the most original men I ever saw—nothing characteristic *externally* of genius or science; extremely silent, and in a few words, a bad companion. Mrs. Beddoes is the reverse of Dr. Beddoes—extremely cheerful, gay, and witty. She is one of the most pleasant women I ever met with." After Dr. Beddoe's death in 1808, Anna and her children, Thomas Lovell, the poet (1803–49), Charles Henry, a sailor, Anna Frances Emily, and Mary Eliza, were frequent guests at Edgeworthstown. Anna Edgeworth Beddoes died in Florence in 1824 and her daughters went to live at Edgeworthstown.

Richard Lovell Edgeworth married second, in June 1773, Honora Sneyd, daughter of Major Edward Sneyd of Lichfield, England. Her name had been associated romantically with that of Major Andre, the British spy hanged in America. By his second wife Mr. Edgeworth had one son and one daughter:

Honora (1774–90). Not the Honora mentioned in the letters.

Lovell (1775–1842), died without issue. During the Napoleonic Wars, British subjects resident in France were treated as prisoners of war; Lovell was an internee for eleven years and his health was impaired. He inherited his father's estate in 1817 and became trustee for his younger brothers and sisters as well as for Maria. His school (1818–28) at Edgeworthstown was something of a miracle in its time, an Irish school that knew no distinction of class or creed. Unknown to his family, however, he had become an alcoholic in France, and by December 1825 his financial affairs were in a disastrous state. He appointed Maria his agent, and she desperately strove to hold on to the family estate, never allowing the first piece of property to go outside the family. Lovell finally was forced to give up his school and to retire to England where he lived on a small annuity until his death.

Richard Lovell Edgeworth married third, 25 December 1780, Elizabeth Sneyd, sister of his second wife, and by her had five sons and four daughters.

Elizabeth (1781–1800).

Henry (1782–1813). He was a physician, educated at Edinburgh. He died of tuberculosis after a long illness.

Charlotte (1783–1807).

Sophia (1784), died an infant.

Charles Sneyd (1786–1864), married (1813) Henrica Broadhurst. Educated at Trinity, he practiced law in Dublin for a time and helped Maria save the Edgeworth estate from Lovell's mismanagement, but he early abandoned his profession to wander with his wife to various watering places for their health, their primary interest. He wrote a life of the Abbé Edgeworth (1745–1807), *Edgeworth's Memories* (London, 1815), based on the letters of the final confessor of Louis XVI and Marie Antoinette.

William (1788–90).

Thomas Day (1789–92), named for Mr. Edgeworth's eccentric friend Thomas Day (1748–89), author and sympathizer of the American side during the Revolution.

Honora (1791–1858), married (1838) Admiral Sir Francis Beaumont. She helped Maria with the children's books written in the 1820s, copying, editing, and correcting proofs. She is mentioned frequently in ME's letters to RML, and ME wrote Mr. Lazarus of Honora's marriage the year following RML's death.

William (1794–1829). He was a rail and road engineer, laying out the spectacular road from Killarney to Glengariff. Especially close to his father during the latter's last years, William suffered a nervous breakdown after RLE's death, but he recovered completely. The rest of his brief life is recounted in these letters.

Richard Lovell Edgeworth married fourth, 31 May 1798, Frances Anne, daughter of the Reverend Daniel Beaufort, rector of Collon, County Louth, and by her had two sons and four daughters:

Frances Maria (1799–1848), married (1829) Lestock Peach Wilson. Fanny, as Maria's favorite, is treated fully in the letters.

Harriet (1801–89), traveled extensively with Maria in Europe, England, and Scotland where she made a favorable impression on Sir Walter Scott. She was unique in the Edgeworth family as the one strong daughter, even relatively late in life a handy carpenter. She married (1829) the Very Reverend Richard Butler, Dean of Clonmacnoise, and lived at Trim, a day's journey from Edgeworthstown. With no children of their own, she and her husband happily raised the four children of her sister Sophy when the latter died at the age of thirty-four. Upon her husband's death in 1862, Harriet returned to live with her family at Edgeworthstown, and after her mother's death in 1865 continued the correspondence with the Mordecais until her own death at eighty-eight in 1889.

Sophia (1803–37), married (1824) her cousin Major Barry Fox of Annagmore, King's County, and left four children, Maxwell, Waller, Mary Anne, and Charlotte. Sophy and her children appear frequently in these letters, and Alfred Mordecai made their acquaintance on his visit to Edgeworthstown in 1833.

Lucy Jane (1805–97), married (1843) the Reverend Thomas Romney Robinson, D.D., and lived in the Observatory at Armagh. "Poor, invalid Lucy," the subject of commiseration in so many of ME's letters, outlived all her brothers and sisters. She continued the correspondence with the Mordecais after her sister Harriet's death. She died at the age of ninety-two, 153 years after her father's birth.

Francis Beaufort (1809–46). Despite Francis Edgeworth's early promise at Charterhouse, as recounted in these letters, he did not do well at Cambridge. Taking the advice of his cousin Thomas Lovell Beddoes, he planned to study philosophy in Germany. En route to France, he chanced to pass a house in Hampstead (near London) where he had once lodged. On an impulse he called to ask for his old landlady but by mistake was shown into a room full of ladies with beautiful dark eyes and charming manners. They were the wife and daughters of General Eroles, a Spanish exile. Within a month Francis had proposed to Rosa Florentina, aged sixteen. His family hoped he would be refused for his small income and lack of a profession, but within another month he was married, 18 December 1831. After some years in Florence, he and his wife returned to England where he maintained his family by preparing pupils for the universities. Finally in 1841 he took over the management of the estate at Edgeworthstown until his death in 1846. He left five sons and one daughter: William, Antonio Eroles, David Reid, Richard Lestock, Ysidro Francis, and Mary. Ysidro Francis Edgeworth (d. 1926) was the last Edgeworth to own the family estate.

Michael Pakenham (1812–81) made a distinguished record at Haileybury in oriental languages and botany and went to India in the civil service. While on leave in 1846, he married Christina Macpherson of Aberdeen and returned to India. His chief publications were in botany, but he also published a grammar of Kashmiri. He died suddenly in the Island of Eigg, Scotland, 30 July 1881, leaving one daughter, Harriet Jessie.

Margaret Edgeworth Ruxton (1746–1830), Richard Lovell Edgeworth's sister, resembled him in looks and manner. She married (1770) John Ruxton, a retired army officer of Black Castle in Navan, County Meath, some forty miles from Edgeworthstown. When Maria came to live in Ireland at the age of fifteen, her Aunt Ruxton became her closest confidant, whom she visited frequently and wrote to at length throughout her life. On the death of her husband, Mrs. Ruxton with her two daughters, Margaret and Sophy, moved to Bloomfield, near Dublin. When she learned of her aunt's death, Maria wrote: "I thought my mind was prepared—we always deceive ourselves."

Mary Snead (1750–1841). The Misses Charlotte and Mary Sneyd, sisters of Richard Lovell Edgeworth's second and third wives, came to Edgeworthstown in 1795 to make their home. They were well-to-do and became widely respected for their good works in the village. Aunt Mary became Maria's "copier in chief." After their brother-in-law's death in 1817, they returned to Lichfield, England, to live with their brother Edward Sneyd. Two years later they came back to Edgeworthstown, their "heart's home." Charlotte Sneyd died in 1822, and Mary Snead became the venerated senior member of the family, happily interested in all its multiple activities until her death in 1841 at the age of ninety. Maria, in London, mournfully wrote: "That poor, *uncentered*, desolate home at Edgeworthstown!"

Thomas Lovell Beddoes (1803–49), English dramatist and poet, son of Anna Edgeworth and Dr. Thomas Beddoes. While a student at Oxford he published *The Bride's Tragedy* (1822), a play in verse. In 1825 he went to Germany to study medicine and, except for brief visits to England, lived abroad for the rest of his life, adopting German thought and manners. Because of his liberal views, he moved to Switzerland where he practiced medicine for a time. He contributed political poems and articles to German and Swiss papers. He committed suicide in a fit of depression over the breakup of a close friendship with a German baker. Maria appears to have been unimpressed with her nephew's talents, referring to him in early letters casually as "little Tom" and perhaps significantly not at all in her later letters. Northrop Frye in his *A Study of English Romanticism* (New York: Random House, 1968) accords a rather high place to Beddoes as a poet.

Appendix B
The Mordecai Family

Printed records on the Mordecai family are fairly numerous. Among these publications are Caroline Cohen, *Records of the Myers, Hays, and Mordecai Families from 1707 to 1913* (Washington, D.C.: Published for the family, n.d.); Gratz Mordecai, *Notice of Jacob Mordecai, Founder and Proprietor from 1809 to 1819, of the Warrenton (N.C.) Female Seminary*, Publications of the American Jewish Historical Society, No. 6, 1897; Ellen Mordecai, *Gleanings from Long Ago* (Savannah: Breid & Hutton, 1933); Gaston Lichtenstein, *A History of the Jews in Richmond* (Richmond: H. T. Ezekiel, 1917); Lizzie Wilson Montgomery, *Sketches of Old Warrenton, North Carolina* (Raleigh: Edwards & Broughton Printing Co., 1924). Numerous Mordecai letters and other family papers are held by the Department of Archives and History in Raleigh, and in the manuscript collections of the University of North Carolina and Duke University. The State Archives in Richmond holds Mordecai family records.

For brief sketches of the various members of the Mordecai family, the genealogical notes compiled by Ruth K. Nuermberger, formerly curator of manuscripts at the Duke University Library, cannot be improved upon. They were published as "Some Notes on the Mordecai Family," in the *Virginia Magazine of History and Biography* 49 (October 1941); 364–73. They are reproduced here, with minor excisions, by permission of the editor of that publication, William M. Rachal.

The Mordecais were a distinguished and brilliant Jewish family whose members contributed to the cultural advancement of North Carolina and in later years graced the society of Richmond, Virginia. Jacob Mordecai was head of the family during its years in North Carolina. Jacob's father, Moses Mordecai (1707–81) was born in Bonn, Germany, married Elizabeth Whitlock in England, and moved to Philadelphia prior to 1762. Elizabeth changed her name to Ester and adopted the Jewish faith. In Philadelphia, Jacob, the eldest of three sons, was born on 11 April 1762. He was one of the large schoolboy delegation that escorted the first Continental Congress into Philadelphia in September 1774, and as a youth he witnessed many stirring scenes of the Revolutionary War. In 1782 Jacob's widowed mother married Jacob I. Cohen of Richmond, Virginia, thereby initiating Jacob's association with the South.

At the age of twenty-two Jacob married, on 16 June 1784, Judith Myers of New York. She was the daughter of Myer Myers (1723–1795) and Elkaleh Cohen. Jacob and Judith (Myers) Mordecai lived successively in Goochland County, Richmond, Petersburg, Virginia, and Warrenton, North Carolina. To this last place they came about 1792, where for several years Jacob carried on a mercantile business. Judith Mordecai died on 9 January 1796, leaving six small children. In 1798, Jacob Mordecai married Rebecca Myers, a half sister of his first wife, whose mother was Joyce Mears Myers.

For a time Jacob's mercantile business in Warrenton flourished, but unfortunate speculations in tobacco brought reverses. It was then that Jacob Mordecai embarked upon the most distinguished part of his career when in 1809 he opened his school for girls in Warrenton. The teaching was done by his older children, together with one or two outside assistants to teach music, drawing, and dancing. Reverses were not lacking here, however, for in 1811 a fire destroyed the school building. New quarters were obtained quickly and the session went on. Good teaching and wise management soon gave the school a wide repute, so that for many years enrollment had to be limited to the available accommodations. The school flourished until November 1818 when it was sold, the Mordecais having accumulated a sufficient profit (some $40,000) from their decade of schoolteaching to retire from its labor.

They purchased a farm (Spring Farm) near Richmond, Virginia, to which they removed early in 1819. Their money was invested in various securities, probably chiefly in bank stock. Whatever the investment, it turned out badly, so that by 1827 the family had lost most of its hard-earned wealth and was reduced to the most economical living. In 1832, Spring Farm, which had never been profitable, together with some of the slaves, was sold and the family moved to a house on Church Hill in Richmond. In this city they remained until 1863, although they occupied two or three other houses.

Jacob Mordecai was in declining health for two or three years before his death on 4 September 1838. Because of his ill health all the children except one were at home on visits during the summer of 1837.

His widow survived until 1 October 1863, although she was an invalid and blind from 1855 onward. Some account follows of Jacob Mordecai's thirteen children: Moses, Samuel, Rachel, Ellen, Solomon, and Caroline of the first marriage; Julia, George W., Alfred, Augustus, Eliza K., Emma, and Laura of the second marriage.

Moses (4 April 1785–1 September 1824), the eldest of the family, was born in New York, educated in Warrenton, began to study law in 1807, and was licensed to practice in 1808. After a few years at Petersburg and Tarboro, he settled in Raleigh. He rode circuit for many years, probably impairing his health thereby. On 9 December 1817 he married Margaret Lane, daughter of Henry Lane and Mary Hinton, one of Raleigh's prominent and wealthy families. Their first child, Henry, was born in 1819; the second, Judith Ellen, was born on 14 April 1820; and the third, Jacob, early in December 1821. On 11 December 1821 Margaret (Lane) Mordecai died. Two years later (6 January 1824) Moses married her sister, Anne Willis Lane (called Nancy). During the following summer Moses's health grew increasingly worse; in July he, accompanied by his brother Samuel, went to the White Sulphur and the Sweet Springs, and at the latter place Moses died on 1 September 1824. On 10 October 1824, Moses and Nancy's daughter, Margaret, was born. Moses made his brother George the guardian of his children.

Samuel (24 July 1786–9 April 1865) was born in New York. He received a good education, but was early put upon his own resources and began business in Richmond perhaps about 1802. During the War of 1812 he served for a short time (1814) in the Richmond militia. In 1821 he transferred his business to Petersburg where he dealt in both tobacco and cotton. The bad crop year of 1826 caused such serious reverses in his business that he had to bring it to a close. The family's money had been placed in his hands for investment and it was due largely to his reverses that their circumstances were straitened shortly after this time. These and later misfortunes rather embittered Samuel, who, as he grew older, could see little pleasure or satisfaction in his life. He always began afresh, however, and witnessed many periods of prosperity. In later years he invested extensively in Arkansas, Texas, Michigan, and Wisconsin lands.

Sometime prior to 1849 he again transferred his business operations to Richmond where he lived until 1863. In 1856 he published *Richmond in By-Gone Days*, a book of reminiscences, but very valuable for the early history of the city. A second and revised edition appeared in 1860. From about 1855 onward Samuel's health was failing, he was no longer active in business, and after 1860 was almost an invalid. He died in Raleigh.

Rachel (1 July 1788–23 June 1838). After her mother's death in 1796, Rachel together with some of the other children lived with their aunt in Richmond, where they were educated. When her father opened his school at Warrenton in 1809, Rachel became one of the chief teachers and continued in this capacity until they closed the school.

With considerable hesitancy Rachel agreed to marry Aaron Lazarus of Wilmington, a widower with seven children. The wedding took place on 21 March 1821. Lazarus was engaged in the shingle and naval stores business. Rachel's four children were: Marx Edgeworth, born on 6 February 1822; Ellen, born on 13 July 1825; Mary Catherine, born on 12 September 1828; and Julia Judith, born on 9 October 1830. As Rachel was travelling from Wilmington to Richmond to be with her invalid father, she died suddenly at Samuel's house in Petersburg on 23 June 1838.

Rachel's younger children were educated by their aunts. Her son, Marx Edgeworth, was a student at the University of North Carolina in 1838 and later studied medicine in Philadelphia. His later life, however, was very unsatisfactory to his Mordecai relatives, for he became an eccentric man, interested in all kinds of quack medical schemes upon which he squandered his inheritance. He was a follower of Fourier, participated in a minor way in the Brook Farm movement, and published several books on scientific and social questions. He served as a private in the Confederate army and spent his later years as a recluse in Georgia, where he died in 1895.

His sisters, Ellen and Julia, became almost equally eccentric, spending many years at various health cures where (so the Mordecais thought) they came under the vicious influence of feminists and radicals. Julia died in 1873 in South Carolina. About 1848 Ellen married a John Allen of Terre Haute, Indiana, and lived there, in Cincinnati, and at other places in the West. Allen was interested in Brook Farm and other reform movements; it is believed that he died in 1857. Ellen later married an Englishman named Shutt and was beset by poverty and misfortunes in educating a large family. As the result of a visit to her Uncle Solomon in 1848, Mary Catherine Lazarus was married in October 1849 to Drury Thomson, a planter near Mobile and a widower with seven children. This match met with universal opposition among the family, and rightly, for Thomson soon turned out to be a cruel husband, and Mary Catherine died 5 July 1850 when her child was prematurely born.

Ellen (10 November 1790–October 1884). Like Rachel, Ellen spent her early childhood at her aunt's in Richmond and there received her education. She became one of the teachers in her father's school in 1809. Even after the family moved to Richmond, Ellen's teaching days were not over, for she spent much time instructing her young half sisters and later her nieces and nephews. Between 1822 and 1827 she lived chiefly at Warrenton where she aided her sister Caroline both in teaching and housekeeping. While there Ellen developed a strong attachment for John D. Plunkett, her brother-in-law's son, and planned to marry him in November 1823, but Moses Mordecai objected. In later years Ellen rejoiced that she had followed her brother's advice, nor did she ever marry. During 1831–32 Ellen visited her brother Solomon in Mobile. From her childhood there had been a very strong attachment between this brother and sister, and she never ceased to lament their separation. In 1834, Ellen went to Petersburg to keep house for her brother Samuel and remained there for several years.

As she grew older Ellen increasingly felt the need of an income definitely her own, and so for the purpose of laying up a competency she began in 1848 to teach, probably as a governess, in the family of Denning Duer in New York City. Some four years there sufficed to provide the sum she desired. Thereafter she remained at home helping to care for her invalid mother, until 1858 and 1859, when she went to Mobile to be with her afflicted brother Solomon. Her later years were spent in Richmond and North Carolina.

Solomon (10 October 1792–1869). Solomon was born and educated in Warrenton, where he attended George's Academy from 1801 to 1806 or longer. He probably cut short his own education to assist in his father's school, where he also kept the accounts and managed the business part of the enterprise. Besides this he and his father arranged many of their own textbooks in geography and grammar. He was an unusually steady and serious as well as brilliant youth. Constant work so impaired his health that in 1817 he was forced to go off on a long vacation while his place in the school was filled by George and Julia, his younger half brother and sister.

After the conclusion of the family's scholastic labors Solomon went to Philadelphia in October 1819 to study medicine. In 1821 he began what amounted to an internship at the Almshouse, a hospital for the poor in Philadelphia. In the spring of 1822 he graduated in medicine and after several months at home he decided, following much family debate, to begin practice in Mobile, Alabama. He sailed for that city on 2 December 1822 and arrived on 25 January 1823. This decision met with opposition from the family who considered Mobile too unhealthful a location, as well as a raw village in the frontier wilderness. On 22

April 1824, Solomon married Caroline Waller, daughter of a planter near Mobile. Solomon had several reverses, but on the whole his medical practice was quite successful. For a time he and a Dr. Cheusse united a drug business with their practice.

Solomon's large family included Edward, born 27 April 1825; William W., born in March 1827; Samuel Fox, born in January 1829; Mary Ellen, born on 25 August 1830; Thomas Waller, born probably in 1832; Laura, born in August 1834; Susan, born in 1837; Jacob Granville, born about 1839; and Caroline, born in 1844.

Impaired vision due to cataracts forced Solomon to seek medical aid at Philadelphia in the summer of 1854, when he also visited his brothers and sisters in Richmond and Raleigh. It was his first and only trip back since settling at Mobile in 1823. An unsuccessful operation was performed on one eye, with the result that Solomon was almost totally blind for the remainder of his life. His sister Caroline, who was living in Mobile, did what she could to assist and entertain him. Solomon Mordecai's affliction brought his sister Ellen to Mobile in 1858 where she remained until 1860.

Caroline 27 August 1794–1862). Caroline passed her early childhood in Richmond at her aunt's, but was taken back home after her father's second marriage. She also taught in her father's school and about 1814 fell in love with Achilles Plunkett who taught music, drawing, dancing, and French in the Mordecai academy. Plunkett was a member of a Santo Domingo French family which had been forced to flee during the insurrection of 1802. He had come to the Mordecai school from Williamsburg in 1812. Caroline's father and brothers frowned on the attachment, and it was not until her mental and physical health were threatened that they gave a grudging assent. Caroline and Achilles Plunkett were married on 19 December 1820, and she returned to teaching in Warrenton, for he had been one of the purchasers of the Mordecai school. Plunkett had been married previously and had three children, John D., Louisa, and Achilles, who were grown or adolescent.

Caroline's first child, Charles Edward, was born on 24 September 1821 and died on 10 May 1823; the second, Alfred Charles, was born on 2 March and died on 15 May 1823. Misfortunes then beset her in earnest, for on 26 January 1824, Achilles Plunkett died. Caroline and her stepson, John D. Plunkett, continued the Warrenton school for a time. On 2 April 1824, Caroline's third child, Frank Alfred, was born. He died on 2 January 1825. In November 1825, Caroline sold the school for $7,000. J. D. Plunkett ceased teaching and left for Santo Domingo to try to recover some of the family property there. In 1827 Caroline began to teach again, keeping a small private school in Warrenton. Mrs. Bourdet, Caroline's mother-in-law who had resided with her for some eight years, died in 1830. Late in that year Caroline moved to Raleigh where she was to devote herself to the education of Moses's children. This arrangement proved unsatisfactory, however, and so in September 1831 she went to Wilmington where she opened a school and assisted with the education of Rachel's children. Yielding to her friends' advice Caroline in 1833 decided to go to Tennessee where she spent one year at La Grange. She then taught in Brownsville until 1836 when she proposed going to Mobile to teach her brother Solomon's children. This she did and remained there until 1861, teaching a school most of the time, though it is doubtful whether she gave much instruction to her brother's children. About 1861 she returned to the family home in Richmond and in 1862 went to Raleigh where she died.

Julia Judith (17 May 1799–15 March 1852). Julia, the eldest child of the second marriage, figures less prominently in the correspondence than most other members of the family. She assisted in the management of the school and was one of the teachers in 1817 when Solomon's ill health forced his temporary cessation. Julia spent most of her time at home, occupied with housekeeping and the education of the younger children, but from time to time she had a respite when she made visits to Richmond, Raleigh, Wilmington, and elsewhere.

About 1847 Julia's health began to fail, and the deaths of her brother Augustus in that year and of his daughter Rebecca in 1849 increased her melancholia. She was very ill during the spring of 1852 and died shortly thereafter. She was never married.

George Washington (27 April 1801–19 February 1871). George, the eldest son of the second marriage, was educated at Warrenton and in 1817 went to Richmond where he joined Samuel in his business operations. A few months later it was necessary for him to return to Warrenton where he temporarily took over Solomon's teaching duties. In 1818 George went to Kentucky where he engaged in the tobacco business. This arrangement did not last long, for two years later he joined his brother Moses in Raleigh and began to read law under his supervision.

George was admitted to the bar in 1821 and practiced for some fifteen years. In 1836 he was made president of the Raleigh and Gaston Railroad, a position which he held until 1852, and remained one of its directors until his death in 1871. At the beginning of 1849 he became president of the North Carolina State Bank. Among his many activities of later years, he was in 1860 president of Forest Mill, a paper mill on the Neuse River.

George was married on 1 July 1853 to Margaret Cameron. Their only child was born in 1855 and died in infancy. George's wife was a semi-invalid for most of her life. The family lived in Raleigh and George died there. George Mordecai visited Edgeworthstown in 1839.

Alfred (3 January 1804–23 October 1887). Alfred was born in Warrenton, North Carolina, educated first in his father's school and by his brothers and sisters, and entered West Point on 24 June 1819. His standing was high, and he graduated first in his class (1823), returning immediately as an instructor in engineering. He was later stationed successively at Fortress Monroe, Virginia, Washington, D.C., and the Frankford Arsenal near Philadelphia. As major of ordnance he was one of a commission sent in 1855 to the Crimea to study military operations there.

On 2 June 1836 he married Sara Hays of a Philadelphia family. Alfred had for some time been dissatisfied with army life, so that within a year after his marriage he had about decided to resign. He was deterred, however, by the panic of 1837, and did not resign until 1861. Alfred and Sara Mordecai's children were: Laura, born on 5 June 1837; Rosa, born in 1839; Frank who was born probably in 1841, died in 1843; Miriam, born in 1843; Alfred, born in 1844; Augustus, born in 1848; and Gratz, born early in 1850. The son Alfred also became an army man, after graduating from West Point in the class of 1861, fought with the Union forces, and became a brigadier general.

In 1857 the elder Alfred was transferred to Watervliet Arsenal near Albany, New York. Secession caused his resignation, as he felt unable to fight either against his own family in the South or against that of his wife in the North. He began to teach mathematics in Philadelphia, soon became assistant engineer of the Mexico and Pacific Railroad (1863–66), and for the remainder of his life was connected with canal and coal companies owned by the Pennsylvania Railroad.

Augustus (5 October 1806–25 July 1847). After receiving his early education in Warrenton, Augustus went to Raleigh where he was under the eye of his two brothers, Moses and George. After a few years in Raleigh, Augustus returned to Spring Farm where, as his father grew older, he took charge of the farming operations. In 1830 he investigated gold mining prospects in North Carolina, but did not venture very heavily on the project. His restlessness and lack of definite occupation during the next years were a matter of concern to the family, for he, the youngest son, had borne the brunt of staying at home with his parents while the other boys had been trained for a profession. In March 1835, Augustus married Rosina Ursula Young of

Westbrook, an estate adjoining Spring Farm. The young couple moved to a farm near Raleigh. After a few years they returned to Rosewood which also adjoined Spring Farm. Augustus entered the ice business and in 1846 had the largest ice storage plant in Virginia. A year later Augustus died.

Augustus and Rosina Mordecai's children were: William Young, born on 28 March 1836; Mary Brooke, born on 15 August 1837 and died in infancy; John Brooke, born on 14 October 1839; Rebecca, born on 9 January 1842; George Washington, born on 18 April 1844; another daughter named Mary Brooke, who was born on 28 July 1846, also died in infancy; and Augusta, born 30 September 1847 subsequent to her father's death.

Eliza Kennon (10 August 1809–8 November 1861) was named for Mrs. Eliza Kennon, a distinguished woman and a great friend of the family. Eliza Mordecai was educated first in her father's school, after 1818 by her half sisters, Rachel and Ellen, and then went to live with Rachel in Wilmington. In the winter of 1825–26 she was introduced to society in Wilmington. On 21 November 1827, Eliza married her cousin, Samuel Hays Myers (1799–1849), and went to live in Petersburg where he had been in business with Samuel Mordecai since 1825. In 1832 this connection was dissolved and Sam H. Myers entered the tobacco business exclusively. He suffered much from gout and other ailments and died on 2 October 1849, at the age of fifty. Thence forward Eliza lived in the family home at Richmond. Eliza and Samuel Myers's children were: Edmund Trowbridge Dana, born on 13 July 1830; and Caroline, born on 5 December 1844.

Emma (9 October 1812–8 April 1906). Emma was educated chiefly by her half sister Ellen and in her sister Caroline Plunkett's school at Warrenton. She lived for some time with her sister Eliza in Petersburg and was introduced to society in Wilmington. Between 1841 and 1849 Emma was chiefly engaged in teaching, part of the time conducting a small school at home and in other years acting as governess for nearby families. After 1849 she remained at home, taking charge of the housekeeping after Julia's health failed, and caring for her invalid mother, until the latter's death in 1863, when the family home in Richmond was broken up. Thereafter she taught for many years, sometimes in private schools and sometimes as governess. Emma never married. She died in Brevard, North Carolina.

Laura (23 April 1818–4 July 1839). Laura, the youngest child, was born in Warrenton. She was considered by the family as its most promising member, for she had both beauty and unusual mental endowments. Ellen took charge of her education. After successive winters spent in Petersburg, Raleigh, and Wilmington, and a visit to Philadelphia on the occasion of Alfred's wedding, Laura returned home and was soon engaged to John Brooke Young, of Westbrook, and brother of Rosina Ursula (Young) Mordecai. The wedding date was set and their house under construction when Laura died very suddenly on 4 July 1839. This was a crushing blow to the family, following, as it did, so closely on Rachel's and their father's deaths the preceding year.

Aaron Marks Lazarus (26 August 1777–2 October 1841) was born in Charleston, the son of Marks Lazarus (22 February 1757–1 November 1835), a soldier in the Revolution, and Rachel Benjamin (?–6 November 1847). By his first wife, Esther Cohen, Aaron Lazarus had eight children: Gershon (10 April 1801), Benjamin (30 July 1805), Phila Cohen (8 September 1806), Rachel A. (8 October 1807), Washington (20 September 1808), Angelina Green (8 October 1807), Maria Cecilia (20 January 1811), Almira Emma (20 September 1814). Esther Cohen Lazarus died in 1816, and Aaron Lazarus doubtless met Rachel Mordecai in Warrenton, North Carolina, where his daughter Phila was a student at the Mordecai School. (These notes on Aaron Lazarus are from the Calder Family Papers by Phila Calder Nye in the possession of Robert Calder of Wilmington, North Carolina.)

Index

V
Van Halen, Jan, 158, 175, 177
Vaux, Roberts, 136, 140
Vicar of Wakefield, 159, 292
Victoria, Queen, 297, 302, 317
Vigne, Godfrey, 250
Vivian, 17
Vivian Gray, 141, 152

W
Ward, Robert Plumer, 141n, 152
Warrenton, N.C., 11n, 326–34
Washington, Bushrod, 130
Washington, D.C., 248
Washington, George, 64, 124, 130, 279
Waverley, 65
Wellington, duke of, 96, 238, 297
Whewell, William, 311
Whitbread, Lady Elizabeth, 37, 180
White, Joseph Blanco, 58
Wilberforce, William, 274, 305
Wilmington, N.C., 26, 126, 132, 161,
    163; cold winter in, 114
Wilson, Alexander, 170
Wilson, Lestock Peach, 180–82, 201,
    217
Wilson, Mrs. *See* Edgeworth, Fanny
Wolfe, Charles, 83n
Wollaston, William Hyde, 188

Y
Yates, Miss (of Liverpool), 199, 218
York, Frederick Agustus, duke of, 88

Z
Zeluco, 57, 66–67
Zoology, 51, 61, 86–87, 104–5, 119,
    124, 150, 156–57, 169–70, 173